Presidential Mandates

American Politics and

Political Economy

A series edited by Benjamin I. Page

Patricia
Heidotting
Conley

Presidential Mandates

How Elections
Shape the
National Agenda

The University of Chicago Press
Chicago & London

PATRICIA HEIDOTTING CONLEY is assistant professor of political
science at Northwestern University.

THE UNIVERSITY OF CHICAGO PRESS, CHICAGO 60637
THE UNIVERSITY OF CHICAGO PRESS, LTD., LONDON

© 2001 by The University of Chicago
All rights reserved. Published 2001
Printed in the United States of America

10 09 08 07 06 05 04 03 02 01   5 4 3 2 1

ISBN (cloth): 0-226-11482-1
ISBN (paper): 0-226-11484-8

Library of Congress Cataloging-in-Publication Data

Conley, Patricia Heidotting.
    Presidential mandates : how elections shape the national
agenda / Patricia Heidotting Conley.
        p.   cm. — (American politics and political economy)
    Includes bibliographical references and index.
    ISBN 0-226-11482-1 (cloth : alk. paper) — ISBN 0-226-
11484-8 (paper : alk. paper)
        1. Presidents—United States—Election.   2. United
States—Politics and government.   I. Title.   II. Series.
JK528.C72   2001
973'.09'9—dc21

00-012822

For Goldie and Russell Benton,
Alice and Albert Heidotting

Contents

Illustrations

Preface

After every presidential election, no matter how large or small the margin of victory, politicians and journalists try to determine whether or not the new president has a mandate. The recently concluded contest for the American presidency in the year 2000 is no exception. Most observers do not believe that President George W. Bush received a mandate for any of the policy proposals on which he campaigned. Some have gone so far as to suggest that he should appoint Democrats and moderates to his cabinet in order to shore up his weak electoral base. For only the fourth time in our nation's history, the new president failed to win a plurality of the popular vote. The controversy over the counting of ballots in Florida left questions about whether Bush was even the rightful winner of the Electoral College vote. Bush detractors in attendance at his inauguration ceremony could only wave placards that read, "Hail to the Thief" and "Reelect Gore in 2004."

Though the resolution of the election in the courts was unprecedented, the analysis that came afterward about whether the new president enjoyed a mandate is part of an ongoing tradition of interpreting presidential elections in the United States. As in past elections, the 2000 race was mined by politicians and journalists alike for the information that it offered about public preferences. Like other politicians, presidents search for the reasons behind their victory and adjust their policy behavior on the basis of their beliefs about voters. Presidents who believe that they represent the voice of the people will claim a mandate and work to change the national policy agenda. Though there appears to be no mandate, the 2000 election does force us to question the accuracy of the vote count on which politicians routinely base their postelection interpretations.

George W. Bush's initial 1,784-vote margin of victory in Florida dropped to a mere 327 votes after a machine recount of ballots in all 67 Florida counties. The Gore campaign immediately asked for a manual recount of votes in four Florida counties; the Bush campaign sued to bar the manual recounts. Thus, the major controversies focused on the mechanics of the voting process and the proper counting of ballots. In Palm Beach County, for instance, it was revealed that more than 19,000 ballots were invalidated and not counted because voters had "over voted"—that is, voted for more than one presidential candidate. Democratic voters in that county claimed that they had been confused by the design of the ballot (the so-called "butterfly ballot"), causing them either to vote mistakenly for Reform Party candidate, Pat Buchanan, or to punch their ballot twice. In counties that used a punch card system, voting machines did not count large numbers of presidential votes because the hole on the ballot was either only partially punched through (a hanging chad) or merely indented (a dimpled chad). Voters also charged that the machines were either old or clogged with chad so that they could not fully punch out the appropriate hole in their ballot. The Gore team argued that a manual inspection of these ballots would allow the examiner to determine clearly the intent of the voter, and therefore to count these votes, even if a machine would not count them. The Bush campaign maintained that it would be unfair to carry out manual recounts in only a small number of counties where a majority of voters favored Gore. They also argued that hand recounts were highly subjective and would inject partisan bias into the counting process.

The astonishingly small margin of victory in Florida, and the fact that both candidates needed Florida's 25 electoral college votes to win the presidency, focused attention on issues of ballot design and the mechanics of voting as never before. Indeed, most Americans had no awareness of these kinds of problems, and took for granted that votes they cast on Election Day were routinely counted. In addition to mechanical problems in the casting and counting of ballots, members of both political parties raised serious charges of improprieties in the voting process. Republicans chastised the media for calling the state of Florida for Gore before the polls closed in the heavily

Republican Florida panhandle. African American voters in Duval County told reporters that they had been harassed and intimidated at the polls. Democrats expressed outrage that Republican Party workers had been allowed to correct errors on Republican applications for absentee ballots to ensure that their partisans would receive ballots, while the Democrats had not been given the chance to do the same for Democratic applicants.

Americans' beliefs about the fairness of the electoral process were challenged further when the outcome ended up being decided by the Supreme Court. Florida's Republican secretary of state used machine-tabulated vote counts to certify the vote and assign the Florida electors to George W. Bush. The Gore team contested the result, arguing that all of the votes had not been counted. Manual recounts that had been completed showed an overall net gain in votes for Gore. On December 8, the Florida Supreme Court ordered an immediate manual recount of all 45,000 ballots where no vote for president had been recorded by machine count. The Bush team immediately appealed to the U.S. Supreme Court, which ordered a halt to the manual recount and agreed to hear the case. On December 12, five weeks after the election, the Supreme Court of the United States ruled by a vote of 5 to 4 to stop the Florida recount, which meant that the presidency would go to George W. Bush. In the end, Bush won the Electoral College vote by a margin of 271 to 267; he lost the popular vote by a little over 300,000 votes.

Both during and after the protracted legal battles over the Florida vote count, partisans on both sides questioned the legitimacy of the process and, therefore, the legitimacy of the eventual winner. Because voters and politicians were engaged in a contest about the *identity* of the winning candidate, postelection coverage did not focus on the usual analysis of the vote and potential policy interpretations for victory. Little time was spent explaining why Gore fared so poorly as a member of an incumbent administration in a time of peace and economic prosperity. Nor was there much analysis of the types of voters that chose Bush over Gore in order to uncover the issues that formed the basis of his support. Instead, analysis rightly focused on the electoral process: the utility of the Electoral College, the role of the Courts, and what it means to say that every vote counts.

Given the controversy in Florida and the disparity between the popular vote and Electoral College results, it seems rather obvious to say that George W. Bush has no mandate. This view was reinforced by the results of the congressional elections. In the House of Representatives, Republicans lost only two seats, leaving a total of 221 Republicans to 212 Democrats. In the Senate, Democrats gained four seats, making that chamber evenly divided between the parties. The parity of the political parties in Congress seemed to reflect the closeness of the race between the presidential candidates.

But let us not forget that this election was unlikely to produce a mandate for either candidate even if the popular and Electoral College votes pointed in the same direction and even if we had not faced ballot problems in Florida. With a lackluster campaign, low enthusiasm for both candidates, a small margin of victory, and an almost evenly divided Congress, the winner would have been hard-pressed to attribute his victory to a desire for change on the part of the electorate. Right up until Election day, Bush's lead in the polls fell within the sampling margin of error and twelve states with nearly a quarter of the electoral college votes were too close to call. A slim victory for either candidate would have been no real surprise.

In the pages that follow, I look at elections from the perspective of politicians who face the difficult task of making inferences about the electorate. Mandates imply that politicians receive direction from the voters who elected them. In practice, however, the voice of the people is not so easy to decipher, even if all votes are accurately counted. When we cast our vote for a person rather than for a single-issue referendum, politicians have many potential hypotheses about the reasons behind our choice. Perhaps we liked the candidate's stand on a single issue and we want him to change the direction of public policy. Then again, perhaps his opponent ran a poor campaign.

By examining the margin of victory, the behavior of coalitions of voters, public opinion polls, and shifts from historical precedent, politicians attempt to determine whether a majority of voters support the president's major campaign pledges. They are backward looking—using the election outcome to gauge current voter preferences—and forward looking—estimating how voters will react in the future and determining how their own actions will affect their chances for reelection. A president will only claim a mandate—and change the policy agenda—if he believes that he can mobilize voters and then members of Congress to support his point of view. Mandates are perceptions of political opportunity.

As our recent election shows, not all presidents have an incentive to ask for major policy changes. If political opportunity is a continuum, then the outcome of the 2000 presidential election surely anchors the low end of the scale. George W. Bush enters office without the ability to claim a popular mandate for his policy agenda. But he is hardly alone among recent presidents. John Kennedy, Jimmy Carter, and George Bush, Sr., did not claim mandates either, even though the circumstances surrounding their election were quite different from Bush's. On the other hand, Harry Truman, Lyndon Johnson, Ronald Reagan, and Bill Clinton *did* claim mandates. Substantial variation exists among presidents with respect to their initial agenda-setting behaviors, even when the basic legitimacy of their selection is not in question. This book is an attempt to explain that variation.

Perhaps the 2000 election was disappointing because it so clearly violates our beliefs about how elections *should* function in a representative democracy. In this ideal world, voters understand and care deeply about the issues, and the winner of a fairly conducted election acts to change policy according to his clearly enunciated campaign promises. This is a view articulated repeatedly by normative theorists and politicians. Here, for instance, a Republican senator responds to Democrats in Congress after the election of 1860:

> Sir, I am one of those who went forth with zeal to maintain the principles of the great Republican Party. In a constitutional way, we met, as you met. We nominated our candidates for President and Vice-President, and you did the same for yourselves. The issue was made up; and we went to the people on it. Although we have usually been in the minority; although we have been generally beaten, yet, this time, the justice of our principles, and the maladministration of the Government in your hands, convinced the peo-

ple that a change ought to be wrought; and after you had
tried your utmost, and we had tried our utmost, we beat
you; and we beat you upon the plainest and most palpable
issue [slavery], that ever was presented to the American people and one that they understood the best . . . with the
verdict of the people given in favor of the platform on
which our candidates were elected, so far as I am concerned,
I would suffer anything to come before I would compromise
that away.[1]

In this narrative, standing up for policy or principle is equivalent to
standing up for one's constituents, since voters chose on the basis
of the issues. The Senator explains his unwillingness to compromise
in the legislature by reminding his opponents that his point of view
prevailed in a fair contest, under previously agreed upon rules of the
game. The parties held strongly opposing views and campaigned on
their differences. The winning party upset the conventional balance
of political power. The nature of the contest and the outcome allowed the voice of the people to be heard.

Rarely are elections so perfect, and not even the election of 1860
could be characterized as such. In the modern era, campaign finance,
media coverage of campaigns, voter apathy, and vote fraud are just
a few of the ways in which our elections fall short of the ideal. Yet
we never fail to measure real outcomes against this optimistic view
of elections in order to evaluate how well elections communicate
popular sentiment. Our reform efforts are directed at ensuring that
voters know the ideas of the candidates and parties and have the
ability to register their choice and select their representatives. If anything, our most recent election will push reform efforts further in
this direction, eliminating any ambiguity caused by the sheer mechanics of voting. Elected officials cannot represent us unless they
can learn about our preferences. We cannot trust them as our representatives unless we are confident that they are the leaders that we
intended to select.

1. Senator Ben Wade, quoted in Bruce Ackerman, *We the People 2: Transformations* (Cambridge: Harvard University Press, 1998), 128.

Acknowledgments

Early in my graduate training, I became curious about philosophical notions of the general will and public interest, as well as theories of political representation. As I pursued my interest in American electoral politics, presidential mandates caught my attention because they seemed to epitomize the notion of a coherent public will that is expressed through elections. Presidential mandate claims became an obsession for me when I discovered that academics dismissed them as random and inconsequential or as the rhetoric of evil presidents trying to claim legitimacy for their own selfish aims. I was convinced that this was not the case.

When I began examining the historical evidence, I observed that mandate claims were not random and that politicians took these claims seriously. I found that little attention had been paid to the psychology of how politicians read electoral outcomes, even though their interpretations appeared to condition their behavior in office. It occurred to me that presidential mandates are perhaps best understood in this context—as summary judgments of political possibilities, made in an environment of uncertainty and limited information. If this is so, then political representation becomes a story of signals sent and received, and the conditions under which a new president sees a political opportunity.

I am grateful to the scholars in American politics, political theory, and methodology who have shaped the way that I think about politics in general and mandates in particular. At the University of Kentucky, I was fortunate to be able to work with Stanley Feldman, Malcolm Jewell, and Mark Peffley; they first encouraged my interests in political psychology and institutions. The intellectual atmosphere at the University of Chicago left a lasting impression on the questions that I ask and the ways that I search for answers. I benefited enormously from the instruction and advising of Chris Achen, Henry Brady, Joseph Cropsey, Jon Elster, J. David Greenstone, Bernard Manin, and Gerald Rosenberg. I owe a special thanks to Mark Hansen for his continued support and for his collaboration on a project on political inference. Some of this material has been incorporated into chapter 3.

I am indebted to those individuals who provided comments and advice at various stages in the writing of the manuscript: David Austen-Smith, Jay Casper, Fred Greenstein, Susan Herbst, Jenny Mansbridge, Terry Moe, Sara Monoson, and Ken Shotts. I am grateful to Ken Janda for directing me to various archival resources on the presidency. I would especially like to thank Ben Page for his substantive comments and his enthusiasm for the project. The manuscript also benefited enormously from the comments of two anonymous reviewers at the University of Chicago Press. Their insights and suggestions were invaluable. I am also grateful to John Tryneski and Claudia Rex for their assistance and patience at all stages of the production process. Most of all, I would like to thank Dennis Chong. He has been an unfailing supporter of my research and a good friend. He has alternately encouraged and chided me, and even copyedited the manuscript in his efforts to help move this project forward. I could not have a better colleague or mentor.

On a more personal note, I thank my husband David and the rest of my family for believing in me and for kindly enduring my work schedule. I could not have completed this project without their support. I would like to thank my daughter Rachel for her curiosity and heart, and for constantly reminding me of what is most important in life. Finally, I dedicate this book to my grandparents. Through the Depression and the Second World War, they worked and fought so that their children and grandchildren would have a better life. They were determined that I should have the education and the opportunities that they did not have. They didn't even waver in their belief in my education when my graduate training seemed never to end. I dedicate this book to them to thank them for a lifetime of love and hard work.

Chicago, Illinois
March 2001

O N E | Rethinking Presidential Mandates

No concept invokes the connection between the public and a president more than the electoral mandate, for it implies that the president shall work to make the will of the people into law. For over a hundred and fifty years, American presidents have claimed to represent the will of the American people rather than simply execute the laws passed by the legislature. In this period, they have used their role as representative of the people to expand the power of the office and to make the president central to policy making. They have used their electoral victories to claim legitimacy for their efforts to shape the national policy agenda. Thus, whether presidential mandates exist and whether they are expressed and affirmed through elections is of great importance for evaluating representative democracy in America.

The ignorance of the American voter and power of the modern presidency have called into question the validity and wisdom of presidential electoral mandates.[1] How can elections convey information about public preferences given the current state of voters and campaigns? Candidates are often ambiguous; voters are uninformed; and the motivations behind the final choice of a president are many. Could not an ambitious president use the rhetoric of a mandate to legitimize his own policy agenda, even if this mandate has no basis in public opinion? Since the president is the only representative of the entire nation and has the ability to set the public policy agenda, he could use his authority to ignore public preferences rather than serve them.

Presidential electoral mandates have therefore been dismissed because they are perceived to be vacuous and self-serving. I argue against this view. Rejecting presidential mandates on these grounds ignores one of the most interesting aspects of political representation: how elections convey information about public preferences to elected representatives so that these representatives know whether or not to adjust the policy agenda. Politicians seek the information that elections provide, and they have an incentive to formulate an accurate portrayal of the public mood. Interpretations cannot be too self-serving in an environment where information is shared and the opposing party is ready to question interpretations and offer up challengers in future elections. A president will claim a mandate only after explanations for victory have been touted and examined and a policy explanation is left standing even after the losers have said their piece. A president will claim a mandate only when he thinks that he can mobilize voters and members of Congress to make a major policy change. The rhetoric alone will not persuade others to go along.

Thus mandate claiming does not necessarily imply that presidents are misrepresenting public preferences or that they are using their authority to get Congress to go along with their own selfish priorities. The president's claims can be checked against empirical evidence; presidents can be punished for having the wrong assessment of the electorate. It is in the president's own best interest to get the interpretation of the election right. Since 1828, roughly half of our presidents have entered office asking for major policy changes on behalf of the electorate. *Half did not.* Presidents are constrained by shared evidence about the election outcome, their own reluctance to make false claims, and the opposing party's incentive to prevent the victor from legitimizing his policy agenda.

This book takes the perspective of politicians who win elections and must make decisions about matters of public policy. Claiming a mandate is equivalent to putting a major policy change on the national agenda. It is also a signal that the president believes he can rally support for his agenda; he will not attempt to change policy if he thinks he will fail. Mandate claims therefore depend upon a subjective reading of electoral and congressional support and upon a calculation of the potential for policy success. They are both empirical statements about voters and strategic political calculations. As I will show, this agenda-setting rhetoric becomes predictable once we understand how politicians read election outcomes and perceive their political opportunities.

THE MEANING OF ELECTORAL MANDATES

The word "mandate" derives from the Latin verb *mandare*, meaning to command or enjoin. It is used most commonly to denote legal imperatives, for instance the mandate of the Constitution to uphold certain rights, or the mandate of the courts to desegregate schools, or the mandate to cut spending by a certain dollar amount to stay in line with budget legislation. In international relations, the term has been used to denote a guardianship in which a nation-state administers a territory until its independence (e.g., under the League of Nations, Palestine was a British mandate).

The notion of an instruction from voters to elected officials first emerged for members of the legislature, since this was understood to be the popular branch of government. Mandates referred either to specific instructions regarding the way a politician should vote on a given policy or very general boundaries outside of which a politician should not stray in dealing with new issues. Thus in the House of Commons, Lord Harrington stated: "I am perfectly aware that there exists in our Constitution no principle of the mandate. . . . But, although no principle of mandate exists, I maintain that there are certain limits which Parliament is morally bound to observe, and beyond which Parliament has morally not got the right to go in its relations with constituents."[2]

It was not until the time of Andrew Jackson that the notion of the American president as representative of the people gained currency among politicians and voters and that presidents began associating their policy agenda with the will of the people.[3] But today, the use of the word "mandate" as well as the underlying story of voters sending presidents a policy message is a familiar one. Politicians and journalists readily label presidential election outcomes according to whether or not they qualify as mandates. When asked if he had a mandate after the 1980 election, President Reagan responded that he would move quickly on his economic policies since "it is what the American people told us with their votes they wanted." President Clinton outlined his version of an electoral mandate in the presidential debates right before his 1992 electoral victory: "You have to vote for somebody with a plan. That's what you have elections for. If the people say, 'Well he got elected to do this,' then the Congress says 'Okay, I'm gonna do it. That's what the election was about.'"[4] Less fortunate presidents have inferred that they did not win electoral mandates. For instance, after the 1988 election, George Bush said that while he had "confidence" in the results, he would not go so far as to claim a mandate.

Academics in the behavioral tradition have scrutinized the mandate claims of presidents as if they were statements of fact about public opinion. Thus they have turned to mass opinion surveys to determine if voters truly hold the preferences that are attributed to them.[5] At a minimum, mandates seem to imply that voters have opinions on policies, know candidates' stands on the issues, and vote on the basis of issues.[6] However, the survey evidence indicates that a large proportion of voters are ignorant of the issues and cannot accurately identify the candidates' platforms.[7] The evidence also suggests that voters are motivated more strongly by partisanship or the personal attributes of candidates than by their policy positions. The limited role of policy in elections, however, may say more about politicians than voters.[8] Candidates have an incentive to be ambiguous or centrist in order to attract a majority of votes. Likewise, it is often advantageous for candidates to emphasize their personal qualities or to use the election as a referendum on the past performance of the parties.[9] But regardless of who is responsible for the lack of policy debate, mandates are viewed with skepticism because they rest on a story about voter intentions and campaign behavior that is not consistent with empirical evidence about voters and elections.

Social choice theorists, on the other hand, take a different tack in denying the plausibility of presidential mandates. For them, a mandate implies a unique public preference for a specific policy.[10] But beginning with Arrow's theorem, scholars have proved that no method of aggregating individual preferences can both satisfy our basic criteria for fairness and also generate a transitive social preference.[11] Methods of aggregation, including majority rule, can yield cyclic or intransitive social orderings. Without transitivity, and a clear social choice, the notion of a public interest is suspect.

The problem of determining the public will is complicated fur-

ther by how votes are counted. For any given set of individual preferences in an electorate, different methods of aggregation, for instance
plurality rule versus a Borda count, will yield different outcomes.
According to plurality rule, the winner is the candidate who receives
the most votes. Every voter votes for one candidate. Other methods
allow voters to rank and give points to all candidates. In a race with
n candidates, the Borda method has voters assign $n - 1$ points to
their favorite alternative, $n - 2$ points to second place, and so forth,
with 0 points for their least favored alternative. The winner is the
candidate with the highest number of points.

Elections can also be manipulated by strategic voting or agenda
setting. For example, suppose we use majority rule as the aggregation
method in pairwise voting on alternatives. The way that we "set the
agenda," by deciding the order in which alternatives are voted on
(and eliminated), will affect the final decision. It is strategic to add
options that create paradoxes in order to achieve desired outcomes,
as in the creation of "killer" amendments in Congress. If aggregate
outcomes are dependent on aggregation procedures and strategic manipulation, then electoral outcomes are not unique. No unique electoral outcome means no unique will of the people.

The normative evaluation of presidential mandate claiming that
follows from behavioral and social choice research is extremely negative. Robert Dahl describes the presidential mandate as a dangerous
"myth" that "elevates the president to an exalted position in our
constitutional system at the expense of Congress."[12] Moreover, "because the myth is almost always employed to support deceptive, misleading, and manipulative interpretations, it is harmful to the political understanding of citizens."[13] In this view, the president does not
deliberate or communicate with members of Congress; he appeals
to and manipulates public opinion. His private interests are hidden
behind appeals to the public interest. "No elected leader, including
the President, is uniquely privileged to say what an election means—
nor to claim that the election has conferred on the president a mandate to enact the particular policies the president supports."[14]

RETHINKING PRESIDENTIAL MANDATES

These critiques are correct about the informational shortcomings
of voters and about the logical problems of identifying the collective

preferences of the electorate. But they do not address why politicians nevertheless persist in using the rhetoric of mandates to diagnose electoral outcomes. Therefore, I propose that we examine mandates from the point of view of presidents who must interpret elections and set policy agendas. Rather than establish whether the public is sufficiently informed to justify a presidential mandate claim, I examine what this rhetoric means to politicians.

In the aftermath of an election, politicians try to figure out what the outcome signifies. In an environment of imperfect information, they must try to distinguish between idiosyncratic events like a weak nominee and long-term political trends like ideological change. If they make inaccurate inferences about the public and pursue these claims through their legislative agendas, they will be punished at the polls in the future. They never have perfect information about voters, and yet they must decide on a policy agenda. The task of studying electoral mandates must therefore focus on explaining when presidents feel they have enough popular support to ask for major policy changes. We need to understand both the institutional incentives that motivate the president to ask for policy change and the ways in which politicians make inferences about voters.

I will argue, first, that mandate claims are the result of strategic calculations based on expectations about congressional responses to the president's initiative and on forecasts about voter reactions in the future. Presidents would like to change the policy agenda to bring it more in line with their own preferences, but they do not have an incentive to try to make changes if they believe that they will fail. The congressional response to the president's agenda depends upon: (1) beliefs about public support for the president's program; (2) the proximity of the president's policy position to that of members of Congress; and (3) the relationship of both to the status quo. Elections supply the data necessary for the president's calculations. They select the new president and members of Congress, thus determining the policy preferences or ideal points of the major actors in the model and the ideological distance between them. Elections also send signals to elected officials about the strength of public support for the president's policy agenda. A president claims a mandate when the election signals strong public support for his agenda or when doing battle with Congress will shift policy outcomes closer to his ideal point. A president does not declare a mandate when he expects that changing the agenda will make him worse off than keeping with the status quo.

Second, I argue that while mandate claims are not statements of fact about fully formed public preferences, this does not imply that politicians disregard the public altogether. Elections constrain politicians by signaling the boundaries of public opinion. Politicians act as if it is meaningful to think of policies favored by majorities of voters. They pay attention to election outcomes, and believe that elections provide useful information. For instance, the interpretation of elections affects how members of Congress construct their policy agendas, committee preferences, staffs, and provisions of constituency services.[15] Politicians make inferences about elections by relying on evidence such as patterns of party support across demographic groups, the magnitude of victory, and comparisons with elections past. Politicians do feel constrained by election outcomes, and they have consistent ways of making inferences about the electorate. But their analysis of voters does not correspond perfectly to those of political scientists because they are forecasting future mobilization as well as current opinion; they recognize that politics is more complicated and dynamic than a single public opinion poll.

Mandate rhetoric is part of a larger dialogue about how politicians view themselves, their political parties, and their future. Elections help a president understand his place in the political landscape, and this understanding conditions his policy behavior.[16] The president is representing his constituents, but this process is complicated by the uncertainties and ambiguities inherent in political life. When we understand mandates from the point of view of the politicians themselves, we see that representation depends upon how voters send signals and how politicians interpret them.

RETHINKING OUR METHODOLOGICAL APPROACH

Rethinking mandates conceptually implies that we rethink our methodological approach. If mandates were understood simply as statements of fact about voter preferences, then a quantitative analysis of public opinion surveys would be the obvious methodological approach. On the other hand, if mandates are based in the interpretation of election outcomes, then we need to see elections as politicians see them. We must examine mandate rhetoric and learn about specific historical cases. If mandates are strategic political calculations, then we should be able to construct a theoretical model that captures the strategy underlying the choices and decisions of politicians independent of place and time. Quantitative data can be employed to test the empirical predictions of this model against alternative explanations.

In this book, I examine electoral mandates using multiple methodological approaches: quantitative, qualitative, and formal.[17] I begin with a formal model of election outcomes and mandate claims, to provide a theory of agenda setting that is parsimonious and generalizable over time. By attending to basic sequences of interaction and simple assumptions about preferences, we can more easily separate the consequential parts of the detailed story of various elections from the parts that have little to do with electoral mandates. I then use quantitative data and case studies to check whether the basic assumptions of the model are reasonable and to test the empirical expectations of the model against alternative explanations. The quantitative analysis shows that mandate claims exhibit regularities over time that make them empirically predictable events. The case studies provide a closer look at the interpretations of politicians and the understanding that they have of their own motivations, choices, and environmental constraints.

CHAPTER OUTLINE

In chapter 2, I present a model that explains postelection agenda-setting behavior as a function of the president's popular support and of his expectations about Congress. If most politicians believe that there is strong public support for the president's initiatives, then the president has an incentive and an opportunity to change the policy agenda. Members of Congress will go along rather than risk being punished in future elections for thwarting the popular will. However, the model also identifies the conditions under which presidents with more moderate public support will still have an incentive to declare a mandate. The presentation of the model remains on an informal level throughout the chapter, while the technical details appear in an appendix at the end of the chapter.

Chapter 3 describes how politicians make inferences about election outcomes. The political psychology of elites is important because a president will declare a mandate only when policy explanations for victory dominate postelection analysis of the outcome. Politicians examine different pieces of evidence, from the margin of victory to an analysis of how different demographic groups cast their votes, to infer how much support the president has on various issues. The motivations of voters may be unclear at the individual level, but politicians readily analyze aggregate data to make forecasts about whether the president can rally majority support behind any issue. In some elections, little information is revealed about the potential for policy mobilization because the outcome is attributed to something like the triumph of negative campaigning, poor strategy on the part of the opposition, or other elements that are unrelated to substantive issues. In others, campaigns oriented around issues, patterns of coalition support, and the magnitude of victory suggest the broad parameters of public support for the president's agenda.

In chapter 4, I provide empirical support for the theory presented in chapter 2 by using aggregate data on presidential elections from 1828 to 1996 to show that mandate claims are predictable events. Presidents have put major policy changes on the national agenda in twenty-four of the forty-three elections, on issues such as slavery, the gold standard, civil rights, war, and taxes. I examine how well these mandate claims are predicted by statistical models based on the president's magnitude of victory, the strength of the president's party in Congress, and his place in the political party system. I conclude that presidential agenda-setting behavior is best predicted by a statistical model that incorporates the basic elements of the formal model.

Chapters 5, 6, and 7 present case studies of eight recent presidential elections. This historical analysis complements the aggregate data analysis by providing evidence of the interpretations and calculations of politicians at the individual level. Chapter 5 presents the elections of Dwight Eisenhower, Lyndon Johnson, and Ronald Reagan, each of whom claimed a mandate after an election in which the estimate of public support on the issues was relatively high.

Chapter 6 analyzes the elections of Harry Truman and Bill Clinton, two presidents whose mandate claims were based upon more modest public support and the benefit of unified government. Chapter 7 describes the elections of John Kennedy, Jimmy Carter, and George Bush, three presidents who did not claim mandates.

In the concluding chapter, I address the normative implications of this theory of presidential mandates. I argue that both shared information about the electorate and party competition keep the president and other politicians within certain boundaries with respect to their policy agenda. A new president cannot create a mandate for himself simply by declaring one. He cannot stray far from public opinion, for a mandate claim is a claim about voters. Yet unless we take the Burkean view that representatives should not be bound to constituency opinion, we are still left with the question of how to make elections better signals. We would do well to reform the process so that all politicians receive higher quality and more representative information about their constituents.

TWO | # Elections and Presidential Agenda Setting

Elections change national policy in two ways. First, turnover can shift the policy preferences of those in office; a new cast of characters yields new policy directions. Second, electoral campaigns and outcomes can signal public enthusiasm for policy change, and elected officials can respond with changes in the national policy agenda, whether or not those changes match their personal policy preferences. Mandate claims stem from both of these mechanisms. Presidents gauge support in Congress, and they look to the election outcome to read public support for their agenda.

REALIGNING ELECTIONS AND POLICY CHANGE

The notion that some elections lead to more significant policy changes than others is not new; both elections and presidents have been categorized according to how much they represent a radical break from the past. Realignment theory is perhaps the most prominent theory of elections and policy change and is a natural place to begin thinking about the impact of elections on presidential agenda-setting. Realigning elections or eras are marked by intense disruptions of traditional patterns of voting behavior, high levels of voter participation and issue-related voting, and ideological polarization between political parties.[1] They result in durable changes in the party balance of the electorate. At these times, congressional elections are national rather than local in character, turnover on congressional committees is high, and party voting increases rapidly.[2] Whether we focus on changes in the terms of political conflict, the balance of partisan identification in the electorate, or shifting coalitions of party support, it is clear that the eras surrounding the elections of 1828,

1860, 1896, and 1932 represented major changes in the structure of party conflict and led to major changes in the national policy agenda.

The elections before and after these four critical elections are by no means dull and uninteresting. V. O. Key, one of the earliest proponents of realignment theory, observed that

> the popular majority does not hold together like a ball of sticky popcorn. Rather, no sooner has a popular majority been constructed than it begins to crumble. . . . A series of maintaining elections occurs only in consequence of a complex process of interaction between government and populace in which old friends are sustained, old enemies are converted into new friends, old friends become even bitter opponents, and new voters are attracted to the cause—all in proper proportions to produce repeatedly for the dominant party its apparently stable and continuing majority.[3]

While realignment theory is focused on critical elections, it also delineates a cycle or pattern of elections. The majority or dominant party has a period of stability often followed by temporary losses of governmental control and a period of decay before the next major realignment.[4] Elections are classified as "converting" if the majority party stays in power, but voter loyalties shift; as "deviating" if a new majority party comes to power, though voter loyalties remain the same; and as "maintaining" if the majority party stays in power and voter loyalties remain the same.[5] Finally, the notion of "dealignment" has emerged, to note elections or eras in which party loyalty has little meaning for the electorate.[6]

ELECTIONS AND PRESIDENTIAL LEADERSHIP

An alternative approach would be to classify presidents according to the political opportunities they face. Stephen Skowronek, for example, argues that presidential leadership is best understood by taking into account two major aspects of the political context: the president's opposition to or affiliation with the dominant political party regime and the extent to which this dominant regime is vulnerable or resilient.[7] Knowing both the president's place in the party system and the stability and strength of that system forms our expectations for presidential leadership. Leaders who come to power as the old regime crumbles make the most changes. They are opposed to an old order that is thoroughly discredited and therefore have the greatest opportunities to build parties, expand the office of the presidency, and enact major policy changes. It is no coincidence that they are also the presidents who win realigning elections—Jackson, Lincoln, and Roosevelt.[8]

In fact, Skowronek's four categories of presidential leadership correspond closely to realignment theory. The "reconstructive" leaders just mentioned are all presidents elected in realigning elections. "Preemptive" leaders come to power after "deviating" elections, when voter loyalties remain the same—the regime is resilient—but voters have nonetheless formed a majority for a candidate of the opposing or weaker party. To broaden their own base of support, preemptive leaders must play upon or redefine partisan and ideological coalitions. "Affiliated" presidents are those who follow "maintaining" elections. Since they are affiliated with the dominant party regime and since that regime is resilient, they draw upon current configurations of ideology and interest rather than create new coalitions. They move policy by demonstrating the continued vitality of the ideas and solutions of the dominant party regime. Finally, "disjunctive" presidents rule after "converting" elections in which the majority party wins at the same time voter loyalties are shifting. Since they are aligned with a party regime that is increasingly discredited, they have trouble gaining credibility for policy leadership.

A MICROLEVEL MODEL OF ELECTIONS AND POLICY CHANGE

From the campaign to the outcome, elections send signals about the vulnerability of political parties and their policies and the place of the winning candidate in the party system. However, it remains unclear how to predict where a new president should be placed without an understanding of how politicians themselves assess the vulnerability of partisan regimes. In addition, the concept of "dominant" parties is complicated by periods in which the two parties are fairly competitive below the presidential level and by periods in which partisanship in the electorate is waning.[9] Finally, if our goal is to understand when presidents will ask for major policy changes, and when they will link these to their understanding of voters, then neither realignment theory nor existing theories of presidential leadership will suffice.

In particular, while all realignments are mandates, not all mandates are realignments. Several presidents (Eisenhower, Johnson, and Clinton, to name a few recent examples) placed major policy changes on the national agenda after *non*-realigning elections. Some, like Clinton, asked for major policy changes after winning with less than 50 percent of the popular vote. Furthermore, presidents who are grouped together in Skowronek's leadership categories vary with respect to their agenda-setting behavior. For instance, Lyndon Johnson and John Kennedy were both presidents affiliated with a resilient political regime; nevertheless Johnson placed major policy changes on the agenda while Kennedy did not. Presidential personality might be offered as an answer, but there does not seem to be a clear difference between those personality types who ask for policy changes and those who do not.

In this chapter, I present an alternative theoretical framework for examining the relationship between elections and presidential policy behavior. This microlevel model describes the logic of post-election agenda-setting behavior and the ways in which this behavior is dependent upon forecasts of popular and legislative support for new initiatives. In the context of this model, presidential mandates are both statements about political reality and strategic calculations. They are statements about political reality in the sense that elections are the major and most pertinent opportunity for politicians to take the pulse of the electorate. They are strategic political calculations because the institutional environment shapes when it is or is not in the president's best interest to place a policy change on the agenda. Although my discussion of the model will remain informal, the technical details are appended to the end of the chapter. In chapter 3, I describe how politicians interpret election outcomes and estimate the likelihood that the president has majority support for a policy initiative. In subsequent chapters, I test the predictions generated by the model using aggregate data from elections since 1828 and case studies in the post-Roosevelt era.

The Logic of Agenda Setting

When presidents claim mandates, they are taking the first step toward capitalizing on the political opportunities created by their election victory. Naturally, some presidents will enjoy a more favorable alignment of political forces and will have better opportunities than others. To understand how elections shape the president's agenda-setting power, I propose that we take the perspective of an individual president. What are the calculations that he must make in deciding on a course of policy? How do his inferences about public opinion shape his decision to place a major policy change on the agenda? How might Congress respond to his initiatives? Does he risk asking for a policy that is at odds with what the public seems to want?

Presidents as well as congressmen and women make inferences about election outcomes in order to learn what voters think and care about.[10] As David Mayhew observed, "Nothing is more important in Capitol Hill politics than the shared conviction that election returns have proven a point."[11] The lessons that politicians take away from the election determine whether presidents are willing to take bold initiatives, as well as whether legislators are inclined to support them. The model that follows shows how forecasts about public and congressional preferences affect the payoffs that the president receives for different courses of action. It exposes the logic of postelection agenda setting and predicts agenda-setting behavior across presidencies.

Players and Preferences

For the discussion that follows, I assume there are two major actors, the president and Congress, where the latter may be thought of as the median voter of the majority party of Congress. Obviously, neither the president nor Congress is a unitary actor in a strictly descriptive sense. Many of the president's decisions involve his advisors and other actors in the executive branch of government. Congress consists of 535 individual members and two distinct chambers. Nonetheless, the goal of the following exercise is to derive the logic of postelection agenda setting from simple assumptions.

The president's decision to claim a mandate is based upon a fundamental calculus: whether the ultimate policy outcome will reflect his own preferences or at least shift public policy away from the status quo in his direction. To make this calculation, he uses four pieces of information: his own policy preferences, the location of the status quo, the preferences of Congress, and his perception of public support on the issue at hand. Whether he has an incentive to proceed depends upon these parameters. He has a strong incentive to avoid claiming a mandate if it looks like he will fail to move the status quo toward his ideal point.

We should not assume that the preferred policy positions of a new president and Congress are identical. The electoral system is designed so that it is likely the president and Congress will differ. The aggregation of district medians is not likely to match the national median voter. In addition, the president and the median voter in Congress will differ if voters do not consistently evaluate all candidates on the basis of ideology. Voters might vote for the president on the basis of policy but vote for their member of Congress on the basis of pork brought to the district. If the president's party controls both chambers of Congress, the distance between a new president and Congress will most likely be smaller than if the president's party controls only one or no chambers of Congress. Again, however, members of the same party may be elected for different reasons.

The Role of Public Opinion

Let us assume that the status quo and the most preferred policy positions of both the president-elect and the new Congress are common knowledge. This is a reasonable assumption because the president and members of Congress are likely to have staked out positions on any issue for which the president might claim a mandate. The degree of popular support for the president's position, however, is not known with certainty. Rather, policy support is inferred or estimated on the basis of the election outcome. Politicians take an outcome that is a function of many variables and forecast who would win majority support in a policy battle over this single issue. A useful analogy may be to treat the election outcome as an observed dependent variable in an equation in which the independent variables and regression weights on the independent variables are not known with certainty. For the sake of simplicity, assume that both the president and Congress share a common estimate of the likelihood that the president could mobilize a majority of voters. Both sides have an incentive to obtain a reliable estimate of this key parameter because the balance of opinion in the electorate determines the outcome of a legislative showdown between them. But since both the president and Congress remain uncertain about exactly what the public prefers, the contest between them is technically described as a "game" in which the two parties share symmetric information with uncertainty.

When a president declares a mandate, he makes a claim that the people elected him to change policy in a substantial way. The task of both the president and Congress is to forecast the probability that he is right, the probability that, if conflict ensued, mobilization of the public would result in affirmation of the president's preferred position. Both sides must estimate what would happen if the issue were to become salient and voters were mobilized. In other words, who would win in a contest between the two parties if the president or members of Congress "go public"? The likelihood that a president can mobilize voters is large if it appears that he already has the backing of a majority of voters for his policy or if he can make the issue salient or change preferences enough to win support of a majority in the future. Thus, the larger the magnitude of victory, and the more plausible a policy explanation of the outcome, the more confidence he has in his ability to mobilize voters.

Forecasting the outcome of mobilization around a particular issue involves estimates of voter preferences as well as the president's ability to communicate or make good on threats against members of Congress. To the extent that personality matters, it is factored into estimates of the likelihood that the president can mobilize voters in the future. Being a great communicator is of little value if the evidence about public preferences for the president's policy is weak or nonexistent. Empirical studies of presidential success in Congress confirm that the president's personal skills are of peripheral importance. Those presidents reputed to be highly skilled don't win consistently more often than expected given other factors, such as the party balance in Congress and the normal cycle of influence over the term.[12]

Figure 2.1 Presidential Agenda Setting

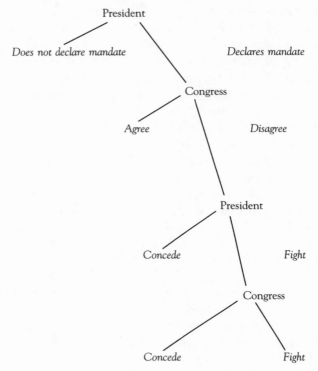

The Basic Model

The agenda-setting process proceeds in four stages (fig. 2.1). In the first stage the new president decides whether or not to claim a mandate, thereby placing a major policy change on the legislative agenda. If the president does not claim a mandate for a large policy change, then there is no large policy change in this area. Either the status quo is maintained or incremental change takes place over a longer period of time.

If the president declares a mandate, the game proceeds to a second stage. Congress either agrees with the president's declaration, in which case the new policy is implemented, or disagrees. The model assumes that the president proposes and Congress disposes. Congress is not able to offer a counterproposal; rather, it must always choose between enacting the president's policy or fighting it. The president suffers no loss of utility whenever his policy is implemented. His best outcome is to enact his policy regardless of whether he actually has an electoral coalition behind him.

For Congress, however, the attraction of the proposed policy depends on (1) the policy's proximity to Congress's ideal point and (2) the state of public opinion toward the policy. In terms of the model, the payoffs from the policy are a function of the distance between Congress's position and the president's position *and* the likelihood that the president's proposal is supported by a majority of the electorate. Whether the president really has a mandate depends on whether he can mobilize voters to his side, but this is a state of the world that politicians can estimate only with uncertainty. When the president truly possesses a mandate and Congress believes this to be so, then Congress is better off agreeing immediately to his proposal. On the other hand, if Congress blunders by agreeing to a shift in policy when there is in fact little popular support, it is punished in the next election for misreading its constituents' preferences.

If Congress refuses to go along with the president, we move to the third stage of the game. In the face of conflict, the president has the choice of either backing down or fighting. If the president concedes, then the status quo results but the president loses some political capital and stature in the process. For its part in calling the president's bluff, Congress gains popularity.

If the president refuses to yield to Congress, we reach the fourth and final stage of the game. The ball is back in Congress's court, as it must choose to back down or fight. Backing down involves accepting the president's policy and suffering a loss in reputation for having delayed the legislative process. As in the second stage of the game, Congress suffers if it opposes a policy that is supported by the electorate or if it supports an unpopular policy. Backing down when there is strong popular support means it loses only the costs of protesting in the first round. Backing down when there is weak popular support means it suffers punishment for agreeing to the "wrong" thing. This is a more severe punishment.

Fighting, on the other hand, means the issue stays on the agenda, and the expected utilities of the actors are dependent upon their forecast about the eventual disposition of the voters. In the last stage, the expected value of the fight, the outcome of the contest, is located somewhere between the preferred positions of the president and Congress. If the likelihood that the president can mobilize voters to his side is greater than 50 percent, then the expected value of the outcome will be closer to the president's preferred policy position. If the likelihood that the president can mobilize voters is less than 50 percent, then the expected value of the outcome will be closer to Congress's preferred policy position.

Popular Mandates, Bargained Mandates, and Winners without Mandates

The president and Congress must select their best strategy by anticipating each other's choices and assessing the outcomes those choices will yield. This process of reasoning from possible outcomes to best choices is know as backward induction. Given the structure of this model, when will the president claim a mandate for a large and new policy change? A formalization of the game between the president and Congress is provided at the end of this chapter. Backward induction yields three types of presidents that correspond to three basic postelection contexts. The first type are those presidents who claim mandates by virtue of their strong popular support; in this case Congress has an incentive to be on the right side of the issue. Any time there is a greater than 50 percent chance that the president can mobilize a majority of voters, the president declares a mandate and he is successful in Congress. The intuition here is quite simple. If the actors believe that the president has strong electoral support and that he can mobilize voters, then it is better for most members of Congress to be on the right side of the issue than fight for the status quo or another alternative. For this type of president, the magnitude of public support trumps consideration of the distance between the president and Congress. Beliefs about the public drive his political opportunity. Though the elections of Dwight Eisenhower, Lyndon Johnson, and Ronald Reagan were certainly different from each other, they all share this basic logic.

The second type are those presidents who declare mandates, knowing they will have a fight (due to only moderate popular support) and forecasting that the outcome will nevertheless be closer to their ideal point than the status quo. We might refer to these as "bargained" mandates, since the outcome lies somewhere between the president and Congress. An example would be the case where the preferences of members of Congress are located between the status quo and the president. Even if Congress gets close to its ideal policy, the president is better off than with the status quo. In general, for presidents whose probability of mobilizing public support is less than 50 percent, the decision to place a major policy change on the agenda will be a tradeoff between the amount of electoral support and the ideological closeness between the president and Congress. Presidents like Bill Clinton or Harry Truman who can make a decent case about the issues behind their election declare mandates partly because of the perceived support of their fellow partisans in Congress.

Finally, there are presidents who have no incentive to declare a mandate because of a postelection climate characterized by a combination of low to moderate popular support and congressional hostility. In this situation, the president has no incentive to place a policy change on the agenda because Congress will always fight, and rather than fight to an outcome worse than the status quo, the president anticipates conceding in the second to last stage of the game. When a president does not claim a mandate for a large policy change, there is either no change or incremental change. John Kennedy, Jimmy Carter, and George Bush all faced this kind of postelection context.

A president whose likelihood of mobilizing a majority is zero will not claim a mandate; Congress never agrees and the president is forced to concede in the end. A president who lies about his public support will fail miserably right at the beginning of his term. On the other hand, when he has less than a 50 percent chance of mobilizing voters in the future, the president may use his ideological closeness with Congress to compensate for the fragility of his electoral victory. And when he has a greater than 50 percent chance of mobilizing voters in the future, the president need not consider Congress at all.

*

Like realignment theory, the model in this chapter presents a framework for viewing elections and policy change. Unlike realign-

ment theory, however, my model focuses on the preferences and perceptions of the politicians who must set the policy agenda. In terms
of the model, a realigning election occurs when estimates of public
support are high and, due to turnover, the new president is close to
his party in Congress. However, the equilibria point to other kinds
of elections after which policy change is likely, though perhaps not
as pronounced as in realigning elections. Bill Clinton's victory in
1992 is representative of the class of elections in which a moderate
level of electoral support may be combined with a friendly Congress
to produce policy change. With Nixon in 1972 and Reagan in
1980, the president and Congress were not close ideologically, but
the estimate of public support was high and the president placed a
policy change on the agenda. Lyndon Johnson had strong popular
and congressional support, and he placed major policy changes
on the agenda. With the possible exception of Reagan's election
in 1980, none of these elections are understood as realignments.
Yet all represent cases where the president asked for major policy
changes.

Similarly, the equilibria of the model remind us that even presidents who are similarly situated in the party system will vary with
respect to the magnitude of their policy initiatives. For instance, according to Skowronek, Presidents Lyndon Johnson and John Kennedy and Presidents Jimmy Carter and Herbert Hoover are pairs of
presidents with the same leadership project.[13] Hoover and Carter
came to power aligned with a regime that was increasingly if not
thoroughly discredited. They had trouble gaining credibility for their
point of view and reified technique (administrative methods, good
government, etc.) as they struggled to lead. Hoover asked for major
policy changes; Carter did not. As mentioned earlier, Johnson and
Kennedy were both affiliated with the dominant political regime yet
Johnson asked for changes while Kennedy did not. Variation in
agenda-setting behavior is best explained by estimates of popular support, the relative ideological positions of the president, Congress,
and the status quo, and the president's incentive to avoid failure at
the beginning of his term.

The agenda-setting model depends on two parameters: the likelihood that a president can mobilize majority support in the elector-

ate and his ideological support in Congress. In order to generate empirical predictions from the model, we must know how politicians draw inferences from election returns. In the next chapter, I address this process of political inference. Election outcomes are noisy and ambiguous as signals of the electorate's concerns and intentions. But politicians have every incentive to learn the right explanation because they need this information to take the kinds of actions that will get them reelected. Their interpretation of the election determines their calculations of the payoffs for different courses of action.

APPENDIX: A GAME THEORETIC MODEL OF PRESIDENTIAL MANDATES
Players and Preferences

I assume there are two players, the president and Congress, where the latter is defined as the median voter of the majority party of Congress. The players have most-preferred policy points denoted X_P and X_C on a unidimensional policy continuum, where the status quo is 0. The policy positions of the president and members of Congress are a function of relatively stable partisan and ideological considerations. The utility for a particular policy position is a function of both sincere preferences and an understanding of how constituency policy preferences will affect the individual's prospects for election. The president's utility does not incorporate expectations about congressional reaction; he does not endorse what Congress would do anyway, in order to make himself look good. The preferred policy positions of a new president and Congress are not identical, though $(X_P - X_C)$ will likely be smaller under unified government.

The basic utility of each actor is the absolute value of the distance between his or her own preferred position and the status quo. I make two further assumptions without loss of generality. The ideal point of the president is constrained to be positive ($X_P \geq 0$). In addition, Congress's ideal point is constrained to be to the left of or equal to that of the president ($X_C \leq X_P$). If the status quo remains, the president's utility is $-X_P$ and Congress's utility is $-|X_C|$. If the president gets the mandate policy he most prefers he loses nothing, but Congress loses the distance between its preferred position and that of the president, $(X_P - X_C)$. If Congress gets its ideal policy, it suffers no utility loss, while the president loses $(X_P - X_C)$.

Either a majority of voters prefer the president's policy position or a majority do not. This preference is generally not known with certainty. Let the parameter alpha (α) denote the probability that the president has the support of a majority of voters. Though I use "strength" and "probability" interchangeably, the underlying popular support variable is assumed to be dichotomous. Alpha is a summary statistic gleaned from the election that determines the expected value of conflict when the issue is made salient and voters are mobilized. Alpha attenuates the utility of the actors, depending upon the credibility of the president's assertion that he has the support of the voters.

The president suffers no utility loss whenever his policy is implemented. For Congress, however, the payoffs from agreeing to the mandate policy are a function of both the distance between its position and the president's position $(X_P - X_C)$ and the likelihood that the president has majority popular support (α). If the state of the world is such that the president can mobilize voters to his side, then the Congress is better off in the future agreeing to the president's position now. On the other hand, if Congress agrees when there is little popular support, it will be punished by constituents. Thus, the expected utility of Congress for agreement is:

$$(1 - \alpha) [-(X_P - X_C)] + \alpha [0]$$
$$(1) \qquad = -(1 - \alpha)(X_P - X_C)$$

When $\alpha = 1$, equation 1 is equal to 0. When $\alpha = 0$, equation 1 is the loss $-(X_P - X_C)$.

Legislators estimate not only constituent preferences but the likelihood that these preferences will actually matter in future evaluations. The credibility of the president's assertion affects both of these calculations. X_C is the result of sincere preferences and Congress's estimate of constituency preferences during the election campaign. Alpha then modifies their overall utility by forecasting the issue's importance in the future.

If Congress challenges the president, the balance of opinion in the electorate determines the outcome in a fight between the two actors. The expected value of this conflict is a point in the region between the policy preferences of the two actors. The expected value of that conflict, X_F, is equal to $\alpha X_P + (1 - \alpha)X_C$. When $\alpha = 1$, then $X_F = X_P$, and the president's policy results. When $\alpha = 0$, then $X_F = X_C$, and Congress's policy results. Therefore, if α is greater than 0.5, this point will be closer to the president's preferred position (X_P) than to the Congress's preferred position (X_C). If α is less than 0.5, then the president suffers more, because X_F is located closer to X_C than X_P.

The utility of each actor when X_F results is the difference between his or her preferred position and X_F. For the president, this difference is ($X_P - X_F$), and for Congress it is ($X_F - X_C$) since $X_C \leq X_F \leq X_P$. Fighting means the following expected policy utility loss for the president:

$$-(X_P - X_F)$$
$$= -(X_P - [\alpha X_P + (1 - \alpha)X_C])$$
$$= -(X_P - \alpha X_P - (1 - \alpha)X_C)$$
$$(2) \qquad = -(1 - \alpha) \, (X_P - X_C)$$

The utility loss for Congress is:

$$-(X_F - X_C)$$
$$= -([\alpha X_P + (1 - \alpha)X_C] - X_C)$$
$$= -(\alpha X_P + X_C - \alpha X_C - X_C)$$
$$(3) \qquad = -\alpha \, (X_P - X_C)$$

The Basic Model

Figure 2.2 reproduces the agenda-setting game with the payoffs for each actor. In this model, the most preferred policy positions of both the president-elect and Congress are common knowledge. Alpha, the indicator of the strength of the president's popular support on a specific policy, is inferred on the basis of the election outcome. The utilities of the actors depend upon a state of nature, where the president has majority popular support with probability α and less than majority support with probability $(1 - \alpha)$. I assume that both the president and Congress share a common estimate of α. I

Figure 2.2. Presidential Mandates: Extensive Game Form

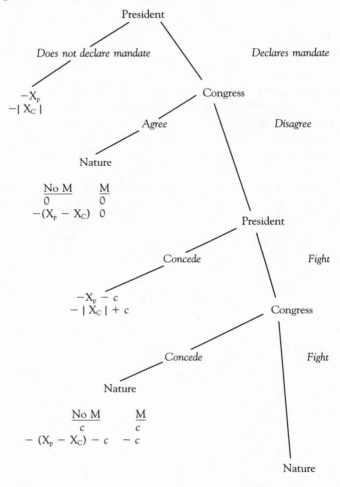

X_p = President's ideal point for mandate policy
  $X_p \geq 0$; $X_p \geq X_C$

X_C = Congress's ideal point for mandate policy
  Congress = Median voter of majority party

Nature:
The probability that a president has an electoral mandate (M) is α.
The probability that the president has no electoral mandate (No M) is $(1 - \alpha)$.

c = resource/reputation costs

also assume that estimates of α are not a function of the distance between the actors' preferred policy positions ($X_P - X_C$). For the purposes of the model, it is irrelevant if the president and members of Congress share inaccurate information.

The final set of parameters are political costs, such as the time, energy, and resources involved in arguing and fighting. These costs ensure that the actors are never indifferent to the choice between early acceptance of an outcome that they are certain will result after a fight and fighting for the outcome. For example, Congress will always prefer agreeing that the president has a mandate to wasting resources on a fight with the same end result. Political costs may also include the price of having the other actor call your bluff in front of colleagues and constituents. For the president, for example, it would be better never to declare a mandate than to declare a mandate and be forced to concede that the claim was unfounded. I assume for convenience that political costs (c) are equivalent at all stages of the game, for both actors.

In the first stage of the agenda-setting game, the new president decides whether to claim a mandate. If he does not place a policy change on the agenda, the status quo is maintained. As noted above, acceptance of the status quo means the president's payoff is $-X_P$ and Congress's payoff is $-|X_C|$. Either or both actors' ideal points could be at the status quo. Empirically, it is unlikely that the president will advocate a status quo policy since mandates are by definition large policy departures.

If the president declares a mandate, the game proceeds to a second stage where Congress either agrees with the president, in which case the new policy is implemented, or Congress disagrees. In this model, Congress does not have the ability to offer a counterproposal. Once the agenda has been set by the president, Congress cannot propose a compromise; it must always choose between enacting the president's policy or fighting it. If Congress agrees, its payoffs are given by equation 1 above; the president suffers no loss of utility no matter what the value of α.

If Congress refuses to go along with the president, we move to the third stage of the game, where the president has the choice of either backing down or fighting. If the president concedes, then the status quo is maintained; Congress objected to his claim but did not offer an alternative. If he concedes, the president suffers a loss of reputation and has exhausted some political capital, while Congress gains reputation for calling his bluff.

If the president chooses to fight, we reach the fourth and final stage of the game where Congress must again decide whether to accept or contest the president's claim. As in the second stage, Congress suffers if it fights against strong popular support *and* if it agrees when popular support is weak. Backing down when there is strong popular support means Congress loses only the costs of protesting the original claim. Backing down when there is weak popular support means it suffers punishment for agreeing to the "wrong" thing in addition to the political costs.

The expected utilities of the actors depend on the state of nature, whether or not the president has popular support. The expected utility of Congress for concession is:

$$(1 - \alpha)[-(X_P - X_C) - c] + \alpha[0 - c]$$
$$(4) \qquad = -(1 - \alpha)(X_P - X_C) - c.$$

The expected utility of the president when Congress concedes is (c). He gets his policy and a reputation "bonus." Fighting, on the other hand, means the issue stays on the agenda. The expected value of the fight, X_F, is located between the preferred positions of the president and Congress. Each actor also loses political capital (c) in a fight. The expected utility of fighting for the president across the two states of nature is:

$$(1 - \alpha)[-(X_P - X_C) - c] + \alpha[0 - c]$$
$$= -(1 - \alpha)(X_P - X_C) - (1 - \alpha)c - \alpha c$$
$$= -(1 - \alpha)(X_P - X_C) - c + \alpha c - \alpha c$$
$$(5) \qquad = -(1 - \alpha)(X_P - X_C) - c.$$

For Congress, the expected utility of fighting is:

$$(1 - \alpha)[0 - c] + \alpha[-(X_P - X_C) - c]$$
$$= -c + \alpha c - \alpha(X_P - X_C) - \alpha c$$
$$(6) \qquad = -\alpha(X_P - X_C) - c.$$

Except for the inclusion of the cost parameters, these expected utilities are identical to the previously derived utilities for fighting in equations 1 and 2: $(X_P - X_F)$ and $(X_F - X_C)$, respectively.

Results

The president and members of Congress share an estimate of the probability that the president can mobilize a majority. Thus, the game is one of symmetric information with uncertainty. Payoffs for each actor are expected utilities across the two states of nature. In the last section, I presented expected utilities (1) for Congress whenever the mandate policy is implemented, and (2) for both actors when they fight in the last stage of the game. In all other cases, the payoffs do not depend on a move by nature.

Backward induction yields the following subgame perfect equilibria. If $\alpha > 0.5$, the president declares a mandate and Congress agrees. If the actors think that the president has the support of voters, then Congress has an incentive to go along with the president rather than face punishment by constituents in the future. When $\alpha = 0.5$, Congress is indifferent on the last move, but both conceding and fighting in the end are more costly than agreeing before the president fights.

When $\alpha < 0.5$, there are four different equilibrium regions. First, when α is less than $-X_C/(X_P - X_C)$, the president does not declare a mandate because he anticipates being forced to concede in the second to last stage of the game. The president anticipates conceding because he prefers the status quo to the outcome of a fight, X_F, which is to the left of the status quo. At the point $-X_C/(X_P - X_C)$, the expected value of a fight equals the status quo. (Set $X_F = \alpha X_P - (1 - \alpha)X_C$ equal to 0). At this point, the president is indifferent between fighting and conceding defeat in the third stage of the game.

In the second region, the president does not declare a mandate because losses incurred in a fight are higher than the losses incurred by doing nothing and staying at the status quo. This is the only case where the actors achieve an outcome that appears (on the basis of policy preferences) inferior for both of them. If Congress is at the status quo or just to the right of it, then the president may not declare a mandate because the costs of the fight outweigh the utility gained in the small shift from the status quo to the position of Congress. In other words, the president knows Congress most certainly will win, and its position is so close to the status quo that arriving at this outcome is not worth the cost of a fight.

In the third region, where α is greater than $(-X_C + c)/(X_P - X_C)$, the president declares a mandate and the expected value of a fight is better for him than the status quo. This region includes those cases where Congress is located between the status quo and the president ($X_C > 0$). When X_C is positive, even if Congress gets its ideal policy, the president is better off than with the status quo. This equilibrium also includes cases where X_C is to the left of the status quo, but X_F is to the right of the status quo. The point $(-X_C + c)/(X_P - X_C)$ is the point at which the president is indifferent between declaring and not declaring a mandate.

Finally, if α is greater than $-c/(2X_P - 2X_C) + 1/2$, then Congress agrees with the president. Congress would rather agree with the president than incur the cost of a fight. In other words, the cost of fighting the president is greater than utility lost by conceding to his position ($c > (X_P - X_C)$). When $\alpha = -c/(2X_P - 2X_C) + 1/2$, Congress is indifferent between agreeing and disagreeing with the president in the second stage of the game.

Elections select the new president and members of Congress, thus determining the policy preferences or ideal points of the actors in the model and the ideological distance between them. Elections also send signals to elected officials about the strength of public support for the president's policy agenda. According to the model, the president's behavior depends upon a tradeoff between the proximity of the actors' ideal points ($X_P - X_C$) and the strength of the president's public support (α). When $0 < \alpha < 0.5$, as α gets larger, the president is more likely to declare a mandate. As α decreases, so must the distance between the president and Congress in order for the president to declare a mandate.

According to the model, a president who is perceived to have strong popular support ($\alpha > 0.5$) has an incentive to declare a mandate. But a president also has an incentive to declare a mandate if placing an issue on the agenda and engaging Congress will shift policy outcomes closer to his ideal point. A president who does not declare a mandate can see that introducing an item on the agenda would make him worse off or no better off than keeping the status quo.

T H R E E | Political Inference

In the weeks following every presidential election, politicians and pundits analyze the meaning of the outcome. Politicians want to understand what happened because they condition their legislative and constituency service behavior on their beliefs about what matters to voters. They want to know how to build a strong case to their constituents for themselves as public leaders; they want to be reelected. But in drawing lessons from elections, politicians confront the problem of causal inference. Elections provide only a noisy and incomplete picture of the electorate's preferences.

In this chapter, I describe how politicians make inferences about election outcomes by addressing three major questions: What are the features of the election outcome that demand explanation? Why are few explanations offered, and, of those offered, why does one explanation tend to dominate all others? When will this dominant explanation attribute the president's victory to support for his policy agenda? The estimate of the president's ability to mobilize public support for policy change will be higher if his victory is attributed to his stand on the issues. This estimate of public support is important because it determines whether the president has an incentive to change the national policy agenda.

I begin with a brief discussion of how the varied perspectives of politicians shape the explanations they offer. I then explain why a conventional wisdom about the election emerges despite this variation. Politicians do offer self-serving explanations. But both publicly shared information about the outcome and the utilitarian incentive to get the story right or be punished at the polls in the future means that there will be a substantial amount of convergence toward a single explanation for victory. Next, I describe how the aspects of the election that demand explanation are those that are historically surprising, either because the margin of victory is large or because old patterns of voting behavior have been upset. Little attention is paid to events consistent with prior expectations. Finally, I argue that policy explanations of unusual or surprising events emerge when they are consistent with the content of the fall campaign and with the voting behavior of subgroups of the electorate. Politicians use patterns of partisan support across groups and comparisons with elections past to evaluate alternative explanations for victory.

FORMING THE CONVENTIONAL WISDOM ABOUT THE ELECTORATE
Participants and Points of View

The process of interpreting elections is conducted primarily inside the beltway. Its main participants are elected officials, their entourages, and the press, with additional contributions from political parties, advocacy groups, and academics. From this group, a collective conventional wisdom emerges. Although there is never perfect consensus about the meaning of any election outcome, there is almost always an understanding of the election that has the support of political actors, commentators, and analysts across the partisan spectrum. This interpretation may be thought of as the modal category of all possible explanations—the explanation that gains the most adherents, usually those in the middle of the ideological spectrum.

Though I speak generically of "politicians," some election interpreters are presidents (and their associates) and some are senators and representatives. The questions of interest to presidents may be broader than the questions that interest members of Congress. Within Congress, some election interpreters represent closely balanced constituencies, and others represent homogeneous constituencies. The view from a safe seat is surely different from the view from a competitive one.[1]

A more crucial distinction may be whether the election interpreter is one of the winners or one of the losers. Winning candidates tend to attribute their successes to themselves and the actions they took; losing candidates tend to blame their losses on impersonal factors beyond their control.[2] Wins are credited to things like constituency service or a good campaign; losses are a function of national trends or the unbeatable name recognition or spending of the opponent.[3]

Winners also tend to favor policy-oriented explanations. After the 1928 election, winner Herbert Hoover and fellow Republicans argued that the victory was the result of a general prosperity and satisfaction with their party's economic policies. Defeated Democrat Al Smith blamed the outcome on his Catholicism. Other Democrats blamed Smith's association with the Tammany Hall machine in addition to religious bigotry. After the election of Whig William Henry Harrison in 1840, Democratic Party newspapers, in reference to the campaign tactics of their opponent, wrote, "We have been sung down, lied down, and drunk down!"[4] The Whigs, on the other hand, referred to Harrison's victory as "the most important event in the political history of a great nation."[5]

Winning and losing factions *within* political parties also offer different kinds of explanations. Members of the losing party who opposed their nominee most vigorously in the primaries tend to offer an interpretation of the election that vindicates their earlier judgment. Often, they attribute the loss to a flawed party message, while others in their party will blame a bad campaign or the nominee himself. For instance, after defeat in the 1988 presidential election, liberal and conservative members of the Democratic Party were split over the meaning of the outcome. One activist, who had supported Jesse Jackson and eventually Michael Dukakis, remarked, "The problem with the Democratic Party this year was the person at the top of the ticket. I don't think it's philosophical. It was a badly run campaign."[6] Another Democrat, who had been agitating for his party to move in a conservative direction, said, "The first thing we've got to understand when you lose five out of six presidential elections, the longest losing streak since the Civil War, is that you need fundamental changes in message."[7]

Defining the Public

For the purpose of forecasting public support, not only those pressure groups and voters participating in this election but those who will participate in the next election make up the relevant public. The president has to forecast how the issues that mattered in this election will affect both his popularity throughout his term and his public support in the next election. In this sense, he must consider what academics have termed "latent publics" or "potential preferences."[8] The potential preferences of constituents are those that "leaders believe might easily be created either by interested parties dissatisfied with legislator's decisions or by future challengers searching for good campaign issues."[9] The president must anticipate the retrospective assessment that voters will make of his action or inaction on major policy changes.

The notion of a "public" that politicians are learning about raises an important normative and empirical observation. There are distinct differences between individuals who participate in politics and those who do not, particularly in terms of socioeconomic status. The least costly and most widely practiced forms of participation, such as voting, give politicians the fuzziest message, while more difficult forms of participation give precise but biased messages.[10] Politicians readily admit that the constituents and supporters that they see are not truly random samples. Outcomes in congressional districts that are viewed as representative of certain types of constituents may be more influential in determining the story of the election than outcomes in districts with less typical constituencies.[11] While a consistently biased electorate may be normatively undesirable, it does not pose any problem for political inference.

Convergence toward a Single Explanation for Victory

The varying perspectives of politicians influence the explanations that specific politicians offer, but they do not inhibit the construction of a conventional wisdom. There is a reason that politicians tend to converge on a single explanation for victory. Most of all, they seek politically useful information. This utilitarian attitude politicians bring to the task of inference creates strong incentives for accuracy. The interpretations are means to ends, to the end of policy enactment or to the end of reelection or to both. If an explanation is to be useful to the pursuit of policy goals, it must be convincing. Before others will go along, they must read the evidence from the election in the same way. Likewise, if an explanation is to be useful to the pursuit of reelection, it had best be right. Interpretations of elections are ideas on which politicians place their gambles. The better the ideas, the surer the bets.[12]

At the same time, in any given election postmortem, most of the interpretations politicians offer for election outcomes are self-serving. Recent decades have raised "spin control" to a high art. But the offer of self-serving explanations must be distinguished from their acceptance. As the dust clears from the election, everybody sends up a trial balloon, but just a few stay aloft. The explanations that endure are still self-serving for some, but they endure because they conform to a common reading of the evidence. The incentives for accuracy make consensus explanations possible.

Competition

Competition shapes the inference-making process, whether the use politicians make of interpretations is legislative or electoral. "Spin doctors" go to work immediately after the election, jockeying for the policy advantage that may be gained from a favorable interpretation of it. But the partisans of one side must contend with the partisans of the other side, putting quite a different light on the results. An incumbent who contents himself with an erroneous understanding of the election, whether out of ignorance, willfulness, or delusion, is always potentially vulnerable to a challenger with a credible argument that the officeholder has "lost touch" with his constituents. Moreover, because there is political benefit to be had from a favorable reading, there is incentive not only to extol the strengths of one's own claim but also to expose the weaknesses of an opponent's case. Competition puts a limit on just how self-serving an argument can be. To succeed in persuasion, and to maintain credibility, interpretations cannot stray too far from the facts.[13] This is a key reason why the interpretations of losing candidates are discounted in constructing a common understanding of the election. Without a clear political future, losing candidates are less constrained by a need to maintain credibility.

Shared Information

A second important feature of the process of electoral interpretation is informational symmetry. Except around the edges, the data that politicians use to construct a story of the election are common knowledge: national, state, and local election tabulations; national, state, and local polls reported in the press; and news accounts of national, state, and local political conditions. Private information exists, of course: private polls, focus groups, field reports from interest groups and parties, and the like. But private information contributes to the development of the conventional wisdom only when it is divulged, at which point it enters the public domain. For all intents and purposes, then, politicians construct explanations out of a shared body of evidence, and the common store of information pushes explanations away from motivational biases.

Contrary to popular belief, politicians cannot simply rely on public opinion polls, because polls do not make other sources of information (e.g., simple patterns of wins and losses) irrelevant. While polls can certainly be used to help test hypotheses about the election outcome, they do not provide perfect information. Often, pre- and post-election polls either do not exist or ask questions that provide only a partial test of an explanation. Below the national level, poll information is scarce and its quality is variable. Even supposing that question wording and order were not misleading, the poll results that are made public tend to be marginals or the simplest of cross-tabulations. Finally, the goal of politicians is to forecast future mobilization. Sources of evidence such as coalition behavior or the pattern of wins and losses for types of candidates according to ideology are easy to remember and use to judge trends. The best way for politicians to forecast the future is to examine multiple sources of data when testing their hypotheses and to rely on behavior such as votes rather than poll results.

Both competition and common information, then, incline politicians toward more rather than less accurate explanations of elections, even against ideological or other motivational leanings.[14] At the same time, competition and common information do not settle the question of the meaning of an election. Even though politicians draw from a common store of information, the evidence is nearly always limited and ambiguous. Likewise, even though politicians submit their positions to a competitive process of interpretation, there is rarely a single potential winner. Elections are complex events; their outcomes are nearly always overdetermined. Thus, there is no objectively most accurate explanation of an election. Ambiguity leaves room for debate.

Parsimony

If politicians have an incentive to be accurate, they also have a need to provide simple explanations. A parsimonious explanation is the account that requires the fewest counterfactual changes in voter behavior to reverse the outcome. In effect, politicians ask what actions might have been undone to yield the results they expected, to put the world right again. Explanations that require fewer actions to be undone are superior explanations.[15]

The preference for parsimonious explanation has greater cognitive justification than logical justification. Scientists almost universally prefer simpler explanations to more complex ones, but as philosophers of science have noted, there is scant logical reason for their prejudice. By all appearances, the scientist's bias toward parsimony rests on the conviction that the basic laws of the natural world are ultimately simple.[16] Politicians would seem to have no such illusions about the political world, which they no doubt see as exceedingly complex. If they, too, prefer more parsimonious explanations they must prefer them for their greater practicality. Politicians are busy people, with limited time and cognitive resources. Their interest in electoral interpretations is almost wholly utilitarian. Simple explanations are easier to conjure and evaluate; they demand less time and thought. Most important, simple explanations also yield clear advice.

For example, take the case where a conservative Republican wins the White House and seven prominent liberal Democratic incumbents in Congress lose their elections (as in 1980). A shift in the ideological orientation of the electorate could explain all of the outcomes. This explanation is preferred to a series of explanations that focus on either causes specific to the individual congressional districts or causes that explain the presidential victory separately from the congressional losses.[17] Moreover, politicians often go back and reinterpret the campaign after the outcome, perceiving electoral events as unfolding "in a regular or linear fashion according to a recognizable pattern with an alleged inner necessity. So that we get the impression that it really could not have happened otherwise."[18]

In general, knowledge of an outcome leads to overestimation of the probability that the outcome was likely to occur.

The simplicity of interpretation is reinforced by practical constraints. Stories about an election circulate within hours after the polls have closed; there is little time to develop a complex theory of the outcome. The set of plausible stories concerning voters and major policy changes is quite limited, since presidential candidates have only a few (if any) major policy changes that are actively promoted in their campaigns. Moreover, there is a decidedly "inside the beltway" character to the interpretation of an election. Journalists tend to rely on Washington insiders, and once a few insiders have spoken, other explanations tend to be ignored. For instance, according to a study of postelection coverage of the 1988 election, four out of five sources cited in major newspapers were Washington insiders, where insiders were defined as candidates, campaign staff, members of Congress, and national party leaders.[19] Journalists do not write at length about alternative explanations for electoral victory, particularly explanations that have not been offered up by an insider.[20]

Framing Questions around Political Change

From past experience, politicians already possess a working model of voting behavior. Therefore many aspects of an election outcome are not noteworthy because they only reinforce long-standing facts and generalizations about elections.[21] On the other hand, politicians are interested in any hint that voting patterns may be changing. Their preoccupation with political change means that two aspects of outcomes get the greatest amount of attention: changes that are surprising, in the sense that they deviate from historical patterns, and changes that are large in magnitude.

The Element of Surprise

Politicians are no different from anybody else in their tendency to focus attention on the unusual features of an event. Both philosophers who have studied causal inference normatively and psychologists who have studied it experimentally underline the salience of the unexpected in the construction of causal explanations. "Satisfactory explanations," the psychologists William Turnbull and Ben Slugoski argue, "resolve puzzles, thereby eliminating contrasts. . . . Events do not require explanation. Rather, contrasts between observed behavior and what would have been considered more normal need to be resolved."[22] People already know what to expect; the aim of explanation is to make sense of outcomes that are at variance with their received understanding of the world. "To explain a thing," notes the philosopher William Dray, "is sometimes merely to show that it need not have caused surprise."[23]

This observation suggests that there might often be elections in which there is nothing unusual to explain. If the overwhelming number of constituencies behave as they have always tended to behave, there are no surprises for which politicians need to account. Traditional patterns of voting and turnout are confirmed. There is nothing more to say. In later chapters, I argue that the presidential elections of 1960 and 1976 fall into this category. In other presidential elections, the element of surprise gives momentum to a president's mandate claims. Much of the significance of Ronald Reagan's 1980 victory was due to the fact that no one had predicted that his party would be a majority in the Senate or that Reagan would win 91 percent of the electoral college vote.

Politicians form their expectations about the election on the basis of historical experience and the events of the current campaign. In order for campaign expectations to significantly shape postelection analysis, the contrast between campaign expectations and the final outcome must be fairly dramatic. Harry Truman's victory in 1948 and the Republican Party takeover of the Senate in 1980 are recent examples. Yet, in most cases, what is unexpected given projections from the campaign is also unexpected given historical experience. It is therefore more common for politicians to define a normal outcome using historical patterns of institutional control and voting behavior. They are more likely to pose questions with a historical frame of reference ("Why did the West swing Democratic this year?") than they are to pose questions that lead to a contemporary comparison ("Why did the Republicans do worse in the West than they seemed to be doing heading into the balloting?"). Historical patterns are weighted more heavily because politicians want to know whether politics is changing in fundamental ways that affect their futures. They are careful to differentiate between idiosyncratic, short-term fluctuations and systematic, long-term changes. Historical evidence that is based on a large number of elections is a better benchmark for analyzing voting returns than are the events of the recent campaign.

In this sense, politicians appear to try to classify elections in the manner of realignment theorists. They seek to distinguish maintaining or deviating elections ("normal" politics and temporary reversals in party balance) from realigning or converting elections (both of which involve major changes in voter loyalties).[24] They have an intuitive sense of what the "normal vote" looks like.[25]

The most recent presidential elections are a convenient and typical basis of comparison. Recent elections may be used because of the similarities in the ideological orientation of the candidates or the characteristics of their constituencies. In 1992, Clinton was compared to Jimmy Carter, his party's last victorious candidate for the presidency and a fellow moderate southern governor. Incumbents running for reelection invariably have their second performance compared to their first. Bill Clinton's performance in 1996 was compared to his performance in 1992. Outcomes are more surprising to the extent that a candidate fares dramatically better or worse than he or his party did the last time around.

The Magnitude of Victory

The idea of "landslide" victories reminds us of the attention that politicians and other political observers pay to the magnitude of victory. Politicians have a tendency to equate large and significant effects with large and significant causes.[26] If big effects do signify big causes, politicians will prefer to concentrate on explaining significant deviations from the past rather than small ones. There is more information about systematic change in politics in larger scale events, both because major changes are less likely to occur than small changes and because small changes to historic voting patterns often cancel each other out. Politicians direct their attention to the most sweeping changes because there is more to learn from them and more to gain from them.

Any election outcome presents several puzzles that are of unequal consequence to politicians. Since politicians care about the policymaking import of the election, they want to understand the source of the most consequential change in the balance of power that results from the election. They will speculate most about the most dramatic institutional changes, and the interpretation they ultimately select will have to account for this change. Therefore, explaining a change in partisan control of a political institution, whether the House, the Senate, or the presidency, will preempt explaining a change in the partisan ratios in a legislative body. Attention to changes in party control or partisan ratios will preempt assessing the reasons for a change in the occupancy of significant positions within a legislature or of explaining a change in the rank-and-file membership of a lawmaking body. Politicians focus their theories on factors that might have produced the most significant changes, neglecting the other changes of lesser moment that might also have occurred.

Similarly, politicians want to identify the causes of shifts in partisan support of the greatest scope. Explaining a change in citizens' willingness to support one party rather than the other dominates speculation about voter turnout. Moreover, at the national level, explaining a change in the pattern of behavior—choice or turnout—across regions or states supersedes understanding the causes of a change in behavior by a demographic bloc, which, in turn, supersedes theorizing the causes of change in the behavior of particular constituencies. Politicians focus their theories on factors that might have produced the most sweeping changes, again neglecting the other changes of lesser scope that might also have occurred in the election.

In most cases, institutional and coalitional change will point politicians in the same direction. Changes in control of institutions, for example, are frequently accompanied by changes in the regional patterns of party support. Often enough, however, the magnitudes of institutional and coalitional change will be different. In such cases, the more significant outcome will dominate the framing of causal interpretations. By selecting one or a few contrasts between outcome and expectations as the subject for analysis, politicians radically reduce the number of causal candidates. The puzzle they choose to explain either holds some potential causes constant or treats some causes as "conditions"—surely necessary to the outcome, but not a point of contrast between the expected and actual outcomes.[27]

Forming Policy Explanations for Victory

Mandate claims are statements that the public wants a major policy change. The president's capacity to achieve his policy goals is enhanced if the conventional wisdom attributes his win to his policy positions. The precise explanation given for his victory—policy, character, negative campaigning, a good economy, etc.—depends on the substance of the campaign and the consistency of that explanation with both public opinion polls and the voting behavior of specific groups of voters. A president may win by a surprisingly large margin, but a policy explanation for his victory will not be compelling unless he campaigned on the issues and group voting patterns are consistent with this policy story.

Campaign Rhetoric

In general, if the president employed a campaign strategy that framed the voters' choice in terms of policy, his election is more likely to be viewed as a mandate.[28] I have already discussed candidate Bill Clinton's preelection attempt to frame the 1992 election as a popular mandate for his economic policies. In 1887, President Grover Cleveland devoted his entire annual message to Congress to the issue of reducing tariffs. He asked, "What is the use of being elected or re-elected unless you stand for something?"[29] Though he was defeated in 1888, he helped to frame the issue of the election. In 1916, Woodrow Wilson and the Democratic Party adopted the slogan "He kept us out of war" and promised that Wilson was the candidate of peace in the future. After Wilson's victory, observers noted that "the United States does not want to go to war, and the elections have clearly shown that the great mass of the Americans desire nothing so much as to keep out of the war. It is undoubtedly the cause of the President's reelection."[30]

Policy interpretations of elections are also more likely when an incumbent president campaigns on his record of policy accomplishments. Incumbents who declare mandates have an opportunity to complete or extend the policy agenda they initiated in their first term.[31] When an incumbent loses, the outcome is often treated as a rejection of his policies and, by implication, an acceptance of the challenger's proposed alternatives. In 1888, when Benjamin Har-

rison defeated incumbent Grover Cleveland, his victory was interpreted as a victory for protectionism because Cleveland had been
devoted to lowering the tariff. When Ronald Reagan won reelection
in 1984, he interpreted his reelection as an endorsement of the economic policy changes he made after his 1980 election.

The election is also more likely to be seen as a mandate for the
victor when opponents present sharply contrasting ideological positions during the campaign. The Democratic Party platform in 1964
was judged by some to be as ideologically moderate as the 1960 Democratic Party platform. However, in the campaign of 1964 the Democrats faced Senator Barry Goldwater and a Republican Party that had
moved markedly to the right since 1960. Therefore, when Lyndon
Johnson won, his victory was more easily attributed to popular support for his policy positions. In 1976, Jimmy Carter could not convincingly portray his election as a choice for a new policy direction
because his platform was similar to that of his opponent, Gerald Ford.
A change in the party controlling the presidency, like the defeat of
an incumbent, is more likely to signal a public desire for a shift in
policy. For this reason, the election of minority party presidents
within a dominant party or realignment regime (e.g., the elections
of Grover Cleveland and Woodrow Wilson in a Republican era) are
often perceived to be significant in policy terms.

Public Opinion and Voting Behavior

In order for policy interpretations of the election to take hold,
they must also be loosely consistent with the behavior of the electorate. It helps if the president's proposal is connected to identifiable
groups of voters whose leaders supported the issue during the campaign, and whose members subsequently voted for the winning candidate. For example, if the issue touches on the interests of labor,
we would expect to see strong support from voters in union households. In addition, the policy story must be consistent with public
opinion polls. Is the policy change consistent with voters' views of
the most important problem facing the nation? Is it one of the major
reasons why voters said they made the choice that they did? What
do a majority of voters prefer when asked directly about the policy
change? Finally, election observers examine the opinions and behav-

ior of swing voters and partisan independents. Since these voters are viewed as crucial in determining the outcome, their reasons for voting must be consistent with an electoral interpretation oriented around the desire for policy change.

Mill's Method of Agreement and Difference

In order to gauge the effect of policy preferences, politicians appear to follow what John Stuart Mill called the "joint method of agreement and difference." To identify the cause of an outcome, politicians discern what is common to all occurrences of the phenomenon (agreement) and what is lacking in all non-occurrences of the phenomenon (difference). They identify the common characteristics of voters whose behavior deviated from expectations and contrast them with the characteristics of voters whose behavior conformed to expectations. The "better" interpretations are those that most sharply define the peculiar constituencies and most sharply contrast them to the normal ones.[32]

The comparisons and contrasts might be made on a number of dimensions, each of which favors a particular kind of explanation. If the characteristics that unite the deviating constituencies and distinguish them from the normal constituencies are demographic, politicians are more likely to settle on an interpretation that centers on a pivotal issue. Politicians sort voters into groups according to age, gender, race, and social class, and they believe in the concept of group interests. When divisions appear along demographic lines, policy positions that appeal to these homogeneous interests must be a cause of the outcome. This is the type of interpretation with the greatest significance for policy.

If, on the other hand, the characteristics common to the odd constituencies and distinct from the regular constituencies are situational (a booming economy, a shared religiosity with the winning candidate, and so forth), politicians are less likely to identify issues as causes and more likely to cite other popular theories of voter behavior. "It was the economy in the industrial states" or "It was Smith's Catholicism" are explanations not lacking in policy content, but they provide a much noisier policy signal. Simply put, there are theories with long pedigrees that explain the outcome equally well without citing policy at all: for example, "The beneficiaries of a strong economy tend to support the incumbent party" and "Catholics tend to prefer other Catholics." Where the patterns of agreement and difference incline politicians to situational explanations, policy implications are diminished.

If, in a third instance, there are no characteristics common to deviating constituencies and distinct from normal constituencies, politicians favor more ephemeral causes internal to the campaign, such as the personal charm of the nominee or the strength of the campaign organization. If there is no relationship between demographics and outcomes or between situations and outcomes, the important causes must be idiosyncratic. Politicians have no strong theories about which types of voters are more or less susceptible to the wiles of a candidate or a media consultant.

Each of these attributions—to policy, to situation, or to idiosyncratic factors—is more or less compelling depending upon the events of the just-concluded campaign. For example, if there is a correspondence between the demographic characteristics of "swung" voters and the policy positions that the winning candidates emphasized in their campaigns, politicians will more confidently attribute the outcome to policy. When the voters' "response" matches the campaign's "stimulus," causal interpretations become all the more authoritative.[33]

Covariation and Positive Test Strategies

Politicians can also gauge the role of issues by comparing the current election outcome with those in the past. Politicians test their explanations by examining other instances in which the event has occurred or is expected to occur, making it less likely that they encounter falsifying evidence. They focus on the co-occurrence of two events, discounting cases in which one event occurs and the other does not.[34] Suppose, for example, it is hypothesized that the Democrats lost control of the Senate because there was an ideological shift on the part of voters. Politicians are likely to test this hypothesis by looking exclusively at past cases of ideological change, to see if party control of the Senate also changed. However, they are likely to ignore past cases in which party control changed without a corresponding ideological shift.[35]

This "hypothesis confirming" or positive test strategy is evident when politicians make historical comparisons on the basis of margins of victory. In 1952, Eisenhower's large percentage of the popular vote—55 percent—was compared to the large popular vote/mandate elections of Roosevelt in 1932 and 1936, as evidence that Eisenhower must also have a mandate. Journalists did not take into account elections like that of Harding in 1920, in which a large popular vote margin (60.3 percent) was not associated with a mandate. Nor did they mention close mandate elections like 1916 or 1892. The same heuristic helps to distinguish elections that do not provide mandates. John Kennedy's election was compared to that of 1888 based on his small margin of victory in the popular vote. His victory was also compared to 1916, when the election was not decided until early the day after the election, with the state of California tipping the balance.[36] Jimmy Carter's victory in 1976 was compared to Kennedy's victory in 1960 because the race was close and voters seemed to break along party and ideological lines.[37]

Such a strategy does not necessarily lead to error or inefficiency.[38] A positive test strategy reveals more false positives than false negatives. It protects politicians from making the mistake of attributing the change in control of the Senate to ideological shifts when in fact it was not caused by ideological shifts but by something else. It does not protect politicians against the mistake of overlooking ideology as a cause when in fact ideology does make a difference. If the former mistake is more consequential than the latter, the heuristic is not inappropriate. In addition, the probability of receiving falsifying evidence may be greater with a positive test strategy in the case where the event to be explained is an outcome that occurs infrequently (less than 50 percent of the time). The historically unexpected outcomes that politicians attempt to explain certainly fit this criterion (or they would not be perceived as abnormal).

INFERENCES ABOUT CONGRESS

According to the agenda-setting model in chapter 2, perceptions of public support are crucial to the new president's decision to claim a mandate. Yet he must also consider the partisan and ideological makeup of the Congress. If his public support is modest and Congress is far away from his own preferences, the president has no incentive to change the policy agenda. On the other hand, a favorable congressional environment can compensate for more modest public support and provide an incentive for the president to claim a mandate.

For the president, perhaps the best indicator of a sympathetic Congress is the strength of his political party. Partisan control of Congress is one of the most important and consistent predictors of a president's success in the legislative arena.[39] When his party has a majority, it controls voting rules and committees, and the party has the numbers to pass legislation. If the president and his party have a sense of shared fate, or party responsibility, the president is even more likely to elicit their cooperation. Political parties, after all, share responsibility for shaping the campaign agenda, and party leaders will likely be involved in the formulation of the president's policies.

Most presidents have governed with both chambers of Congress controlled by their party.[40] Only 30 percent of the presidents since Andrew Jackson have faced opposing party control of at least one chamber of Congress at the time of their own election. However, unified government does not mean that presidents can assume that Congress will go along with any major policy change they desire. Forecasts of congressional support also depend upon the political ideology and absolute number of fellow partisans. Ideological divisions within parties allow interparty coalitions to form (such as Republicans and Southern Democrats). A president might be less optimistic if his vote totals trailed those of his party's congressional candidates in most districts. A president assessing his potential legislative coalition will therefore take stock of the distribution of partisanship and ideology among members of the House and Senate.

The assessment of legislative coalitions differs from that of electoral coalitions in a significant way. While campaigns and elections suggest general issues that need serious attention, the president will have to legislate specific policy solutions.[41] In his 1932 campaign, Franklin Roosevelt promised that the government would take more initiative and responsibility for the economic welfare of the country. While he felt confident that the electorate had given him a mandate to address this issue, he nevertheless had to consider whether he could fashion a legislative majority around specific plans for social welfare and economic reform. In 1980, Ronald Reagan and his advisors assessed reactions of the new Congress to specific tax and spending cuts in addition to its amenability to a general plan of "less government."

Even though he must forecast more specific preferences, the president has several clues about the policy leanings of members of Congress. They may have already taken a stand on policy issues during the election campaign; at the least, the party leadership in Congress speaks out on the major issues. Incumbent members of Congress may have a long legislative history that provides clues as to their likely position on the issues. The president may even consider the ideological orientation of the senior committee members with direct jurisdiction over his policy proposal.

Legislators make their own calculations about how their future electoral fate would be affected if the president or a challenger makes this issue the centerpiece of a campaign against them in the future. Their challenge is to anticipate the reaction of constituency groups and forecast changes in the magnitude and composition of each constituency, depending upon the president's behavior. Like the president, they must forecast the consequences of their policy behavior, though certainly their task is different; they have a different constituency and a different role to play in the constitutional system. But they are just as concerned about the consequences of passing highly salient and visible legislation.

*

Inferences about voters and members of Congress are important because they shape the president's policy decisions. The behavior of the electorate must be consistent with the idea that voters want policy change. With the public behind him, the president can be confident that Congress will react favorably to his agenda. Without strong public support, the president will have to consider the preferences of Congress carefully and gauge whether fighting or bargaining with Congress would be better than the status quo.

Presidential mandate claims are related to the preferences of voters. However, in the last two chapters, I have argued that this relationship is not a simple identity between the two; mandates are not equivalent to poll results. Public opinion at the time of the election is only part of the story. According to the model, public opinion matters, but it is embedded in a game between the president and Congress. Moreover, the public opinion that matters is the public opinion of the future. Politicians use evidence about public opinion at the time of the election to make *forecasts*; they use evidence about how an issue played out in the election to estimate support for the same issue once it is on the legislative agenda.

The structure of the model and the fact that politicians have standard ways of making inferences about Congress and the electorate means that mandate claims should be empirically predictable events. In the next chapter, I examine which of the American presidents since 1828 have claimed mandates, and I describe how these claims vary with indicators of electoral and legislative support. I then predict mandate claims as a function of the magnitude of victory, the president's place in the party system, and his congressional support. The empirical model that incorporates the tradeoffs in the formal model outperforms the alternatives. After establishing that the aggregate evidence is consistent with the model, I present case studies of elections to provide evidence for the psychology of inference outlined in this chapter.

| Presidential Mandates
since 1828

If mandate claims are not random or capricious utterances on the part of presidents, we should be able to predict them. I have argued that presidential mandate claims follow a distinct and predictable pattern because they are made on the basis of inferences about the preferences of the electorate and the new Congress. According to the model I presented in chapter 2, presidents who win by large margins or who upset the status quo should be more likely to declare mandates. The strength of the president's party in Congress should influence the president's decision to claim a mandate only when he is perceived to have weak public support. Presidents with little electoral and congressional support should not declare mandates.

In this chapter, I test these deductions by examining the relationship between election outcomes and presidential mandate claims for every presidential election from Andrew Jackson in 1828 to Bill Clinton in 1996, a total of forty-three elections. While the small number of cases makes it difficult to build an elaborate statistical model, we can nevertheless determine whether there are any regularities in election outcomes that make presidents more likely to ask for policy change. Although an aggregate statistical model cannot directly verify the precise cognitive mechanisms at work in the minds of politicians, we can assess whether the aggregate evidence is consistent with the microlevel account I have provided.

In particular, we can use the data to see whether a statistical model based on the formal model in chapter 2 performs better than statistical models based on alternative theories. For example, the most naïve expectation is that mandates are simply equivalent to big wins. If this is true, then variation in the margin of victory should best predict which presidents declare mandates. Realignment theory, on the other hand, suggests that the president's agenda-setting behavior is best predicted by his place in the political party system. One could also argue that mandate claims are purely a function of partisan strength in Congress. If his party controls Congress, the president is free to place major policy changes on the agenda, irrespective of his popular victory. In that case, Congress-centered variables should best predict mandate claims. (Note, the model in chapter 2 suggests that Congress matters, but only when the president's public support is weak.) I evaluate these alternatives by examining a series of bivariate relationships and logit models.

I use elections after 1828 for three main reasons. First, political party divisions became relatively stable only after about 1828. Second, Jackson is the first officeholder to openly promote the presidency as representing all of the people, on a par with Congress.[1] Third, around this time, the franchise for white males was expanded steadily as voting requirements based upon property ownership and paid taxes were eliminated and the principle of universal white male suffrage took hold. The means of choosing electors for the electoral college (statewide winner takes all popular ballot) was also standardized.

One might argue that the evolution of the institution of the presidency undermines any generalizations that might be offered about presidential politics from the Jacksonian era to the present. Throughout history, presidents have played different political roles.[2] At the time of the Founding, the president was expected to stay above factional disputes. By the mid-1800s, he was at the center of party politics. In the twentieth century, the president started bargaining directly with interest groups and members of Congress, as well as appealing directly to voters over the heads of Congress. Nineteenth-century presidents did not actively campaign or engage in "going public."[3] In the post-Roosevelt era, presidents have had both increased responsibility and more detailed legislative agendas.[4] Many scholars therefore conclude that Roosevelt breaks sharply with the past and begins the era of the "modern" presidency.[5]

Yet I believe that it is entirely appropriate to study pre- and post-modern presidents together because there are basic constitutional and institutional structures and incentives that hold over time. In the case of mandate claims, presidents since Jackson have all looked to election results for clues about public preferences, even though the information available to politicians who wish to make forecasts about electoral and legislative mobilization has changed dramatically. Similarly, throughout history, presidents have always made prospective calculations about the consequences of their agenda-setting plans. They have had to consider what would happen if their policy were placed on the agenda and it encountered congressional opposition. Would the likely outcome be closer to their own policy position or to the status quo? Twentieth-century presidents may have gone public in a fight with Congress, whereas nineteenth-century presidents may have instead mobilized party elites. But no matter what strategy has been employed to do battle with Congress, expectations about the outcome of this contest shape the president's original decision to place a policy change on the national agenda.

Social and political transformations therefore do not change the fact that presidents must make inferences about electoral and legislative coalitions. Nor do such transformations change the logic of how these inferences influence presidential agenda setting. The major pieces of information about electoral and congressional support remain the same: margin of victory, gains and losses in Congress, comparisons with elections past. Presidents since Jackson have claimed a mandate when they assumed that they possessed the popular and congressional support needed to enact a major policy initiative.

PRESIDENTIAL MANDATES SINCE 1828

Table 4.1 lists all presidents from 1828 to 1996 who claimed mandates for the major policy initiatives they sought at the beginning of their terms. To be included in the list, the president must have claimed that the people elected him specifically to enact a major policy initiative. I include politicians who asked for a complete change in policy direction (e.g., Reagan in 1980) and those who asked for large policies that pushed further in a given ideological direction (e.g., Johnson in 1964). Presidents who do not claim mandates do not link their election to any major policy initiative, and the status quo often results by default. This dichotomous variable—

Table 4.1 Presidential Mandates, 1828–1996

	President	Issue
1828	Jackson (D)	national bank; internal improvements; protectionism
1832	Jackson (D)	national bank; internal improvements; protectionism
1840	Harrison (W)	anti-Jacksonian
1852	Pierce (D)	slavery (1850 Compromise)
1856	Buchanan (D)	slavery
1860	Lincoln (R)	slavery; preservation of union
1864	Lincoln (R)	slavery; preservation of union
1892	Cleveland (D)	tariff reform/free trade
1896	McKinley (R)	tariff reform/protectionist
1912	Wilson (D)	tariff and banking reform; Progressivism
1916	Wilson (D)	neutrality in WWI
1924	Coolidge (R)	less government
1928	Hoover (R)	less government; Prohibition
1932	Roosevelt (D)	government intervention to end the Depression
1936	Roosevelt (D)	government intervention to end the Depression
1940	Roosevelt (D)	neutrality in WWII
1948	Truman (D)	New Deal; civil rights; repeal Taft-Hartley
1952	Eisenhower (R)	Korean War; communism
1964	Johnson (D)	Great Society; civil rights
1972	Nixon (R)	Vietnam; Cold War
1980	Reagan (R)	less government, taxes
1984	Reagan (R)	less government, taxes
1992	Clinton (D)	economic policy; health care
1996	Clinton (D)	economic policy; health care

claimed a mandate or not—is the dependent variable in the analysis that follows.

Presidents are coded on the basis of public statements, including their inaugural and state of the union addresses. Presidents from Truman to Clinton have been asked directly about the existence of a mandate at their first postelection news conference—their statements are provided in later chapters. For earlier presidents, I supplement their speeches with newspaper coverage of presidential remarks, memoirs, and private letters. It is not necessary that the president uses the word "mandate," but he must link his electoral victory to the major policy initiative that he intends to place on the agenda.

The case studies provide the text of statements for presidents in the post-Roosevelt era. It is worth quoting a few examples before Roosevelt to see how presidents link their election to popular demands for policy change without necessarily using the word mandate.[6]

GROVER CLEVELAND (1893): "The verdict of our voters which condemned the injustice of maintaining protection for protection's sake enjoins upon the people's servants the duty of exposing and destroying the brood of kindred evils which are the wholesome progeny of paternalism. . . . The people of the United States have decreed that on this day the control of their Government in its legislative and executive branches shall be given to a political party pledged in the most positive terms to the accomplishment of tariff reform. They have thus determined in favor of a more just and equitable system of Federal taxation. The agents they have chosen to carry out their purposes are bound by their promises not less than by the command of their masters to devote themselves unremittingly to this service."

WILLIAM McKINLEY (1897): "The question of bimettalism will have early and earnest attention. It will be my constant endeavor to secure it by co-operation with the other great commercial powers of the world. . . . This was the commanding verdict of the people and it will not be unheeded. . . . There could be no better time to put the government upon a sound financial and economic basis than not. The people have only recently voted that this should be done, and nothing is more binding upon the agents of their will than the obligation of immediate action."

WOODROW WILSON (1913): "There has been a change of government. It began two years ago, when the House of Representatives became Democratic by a decisive majority. It has now been completed. The Senate about to assemble will also be Democratic. The offices of President and Vice-President have been put into the hands of Democrats. What does the change mean? . . . It means much more than the mere success of a party. The success of a party means little except when the Nation is using that party for a large and definite purpose. No one can mistake the purpose for which the Nation now seeks to use the Democratic Party. It seeks to use it to interpret a change in its own plans and point of view. . . . We have itemized with some degree of particularity the things that ought to be altered and here are some of the chief items: A tariff which cuts us off from our proper part in the commerce of the world . . . ; a banking and currency system based upon the necessity of the Government to sell its bonds fifty years ago."

CALVIN COOLIDGE (1925): "This Administration has come into power with a very clear and definite mandate from the people. The expression of the popular will in favor of maintaining our constitutional guarantees was overwhelming and decisive. There was a manifestation of such faith in the integrity of the courts that we can consider that issue rejected for some time to come. Likewise, the policy of public ownership of railroads and certain electric utilities met with unmistakable defeat. The people declared that they wanted their rights to have not a political but a judicial determination, and their independence and freedom continued and supported by having the ownership and control of their property, not in the Government, but in their own hands. . . . When we turn from what was rejected to inquire what was accepted, the policy that stands out with the greatest clearness is that of economy in public expenditure with reduction and reform of taxation."

Presidents declared mandates after 55.8 percent—or twenty-four out of forty-three—elections. The issues ranged from the extension of slavery to the gold standard to civil rights to cutting taxes. Presidents in the twentieth century were more likely to declare mandates than presidents in the nineteenth century (62 percent versus 47 percent). Figure 4.1 plots the probability of claiming a mandate over time.[7] Table 4.2 presents some of the major variables that describe election outcomes for every president from Jackson to Clinton: popular and electoral college vote percentages, gains and losses in Congress, and the percentage of seats held by the president's party in Congress. The unit of analysis here is the election ($N = 43$), not the individual president.

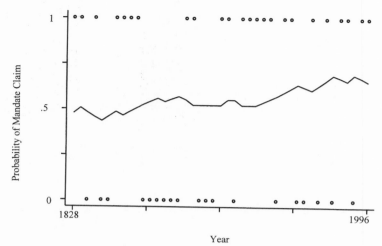

Figure 4.1 Presidential Mandate Claims, 1828–1996. NOTE: Circles indicate whether a president claimed a mandate (1) or not (0). $N = 43$ elections.

While the vast majority of mandate claims involve issues of domestic policy, four presidents claimed mandates either wholly or in part for foreign policy initiatives. Woodrow Wilson and Franklin Roosevelt promised neutrality in times of war. Dwight Eisenhower promised to fight communism and to end the Korean War. Richard Nixon promised to fight communism and end the Vietnam War. I should note that studies of presidential policy success often distinguish foreign and domestic policy realms because the staffs and decision chains for foreign and domestic policy are different, and Congress tends to grant the president more discretion on foreign policy.[8] However, for the purpose of this analysis, I do not separate foreign and domestic policy mandate claims, because the same kinds of inference processes are involved in interpreting an election whether or not the major issue is foreign or domestic. Moreover, since each of the foreign policy mandates pertained to war or protracted military conflict, the presidents who claimed them still had to take into account the preferences of Congress.

Table 4.2 Presidential Election Statistics, 1828–1996

	Winning Candidate	Popular Vote (%)	Electoral College (%)	Gains/Losses		President's Party % Seats			
				Senate	House	Senate		House	
1828*	Jackson (D)	55.97	68	− 2	+ 20	M	54	M	65
1830				− 1	+ 2	M	52	M	66
1832*	Jackson (D)	54.23	77	− 5	+ 6	E	42	M	61
1834				+ 7	+ 2	M	52	M	60
1836	Van Buren (D)	50.83	58	+ 3	− 37	M	58	M	44
1838				− 2	+ 16	M	54	M	51
1840*	Harrison (W)	52.88	80	+ 6	+ 15	NM	54	NM	55
1842	Tyler (W)			+ 0	− 54	M	54	Nm	35
1844	Polk (D)	49.54	62	+ 6	+ 1	NM	55	M	63
1846				+ 5	− 35	M	62	m	48
1848	Taylor (W)	47.28	56	+ 4	− 6	m	42	Nm	47
1850	Fillmore (W)			− 1	− 21	m	39	m	38
1852*	Pierce (D)	50.84	86	+ 3	+ 19	M	61	M	68
1854				+ 2	− 76	M	67	Nm	35
1856*	Buchanan (D)	45.28	59	− 3	+ 48	M	61	NM	55
1858				− 1	− 30	M	58	Nm	43
1860*	Lincoln (R)	39.82	59	+ 5	− 7	NM	63	M	60
1862				+ 8	− 3	M	76	M	56
1864*	Lincoln (R)	55.02	90	+ 3	+ 42	M	81	M	76
1866	Johnson (R)			+ 0	− 2	M	79	M	74
1868	Grant (R)	52.66	73	+ 19	+ 27	M	85	M	70
1870				− 4	− 31	M	77	M	57

Year	President								
1872	Grant (R)	55.63	78	− 3	+ 64	74	M	70	M
1874				− 8	− 96	61	M	37	Nm
1876	Hayes (R)	47.95	50.1	− 7	+ 30	51	M	47	m
1878				− 6	− 9	43	Nm	44	m
1880	Garfield (R)	48.27	58	+ 4	+ 24	49	E	54	NM
1882	Arthur (R)			+ 3	− 33	53	M	37	Nm
1884	Cleveland (D)	48.50	55	− 2	− 18	45	m	56	M
1886				+ 3	− 12	49	m	52	M
1888	Harrison (R)	47.82	58	+ 8	+ 22	56	M	52	NM
1890				+ 0	− 85	53	M	26	Nm
1892*	Cleveland (D)	46.05	62	+ 5	− 11	52	NM	62	M
1894				− 5	− 116	38	Nm	29	Nm
1896*	McKinley (R)	51.01	61	+ 2	− 40	51	M	58	M
1898				+ 7	− 21	59	M	52	M
1900	McKinley (R)	51.67	65	+ 3	+ 13	64	M	56	M
1902	Roosevelt (R)			+ 2	+ 9	64	M	54	M
1904	Roosevelt (R)	56.41	71	+ 0	+ 43	64	M	65	M
1906				+ 3	− 28	68	M	58	M
1908	Taft (R)	51.58	66	− 2	− 3	65	M	56	M
1910				− 10	− 57	54	M	42	M
1912*	Wilson (D)	41.84	82	+ 9	+ 62	53	NM	67	M
1914				+ 5	− 59	58	M	53	M
1916*	Wilson (D)	49.24	52	− 3	− 21	55	M	48	Nm
1918				− 6	− 19	49	Nm	44	m
1920	Harding (R)	60.30	76	+11	+ 63	61	M	69	M
1922				− 8	− 75	53	M	52	M
1924*	Coolidge (R)	54.06	72	+ 3	+ 22	56	M	57	M
1926				− 6	− 10	50	M	54	M

Table 4.2 *continued*

	Winning Candidate	Popular Vote (%)	Electoral College (%)	Gains/Losses		President's Party[a] % Seats			
				Senate	House	Senate		House	
1928*	Hoover (R)	58.20	84	+ 8	+ 30	58	M	61	M
1930				− 8	− 49	50	M	50	M
1932*	FDR (D)	57.42	89	+12	+ 97	61	NM	72	NM
1934				+10	+ 9	72	M	74	M
1936*	FDR (D)	60.79	98	+ 6	+ 11	78	M	77	M
1938				− 8	− 71	72	M	60	M
1940*	FDR (D)	54.70	85	− 3	+ 5	69	M	61	M
1942				− 9	− 45	59	M	51	M
1944	FDR (D)	53.39	81	+ 0	+ 21	59	M	56	M
1946				−12	− 55	47	Nm	43	Nm
1948*	Truman (D)	49.51	57	+ 9	+ 75	56	NM	60	NM
1950				− 6	− 29	50	M	54	M
1952*	Eisenhower (R)	55.13	83	+ 1	+ 22	50	NM	51	NM
1954				− 1	− 18	49	Nm	47	Nm
1956	Eisenhower (R)	57.37	86	+ 0	− 2	49	m	46	m
1958				−13	− 47	35	m	35	m
1960	Kennedy (D)	49.72	56	− 2	− 20	64	M	60	M
1962				+ 4	− 4	67	M	59	M

1964*	Johnson (D)	61.05	90	+ 2	+ 38	68	M	68	M
1966				− 3	− 47	64	M	57	M
1968	Nixon (R)	43.42	56	+ 5	+ 4	42	m	44	m
1970				+ 2	− 12	45	m	41	m
1972*	Nixon (R)	60.69	97	− 2	+ 12	43	m	44	m
1974	Ford (R)			− 3	− 43	38	m	33	m
1976	Carter (D)	50.1	55	+ 0	+ 1	62	M	67	M
1978				− 3	− 11	59	M	64	M
1980*	Reagan (R)	50.8	91	+12	+ 33	53	NM	44	m
1982				+ 1	− 26	54	M	38	m
1984*	Reagan (R)	58.77	98	− 2	+ 14	53	M	42	m
1986				− 8	− 5	45	Nm	41	m
1988	Bush (R)	53.4	80	− 1	− 3	45	m	40	m
1990				− 1	− 8	44	m	38	m
1992*	Clinton (D)	43.0	69	+0	− 10	57	M	59	M
1994				−10	− 52	47	Nm	47	Nm
1996*	Clinton (D)	49.0	70.5	− 2	+ 9	45	m	47	m

SOURCE: *Congressional Quarterly Guide to U.S. Elections*, 3d ed. (Washington, D.C.: Congressional Quarterly Inc., 1994).

NOTE: Presidents who claimed mandates are marked with an asterisk.

[a] I present the numerical gains into percentage of seats for the president's party as well as the total percentage of seats for his party in each chamber of Congress. The translation of numerical gains into percentage of seats is not constant over time, due both to increases in the total numbers of seats in each chamber as states are added to the union and to variation in the number of seats occupied by third parties. The president's party is coded as being the majority party (M), the minority party (m), or evenly matched (E). N denotes whether the party changed to that status with the current election.

Table 4.3 Mandate Declarations by Magnitude of Victory:
Difference of Means

Variable	Mandate (%)	No Mandate (%)
Electoral college votes[a]	77.5	65.3
Popular vote	52.3	51.4
Two-party vote[a]	56.8	53.1
Plurality[a]	12.4	6.7
Third-party vote[b]	6.5	2.0
States won[a]	74.6	63.1
Voter turnout	62.5	67.1
Gains, Senate	.03	.03
Gains, House	.06	.03
Seats, House	59.1	55.9
Seats, Senate	57.3	57.4
N =	24	19

[a] $p < .01$
[b] $p < .05$

Magnitude of Victory

The simplest expectation is that presidents with landslides declare mandates. Table 4.3 presents the difference in means between
presidents who declare mandates and those who do not for various
indicators of the magnitude of victory. While the percentage of the
popular vote is not significantly different across the two groups of
presidents, mandate claimers do win a significantly higher percentage
of electoral college votes—an average of 77.5 percent as compared
to 65.3 percent for those who do not declare mandates. Presidents
who declare mandates also have much larger pluralities than presidents who do not declare mandates.

The reason for the disparity between the popular and electoral
college votes is twofold. First, there is not much variation in the popular vote percentage over time; the winner take all nature of the electoral college, on the other hand, gives it much higher variance over
time (Figure 4.2). Its higher variance and its association with winning states and regions make it a more valuable signal to politicians.

Second, there are several cases—Buchanan (1856), Lincoln
(1860), Wilson (1912), Truman (1948), and Clinton (1992)—
where third-party challenges focused the campaign on the issues at

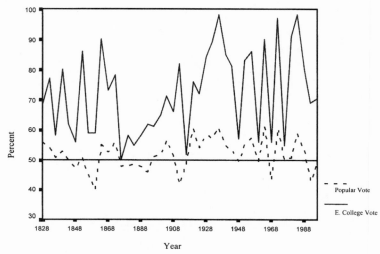

Figure 4.2 The Electoral College and Popular Vote, 1828–1996

the same time that they prevented the victor from receiving a large popular vote victory. The addition of a third candidate explains why both the plurality and the percentage of the two-party vote are significantly different across the two groups while the popular vote is not. Figures 4.3 and 4.4 present the relationship between the popular vote and electoral college vote and the probability of claiming a mandate. The relationship between the electoral college vote and mandate claims is strong and positive, while the relationship between the popular vote and mandate claiming is a U-shaped curve. Presidents are more likely to declare mandates when the popular vote is low (the three-way races) and high, but less likely when it is close to 50 percent.

Place in the Party System

Realignment theory suggests that mandate claims are a function of the president's place in the political party system. New presidents who are able to upset the status quo and turn the tide of recent electoral trends should be more likely to claim a mandate for their policies. According to realignment theory, the presidential elections

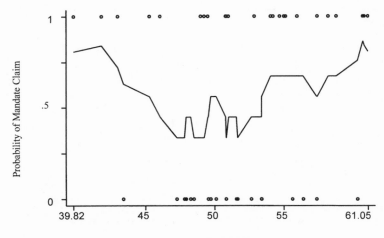

Figure 4.3 Mandate Claims and the Popular Vote. NOTE: Circles indicate whether a president claimed a mandate (1) or not (0). N = 43 elections (1828–1996).

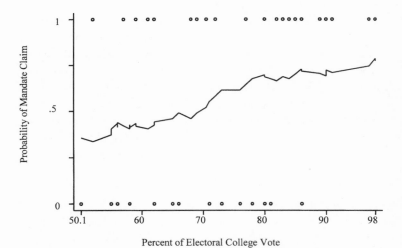

Figure 4.4 Mandate Claims and the Electoral College Vote. NOTE: Circles indicate whether a president claimed a mandate (1) or not (0). N = 43 elections (1828–1996).

Table 4.4 Mandates and Affiliation with Majority Party Regime

Mandate Declared	President Is Affiliated with Majority Party[a]		Row Total
	% No (# of elections)	% Yes (# of elections)	
No	20.0	65.2	44.2
	(4)	(15)	(19)
Yes	80.0	34.8	55.8
	(16)	(8)	(24)
Column Total	46.5	53.5	100
	(20)	(23)	(43)

NOTE: Chi-square = 8.87, p < .003.

[a] I assume the following political party regimes: 1828–1860, Jacksonian/Democratic Party; 1864–1932, Republican Party; 1936–1980, Democratic Party; 1984–present, Republican Party.

of 1828, 1860, and 1932 divide American political history into political party regimes.[9] The assessment of party regimes is based upon changes in the party balance of the electorate, but it also refers to the resilience of a party's philosophy and proposed solutions to political problems.[10] For the purposes of examining the relationship between political party status and mandate declarations, I divide the sample into four party regimes. In the Jacksonian period, the Democratic Party dominates presidential politics, while in the years from the Civil War until the Great Depression, the Republican Party is dominant. The presidency of Franklin Roosevelt marks the return of Democratic Party dominance. Finally, the presidency of Ronald Reagan marks the ascendance of the Republican Party in presidential politics.[11] By definition, a new president is a majority party president if he belongs to the dominant party and a minority party president if he belongs to the minor party.[12] Table 4.4 presents the results of a cross-tabulation of party status and mandate declarations. Minority party presidents are much more likely to declare mandates.

Therefore, if the minority party candidate succeeds when the balance of the partisan forces are aligned against him, he tends to explain his victory as a call for new policies. A victory over a dominant party regime has many parallels with a victory over a sitting president; both represent a rejection of an established record of policymaking. In fact, presidents declared mandates in 77 percent of the cases in which incumbents were defeated and in only 50 percent of the cases in which incumbents were not defeated. Moreover, to the extent that the election of a minority party president reveals weaknesses in the dominant party regime, the new president may have more latitude to push policy in a new direction.

Legislative Support

The relationship between the new president and his party in Congress also affects the frequency with which mandates are declared. Presidents have an easier time getting legislation passed if their party has a majority in the House and Senate.[13] When they have a majority, the president's fellow partisans have more control over the congressional agenda and policy process, and they have the votes to pass his program. Even if the president's party has a majority, however, the number of partisans and their ideological orientation should have a bearing on his policy success.

Table 4.5 presents the distribution of presidents according to their party's control of the House and Senate. Presidents are sorted by whether their party had a majority in both chambers, one chamber, or neither chamber. If the president's party was evenly matched with the opposing party in the Senate, and if the vote of the vice president could serve as a tiebreaker, then the president is coded as having a majority. If the president's party is evenly matched with the opposition, and if the number of independents is large, then the president is coded as having a minority in that chamber.

Sixty-seven percent of all presidents belonged to the party controlling both houses of Congress. With one exception, all of the presidents with a party minority in both the House and Senate held office in the mid to late twentieth century (Eisenhower, Nixon, Bush, and Clinton).[14] Historically, we find only ten cases in which the election brings a change in the partisan control of Congress; usually, the president comes to power with his party sustaining control from past electoral victories.

We would expect that when the party of the new president controls both the House and the Senate, he is more likely to declare a mandate. This is indeed the case: 59 percent of unified government

Table 4.5 Presidents and Party Control of Congress

	President's Party Has:		
	Majority in Both Chambers % and (# of elections)	Majority in One Chamber % and (# of elections)	Minority in Both Chambers % and (# of elections)
	69.8 (30)	16.2 (7)	14 (6)[a]
New Control of Both Chambers	23.3 (10)		
Sustained Control of Both Chambers	46.5 (20)		
Senate Only		9.3 (4)[b]	
House Only		6.9 (3)[c]	

NOTE: N = 43 elections, 1828–1996.

[a] Taylor in 1848, Eisenhower in 1956, Nixon in 1968 and 1972, Bush in 1988, and Clinton in 1996.

[b] Hayes in 1876, Wilson in 1916, and Ronald Reagan in 1980 and 1984. Except for Ronald Reagan in 1980, these Senate majorities were lost in the following midterm election.

[c] Jackson in 1832, Garfield in 1880, and Cleveland in 1884. While Jackson and Garfield had the same number of partisans as the major opposing party, they did not have a majority without the support of "independents" in the Senate.

presidents declared mandates as opposed to only 50 percent of presidents presiding over divided government. Moreover, within the group of fourteen presidents presiding over divided government, mandate claims are more likely when the president's party controls at least one chamber of Congress.

The percentage of seats held by the president's party in the Senate is not significantly different for presidents who declare mandates and those who do not—on average both groups of presidents belong to a party holding 57 percent of all Senate seats. In addition, presidents who have large, close to filibuster-proof majorities do not seem any more likely to declare mandates. On the other hand, there is a significant difference with respect to the percentage of seats held by the president's party in the House of Representatives. Presidents who claim mandates belong to parties that on average hold 59 percent of House seats; those who do not claim mandates belong to parties holding an average of 55 percent of all House seats.[15]

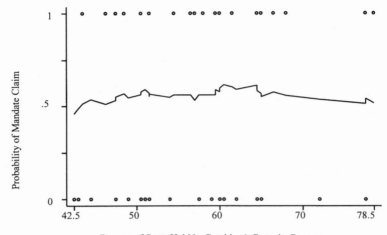

Percent of Seats Held by President's Party in Congress

Figure 4.5 Mandate Claims and Party Strength in Congress. NOTE: Circles indicate whether a president claimed a mandate (1) or not (0). N = 43 elections (1828–1996).

Figure 4.5 shows the probability of claiming a mandate as a function of the percentage of seats held by the president's party in Congress. The probability of claiming a mandate appears to be only weakly related to party strength in Congress. However, according to the model I developed in chapter 2, strength in Congress should be relevant to those presidents with weak popular support because their ability to pass a major initiative depends on whether they can build a legislative majority. In contrast, popular presidents who are confronted with a recalcitrant Congress can always "go public." We can index a president's popularity according to whether his popular vote fell above or below 50 percent. The popular vote total serves as a rough proxy for his capacity to mobilize the electorate behind his policies. Figure 4.6 plots the relationship between congressional strength and mandate claims for presidents who won with less than 50 percent of the popular vote. For this group of presidencies, there is a positive relationship between congressional strength and mandate claiming. Figure 4.7 plots the same relationship for presidents who won with more than 50 percent of the popular vote. In this case,

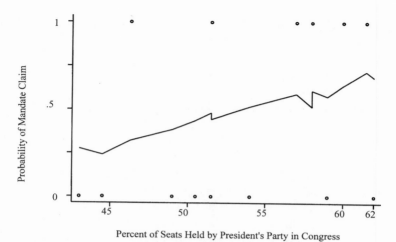

Figure 4.6 Mandates and Party Strength, Weak Popular Support. NOTE: Circles indicate whether a president claimed a mandate (1) or not (0). $N = 19$ elections.

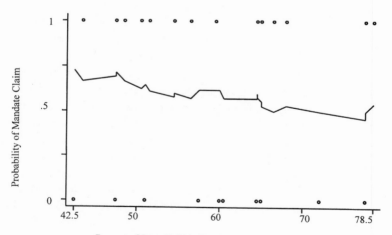

Figure 4.7 Mandates and Party Strength, Strong Popular Support. NOTE: Circles indicate whether a president claimed a mandate (1) or not (0). $N = 24$ elections.

there is little or no relationship between congressional strength and mandate claims. Therefore, presidents claim mandates when they win impressive electoral victories, but some presidents still claim mandates if they calculate that they have enough strength in Congress to pass their agenda. Presidents with little electoral or congressional support do not claim mandates.

Evaluating Alternative Models

The bivariate analysis presented thus far suggests that magnitude of victory, place in the party system, and unified government are related to presidential mandate claims. However, if my theory about the types of presidents who claim mandates is correct, then a statistical model that incorporates the interaction between magnitude of victory and congressional strength should outperform the alternatives.

Table 4.6 presents the results of a series of logit models in which mandate claims are predicted by variables representing (1) the president's magnitude of victory, (2) his place in the party system, and (3) whether his party controls Congress. The dependent variable is coded 1 if the president declared a mandate, and 0 otherwise. The independent variables are coded as follows. The president's magnitude of victory is measured by his percentage of the popular vote and of the electoral college vote. His place in the party system is measured by two dummy variables that summarize his relationship to the dominant party regime. The first variable is coded 1 if the president is opposed to the dominant party regime, and 0 if the president is affiliated with the dominant party regime.[16] This variable is identical to the majority/minority party president variable used earlier in Table 4.4. The second party regime variable is coded 1 if the party regime is "vulnerable" in a given year, and 0 otherwise. This measure is based directly on Skowronek's assessment of regime vulnerability. Election years with vulnerable regimes are those immediately preceding and during realigning elections.[17] To capture the partisanship of Congress, I include two dummy variables that measure the degree to which the president's party controls Congress. The first variable determines if there is a unified government; it equals 1 if the president's party controls both chambers of Congress, and 0 otherwise. The second variable equals 1 if the president's party controls one

Table 4.6 Logit Models Predicting Presidential Mandate Claims

Independent Variables	Model 1	Model 2	Model 3	Model 4	Model 5
Landslide					
% Electoral College Vote	.07[a]				.13[a]
	(.027)				(.05)
% Popular Vote		−2.21[c]			
		(1.23)			
Popular Vote Squared		.02[c]			
		(.01)			
Popular Vote < 50%					−5.4
					(6.5)
Party System					
Majority Party			1.27[c]		
			(.72)		
Vulnerable Regime			1.94[c]		
			(1.14)		
Congress					
Unified Control				1.36	
				(1.3)	
One Chamber Control				1.06	
				(1.18)	
% Seats				−.01	−.02
				(.05)	(.05)
% Seats * Popular Vote < 50%					.14
					(.11)
Constant	−4.9[a]	55.6[c]	−.49	−.009	−8.7[c]
	(1.9)	(31.7)	(.42)	(2.4)	(4.6)
Pseudo R^2	.15	.08	.13	.03	.25
Residual Deviance	50.2	54.4	51.2	57.5	44.5

NOTE: N = 43 Elections, 1828–1996. The dependent variable is coded 1 if the president claimed a mandate, 0 otherwise. See text for coding of independent variables. Standard Errors are listed in parentheses under the coefficients.

[a] $p < .01$ [b] $p < .05$ [c] $p < .10$

chamber of Congress, and 0 otherwise. The baseline category (i.e., presidents who score 0 on both variables) comprises presidents who must contend with opposition party control in both chambers. A third measure of congressional partisanship is the percentage of seats held by the president's party in both chambers of Congress. This variable is simply the average of the percentage of seats held by the president's party in the House and the Senate.

In the first two models, the indicators of the president's magnitude of victory are used to predict mandate claims. The percentage of the popular vote is not a strong predictor, as would be expected given its low variance and the aforementioned impact of third-party challenges. The direction of the coefficients does suggest the nonlinear relationship visible in Figure 4.3. On the other hand, the coefficient for the percentage of the electoral college vote is strong and statistically significant.

Model 3 is a logit analysis of the influence of the president's place in the party system. Opposition to the majority party regime and regime vulnerability strongly increase the likelihood of declaring mandates, though these variables do not quite reach statistical significance. Model 4 is a logit analysis of mandate claims as a function of partisan control of Congress and the strength of the president's party in Congress. While the coefficients suggest that unified control increases the likelihood of mandate claims more than does the control of one chamber, and that control of one or both chambers increases the likelihood as opposed to minorities in both chambers, the coefficients are not statistically significant and the model performs poorly overall.

Model 5 is specified according to the theoretical framework laid out in chapter 2. This logit includes both a measure of the magnitude of victory—the percentage of electoral college votes won—and an interaction term that represents the tradeoff between perceptions of the president's ability to mobilize voters and his party's strength in Congress. Let us assume that the percentage of the popular vote is a rough proxy for the president's ability to mobilize voters. We can then divide the sample into two groups of presidents: those who won less than 50 percent of the popular vote (weak popular support) and those who won more than 50 percent of the popular vote (strong popular support). An interaction term is computed by multiplying this dummy variable (coded 1 if the president has weak popular support, and 0 otherwise) by the percentage of seats held in Congress. The coefficient on the interaction term is positive, as expected on the basis of figures 4.6 and 4.7. Presidents with weak popular support factor in the strength of their party in Congress more than presidents with strong popular support. The coefficient is not statistically significant, most likely because it is highly correlated with the popular vote dummy variable. The electoral college vote has a strong, statistically significant effect on the likelihood of claiming a mandate. Looking at the pseudo R^2 and deviance residuals for all models, the final model appears to have the best fit with the data.

According to the aggregate data, then, mandate claims are not random. The data are consistent with a model that predicts mandate claims under two conditions: (1) when the president's popular support is perceived to be high; and (2) when he enjoys moderate popular support but his party dominates Congress. Mandate claims clearly correspond to various indicators of the magnitude of victory, but a model based upon that factor alone does not perform as well as a fully specified model. Likewise, mandate claims are not reliably predicted if we consider only the strength of the president's party in Congress. A statistical model based on the president's place in the party system does reasonably well, but the measurement of this variable relies on historical information about party regimes that is not available to politicians when they are deciding how to set the agenda following the election. Finally, the statistical model that best predicts presidential mandate claims takes account of the joint influence of electoral strength and congressional strength.

Elections and Presidential Success

The analysis in this chapter shows that political resources—the signals from the election and congressional context—do predict which presidents will place major policy changes at the top of their agenda. But do the presidents with greater political resources have greater policy success than other presidents? Presidents with more political capital should have greater legislative success during their first year in office. Presidents who were elected in contests based on the issues, with strong forecasts of popular mobilization, should be most successful, with the highest success rates going to those who also face their own party in control of both chambers of Congress. Next should be presidents who have strong congressional coalitions (unified government) but who are believed to have limited capacity to mobilize popular support. Last would be presidents whose elections were not interpreted as a call to action on policy issues and who face the opposition party in Congress.

Table 4.7 First-Year Presidential Success Scores

		First-Year Success Score (%)	Concurrence with Own Partisans	
			House (%)	Senate (%)
Eisenhower	1953	89.0	80.0	78.0
Johnson	1965	88.0	83.0	75.0
Clinton	1993	86.4	77.0	87.0
Reagan	1981	82.4	72.0	84.0
Kennedy	1961	81.0	81.0	73.0
Carter	1977	75.4	69.0	77.0
Nixon	1969	74.0	65.0	74.0
Bush	1989	62.6	72.0	84.0
Ford	1975	58.2	67.0	76.0

SOURCES: Phil Duncan and Steve Langdon, "When Congress Had to Choose, It Voted to Back Clinton," *Congressional Quarterly Weekly Report*, 12 December 1993, p. 3428, 3473; Lynn Ragsdale, *Vital Statistics on the Presidency* (Washington, D.C.: Congressional Quarterly, Inc., 1996), 385–386.

In the chapters that follow, I use case studies to describe how well the three types of presidents fare with respect to passing their legislative agendas. As a prelude to that discussion, I present a rank ordering of *Congressional Quarterly* first-year presidential success scores for presidents since Eisenhower that roughly follows the pattern outlined above (Table 4.7).[18] Presidential success scores measure how often the president won roll call votes on which he took a clear position. These scores are not without flaws.[19] For example, they do not take into account presidential positions that never reach a floor vote or the degree of compromise in the final version of a presidential bill that passes. Moreover, bills that are introduced in the first year but are not passed until later in the term are coded as "failures." Presidents may also be joining winning coalitions rather than persuading legislators to their side. Finally, success scores treat all floor votes equally, though some key votes may be more important to the administration's legislative agenda than others. Nonetheless, I have argued that the president's perceived popular and congressional support, informed by the interpretation of the election, form his political capital at the start of his term.[20] The data in Table 4.7 suggest that those presidents who claim mandates are generally more successful than others.

Table 4.7 also lists vote concurrence rates for each president.[21] These rates represent the percentage of the time that a majority of members of the president's own party supported the president's position on roll call votes. Concurrence rates for fellow partisans are broken down by congressional chamber. In general, the mandate-claiming presidents (Eisenhower, Johnson, Clinton, and Reagan) have higher concurrence rates with their own partisans than the presidents who did not declare mandates.

The legislative success measures of other scholars confirm these results. Mark Peterson coded congressional responses to presidential initiatives for presidents from Eisenhower to Reagan.[22] Rather than simply code the success or failure of the president's position, he divided the congressional response into five mutually exclusive categories: inaction, opposition dominance, presidential dominance, compromise, or consensus. This measure gauges how much of the president's program passed and how much conflict it generated. Both Eisenhower and Johnson achieved their respective legislative agendas without serious compromise nearly 50 percent of the time.[23] Compared to other presidents, they were the least likely to run up against congressional inaction in response to their proposals. They were also the most likely to achieve consensus.[24] Presidents Nixon, Ford, and Carter, on the other hand, faced higher rates of inaction in Congress and rarely saw their preferences trump the opposition's; either they had to compromise or the opposing view triumphed over their own preferences.[25] Fewer than half of President Kennedy's initiatives were passed, even in part.[26]

The three chapters that follow are organized around the three kinds of presidents predicted by the model in chapter 2. These groups of presidents differ with respect to the eventual success of their policy agendas. Eisenhower's foreign policy initiatives, Johnson's welfare programs, and Reagan's economic policies were all mandate issues that were enacted essentially without revision. Truman and Clinton claimed mandates and asked for major policy changes, and Congress did act, but these presidents were forced to compromise. John Kennedy, Jimmy Carter, and George Bush did not claim mandates, nor did their first-year result in any kind of resounding success in Congress. I do not mean to argue that the president can summon his electoral support with equal facility on all policy issues. Neustadt pointed out that the quality of prestige is as important as the quantity.[27] We should find not only that mandate-claiming presidents are generally more successful but also that they are more successful on the issues that form the basis of their mandate. If the election was perceived to be a message about voter preferences for a particular policy, the president should be more successful on that policy.

*

A statistical model based upon the parameters of the formal model in chapter 2 predicts presidential mandate claims better than models based upon either the president's magnitude of victory, the strength of his party in Congress, or his place in the political party system. Those presidents who claim mandates have more legislative success in their first year in office than presidents who do not claim mandates. Yet while the aggregate data is consistent with the model, only case studies can provide evidence about the specific causal mechanisms underlying these patterns.

In the next three chapters, I analyze eight recent elections, grouped according to the types of presidencies that represent the equilibria of the model: presidents with strong popular support, presidents with moderate popular support and the benefit of unified government, and presidents with little electoral or congressional support. The cases will not provide the reader with any new historical details; the events of these elections are well known. Rather, the cases should be read as additional evidence for the theory of presidential mandate claims and for the political psychology of elites presented in earlier chapters. For each election, I describe both the campaigns and election outcomes, as well as the corresponding interpretations of politicians. I outline the new president's response to his victory and to the new Congress, as well as his policy agenda. While the aggregate data in this chapter is consistent with the model, the following chapters will make the case at the level of individual perceptions.

FIVE | Popular Mandates: 1952, 1964, and 1980

Elections send signals about the extent of a president's popular and legislative support. The president uses this information to decide whether or not to ask for a major policy change. According to the model in chapter 2, we should see three different kinds of presidents, corresponding to three different political contexts. In this chapter and the two that follow, I present case studies of eight recent elections to illustrate the three kinds of postelection presidencies that are identified by the model. In analyzing these elections, I will focus on how politicians interpret campaign events and voting patterns to estimate the president's popular and legislative support. I will also evaluate whether presidents make the postelection policy choices that are predicted of them by the agenda-setting model.

The elections of 1952, 1964, and 1980, the subject of this chapter, ushered in presidents who began their terms by asking for major policy changes because there was a consensus that they could mobilize the public behind their plans. The elections of 1948 and 1992, the subject of chapter 6, each produced a president who received only moderate popular support but still declared a mandate because his party controlled both chambers of Congress. The elections of 1960, 1976, and 1988, which I turn to in chapter 7, were elections after which the president did not declare a mandate for a major policy change.

The cases are limited to the post-Roosevelt era for two reasons. First, the evidence about elections and the reactions of politicians is readily available in this period. Recent presidents and their advisors issued many more public statements about elections than their counterparts did in the past. Likewise, the modern press has made a habit of reporting virtually all of the information about election outcomes that politicians use to make inferences. Second, it is better to study a series of elections because, as I noted in chapter 3, inferences are based upon historical comparisons, so that every election has implications for subsequent elections. For this reason, covering almost every election during a forty-year period is preferable to picking only one election from every forty-year period of the nation's history. By limiting our focus to the post-Roosevelt era, we have the benefit of observing the interpretation of the same group of political elites over time, as they witness a series of presidential elections and draw inferences about what is unusual or surprising about a particular outcome.

For each election, I reconstruct how politicians interpreted events, using newspaper coverage, public papers and speeches of the candidates, memoirs, polls, and scholarly accounts of the election. Since I am interested in the point of view of politicians, I focus on the words of politicians themselves whenever possible rather than on secondary accounts of an election. To gauge postelection agenda-setting behavior, I use the press conferences and major policy addresses (inaugural, state of the union, and budget messages) of the new president, as well as the legislative record of his first year in office.[1]

In each case, I begin with a brief discussion of the primaries and conventions, because these set the tone for the fall campaign. They provide information about divisions within the parties and give background on the cast of characters who will later interpret the general election outcome. Next, I describe the campaign strategies for the candidates and their parties, paying attention to whether or not they emphasized issues, character, or partisanship. I also review the presidential and congressional election forecasts that politicians and political analysts made at the time, to determine the extent to which they were surprised by the actual outcome. I then examine the subsequent analysis of voting behavior that took place in the weeks immediately after the election, offering the interpretation of both winners and losers. Finally, I examine the president's legislative agenda to see if it corresponds to the dominant interpretation of the outcome.

The cases in this chapter represent some of the strongest presidential mandates in the post-Roosevelt era. In 1952, Dwight Eisenhower won a landslide victory, even though the Republican Party won only a slim majority in Congress. His largely personal victory nonetheless translated into policy because politicians believed that he had a directive from the electorate to end the war in Korea, and because the president is perceived to have more independence from Congress on issues of foreign policy. In 1964, Lyndon Johnson received what is perhaps the most impressive presidential mandate in the post–World War II period: In a contest that posed a clear choice to the electorate, voters gave Johnson a landslide victory of historic proportions and elected a Congress with an enormous Democratic majority. In 1980, Ronald Reagan defeated incumbent Jimmy Carter after a campaign that was focused on the economy. The lessons that politicians drew about the mood of the public from Reagan's large margin of victory, the defection of previously Democratic voters, and the Republican Party's capture of the Senate created opportunities for Reagan to make a sharp turn in economic policy. I provide the most detail for the 1980 election, since the available documentation of commentary and interpretation has grown over the years. In addition, Reagan's election is pivotal in scholars' rejection of the concept of electoral mandates.[2]

The discussion of Reagan, Johnson, and Eisenhower also raises the issue of mandates for incumbents running for reelection. Defeating an incumbent is viewed as a powerful message. Winning reelection by a large margin is also treated as a significant signal from the electorate; a big win is treated as an endorsement of major policy changes that were made in the first term. When presidents claim mandates at the beginning of their first term and then seek reelection, their reelection campaign rhetoric often consists of direct pleas to voters to renew their mandate so that they may extend the changes made in their first term.

The Election of 1952

In 1952, Republican Dwight Eisenhower defeated Democrat Adlai Stevenson Jr. The papers declared it was "Ike in a Landslide," and it seemed that the Republican theme that it was "time for a change" had triumphed over the Democrat's mantra that "you never had it so good."[3] Postelection analysis focused on Eisenhower's competence in handling the Korean War as well as his intention (with Vice President Richard Nixon) to fight communism and rid the government of corruption. The Republicans gained control of the House and Senate by extremely slim margins, so that the Eisenhower mandate was not thought to reach much beyond the candidate and his foreign policy aspirations.

Primaries and Conventions
The Republican Party

Nineteen fifty-two was one of the most contentious primary and convention seasons in the twentieth century. In the 1940s, the Republican nomination had fallen to members of the liberal eastern wing of the party such as Wendell Willkie and Thomas Dewey. The conservative wing of the party hoped to reverse this trend with the candidacy of Senator Robert Taft of Ohio, lawyer, outspoken critic of Democrats and the New Deal, and son of William Howard Taft. Taft was particularly critical of the Truman administration's foreign policy and spearheaded the opposition to both the Truman doctrine and NATO.[4]

Taft's major competition and the hope of moderate Republicans was General Dwight D. Eisenhower. The two men represented the conflict between midwestern isolationists and eastern internationalists within the Republican Party. Eisenhower's supporters had worked to secure victory for him in the first-in-the-nation New Hampshire primary, but the general neither acknowledged his candidacy nor actively pursued the Republican nomination until mid-June, after the primary season had ended and Taft had failed to attain the delegates necessary to win the nomination.[5] Although the Taft organization derided Eisenhower as the "phantom candidate," Eisenhower's refusal to become involved directly in the primaries made him an elusive target. He was especially difficult to attack because no one, including those politicians who backed him early on, was certain just where he stood on most issues.

Eisenhower returned from his NATO command in Europe in early June to seek the nomination in person. At the start of the convention, Taft had more delegates than Eisenhower and was just seventy-five votes short of a majority. Public opinion polls, however, showed that Taft would lose to any of the prominent Democrats running for the presidency (and by large margins), whereas Eisenhower would win. Newspapers, including the *New York Times*, ran editorials claiming that Taft was unelectable. After heated debate and votes resolving disputed delegates, Eisenhower won the nomination on the first roll call. He chose Senator Richard Nixon of California as his vice presidential running mate. Nixon brought geographical balance to the ticket and a strong record of opposition to both communism and corruption in government, which appealed to members of all factions of the party.

The Democratic Party

The fight for the Democratic nomination was also fractious. In March, President Truman announced he would not seek reelection. With the nomination now open, Senator Estes Kefauver of Tennessee entered the contest first, followed by Senator Robert Kerr of Oklahoma, Senator Richard Russell of Georgia, and former ambassador to the Soviet Union, W. Averell Harriman. Kefauver had established a national reputation through his role on the Senate Crime Investigations Committee, and though he was generally opposed by party elites, especially in the South, Kerr and Russell were not strong enough to stop him in the primaries. Harriman was thought to be too closely tied to the unpopular Truman administration to be a plausible nominee. Party leaders tried to draft Illinois governor Adlai Stevenson, but he was initially reluctant to become a candidate, despite being promised the endorsement of President Truman. By the convention, the delegates were split between all five of the candidates, with Stevenson holding the fewest as a result of his refusal to enter the race. After four days and three ballots, however, Governor Stevenson emerged as the convention's compromise candidate. He chose Senator John Sparkman of Alabama as his vice presidential running mate in an effort to appease the southern wing of the party.

The General Election Campaign

The campaign was distinctive for the variety of media that the candidates used to get their message out as well as for the extent of their travels.[6] For the first time in history, the candidates ran television commercials to broaden their name recognition, attack their opponent, and put forward their message. Stevenson relied heavily on thirty-minute talks on television. Eisenhower appeared on "Eisenhower Answers America" spots that featured citizens asking questions or commenting on hard times and Eisenhower answering them by underscoring the need for change.[7] The candidates took to the campaign trail by plane and by train. Though Stevenson initially tried to distance himself from the Truman administration, by late September President Truman actively campaigned on a whistle-stop tour, coordinating his campaign stops and themes with the Stevenson campaign.[8] Both candidates, but particularly Eisenhower, actively campaigned in the South, a region that had seen little campaigning in the past due to its solid record of support for Democratic candidates.

Voters wanted change in Washington at the same time that they wanted to preserve the social and economic prosperity achieved in the postwar era. Thus, the Republicans argued that it was "time for a change," while the Democrats stood by their record and told voters that "you never had it so good." The Republicans promised to change U.S. policy toward Korea, to root out the Communists they suspected of being in government, and to combat high taxes, prices, and inflation. The Democrats pointed to their good relations with labor, their record on civil rights, and the New Deal legislation they had passed to improve the lot of the aged and underprivileged, such as the Social Security plan. They raised the specter of another "Republican depression" if Eisenhower were to be elected.

Poll results made it clear that the Democratic ticket faced an uphill battle. Early in the year, polls revealed that 52 percent of voters felt there was considerable corruption in Washington and that Truman knew about it.[9] Unfortunately for Stevenson, as late as September, 45 percent of the voters thought corruption would continue even if he were elected.[10] While Stevenson obviously had more political experience than Eisenhower, voters thought that Ike was the better leader and was more attractive personally.[11] Voters had more confidence in the Republican Party's ability to end the war and fight corruption, communism, and inflation. They thought Eisenhower better able to handle foreign policy in general, and Korea in particular.[12] By late October, 52 percent of voters claimed that the two-year-old conflict in Korea was the "most important problem" facing the nation.[13] Three-quarters of these voters said that Eisenhower would be able to end the war more quickly than Stevenson.[14]

Perhaps because they had been surprised by the outcome of the 1948 presidential race, pollsters and pundits seemed hesitant to forecast victory for either side in 1952. Instead, news coverage focused on heavy voter registration, the influx of new voters, and an unusually large number of uncommitted voters for an election that was only weeks away.[15] In the final week of the race, in an effort to sway the large contingent of independent and uncommitted voters to his side, Eisenhower gave voters a reason to support his candidacy:

> In this anxious autumn for America, one fact looms above all others in our people's mind. One tragedy challenges all men dedicated to the work of peace. One word shouts denial to those who foolishly pretend that ours is not a nation at war. This fact, this tragedy, this word is: Korea. . . . It has been the burial ground for 20,000 American dead. . . . Where will a new Administration begin? It will begin with its President taking a simple, firm resolution . . . to forego the diversions of politics and to concentrate on the job of ending the Korean War. . . . That job requires a personal trip to Korea. I shall make that trip. . . . I shall go to Korea.[16]

The Democrats tried to dismiss the importance of his claim (as Stevenson said, "If elected, I will go to the White House"), but Eisenhower's message had reinforced his image as an experienced general and world leader. His promise played to his strengths and accentuated his campaign's theme of change from the policies of the Truman administration.

There was no immediate evidence that Eisenhower's dramatic promise touched a chord with voters. The vast majority of states remained too close to call the day before the election, and the outcome appeared certain in only twenty-one states, comprising a total of 173 electoral college votes.[17] The Sunday before the election, campaign strategists on both sides made their forecasts: the Eisenhower camp thought they would win 275 votes, and the Stevenson camp thought they would win 267, both only narrowly passing the 266 votes needed to win.[18] It was unclear which party would win a majority in the House and the Senate.

The Election Outcome

The day after the election, headlines proclaimed, "Eisenhower Wins in a Landslide."[19] Eisenhower won 55 percent of the popular vote to Stevenson's 44 percent. He won 442 of 531 electoral college votes and fared well in all regions of the country, including the South. Eisenhower was more successful in the South than any Republican candidate had been before him, winning Florida, Tennessee, Virginia, and Texas. He even captured Stevenson's home state of Illinois. It was clear that he gained the support of a large proportion of Democrats who had supported Truman in 1948. The papers proclaimed the start of a two-party system in the South.[20]

The congressional races produced a mixed outcome. Republicans gained 22 seats in the House, taking control of that chamber by a slim margin of only 221 to 213. However, they gained only 1 seat in the Senate, making the parties evenly matched in that chamber (48 Republicans versus 47 Democrats plus 1 independent), setting aside the future (Republican) vice president's potential tie-breaking vote.

Interpretations of Victory

The outcome posed an interesting puzzle: Never before had such a presidential landslide been coupled with such tenuous party control of Congress. In order to explain this inconsistency, it was necessary to split the man from his party: "That General Eisenhower and not the Republican party, was the principle reason for the termination of Democratic tenure in the White House that had lasted for twenty years was made evident by the result of the contests for Congress."[21] Yet voters did more than vote for Eisenhower the war hero. The outcome was interpreted as a mandate for Eisenhower's leadership in foreign policy. *Newsweek* commented that "millions of Americans saw in Eisenhower the candidate most likely to find some way out" of the conflict in Korea.[22] On the left, the editors of *The Nation* wrote that "the American people saw Eisenhower and a sweeping change as the likeliest means of getting relief from the tensions generated by Korea and the Cold War."[23] Scholars posited that he was "a symbol of national security much as Roosevelt served as a symbol of economic security in the 1930's."[24] When asked to explain the loss, an aide to Stevenson replied, "Korea, more than anything else."[25]

Forecasts about his general success in Congress were mixed. On the one hand, given the number of fellow partisans: "One thing was certain: that President Dwight D. Eisenhower would not have a comfortable working majority in either house and would require all his gifts of persuasion to win consent for his policies on Capitol Hill."[26] Given past conflict between Eisenhower and the Taft-led conservative Republicans in the Senate and the extremely small Republican majority in the House, he would have to have strong bipartisan support for most of his policies. On the other hand, his "bipartisan" victory with the public might bolster his efforts in Congress:

> His following in the country is tremendous, as the great popular vote he polled demonstrates. Like a famed predecessor in the White House, Franklin Delano Roosevelt, the incoming Chief Executive thus will be able to carry his case directly to the people if hampered by a balky Congress. This is an ace in the hole for the General if persuasion and efforts to achieve reasonable and honest compromise fail. . . . His personal appeal for the people, so clearly manifest in the Tuesday election, transcends party.[27]

Domestic policy would most likely continue to be controlled by a coalition of Republicans and conservative Democrats. Foreign policy was another matter. Eisenhower's popularity was related to his proven leadership in international affairs. And there was one observation consistently made about the new Congress: It would be more internationalist, and more in line with Eisenhower's foreign policy views than the previous one.[28]

Eisenhower's Policy Agenda

Eisenhower's First Inaugural Address focused almost solely on foreign policy, outlining a nine-point program for world peace.[29] He called for a new foreign policy in his first State of the Union Address. In his first year, Eisenhower won seventy-four of the eighty-three roll call votes cast on issues on which his administration took a clear position. His greatest successes came in the realm of foreign policy, where he won 91 percent of the time.[30] He traveled to Korea, as promised, in December 1952, three weeks after his election. Peace talks that had been stalled in the years prior to the election began to move forward; only six months after he took office, an armistice was signed and the Korean conflict was ended.

In Eisenhower's reelection campaign in 1956, the GOP printed leaflets reminding voters that the incumbent president "ended the Korean War and has kept America out of war." Just days before the election, the Suez crisis and the Soviet invasion of Hungary placed the spotlight once more on international relations and helped boost Eisenhower to another victory. In his second victory over Stevenson, Eisenhower won by an even larger margin, 57.4 to 42 percent of the popular vote. He picked up three additional southern states that Stevenson had won in 1952—Kentucky, Louisiana, and West Virginia.

The Republican Party, on the other hand, had lost control of the House and Senate in the 1954 midterm elections. In 1956, they lost two more seats in the House and made no gains in the Senate, leaving them out of power. The 1956 election was not interpreted as a mandate by most observers. Even members of Eisenhower's own party said that "the most obvious reaction is that the President is much more popular than his party, much stronger."[31] In a time of international uncertainty and crisis, voters had stayed with a successful incumbent.

THE ELECTION OF 1964

Like Eisenhower, Lyndon Johnson also claimed a mandate after a landslide election.[32] Unlike Eisenhower, Johnson's victory was accompanied by the election of an overwhelming majority of his own partisans in the House and the Senate. When coupled with a friendly Congress, Johnson's crushing victory over an extremely ideological opponent placed him in an ideal position to make major policy changes. Johnson, who had served as president in the months since

John Kennedy's assassination, promised to continue Kennedy's legislative program. But during the campaign he repeatedly called for new
initiatives:

> Let me make this clear. I ask the American people for a
> mandate—not to preside over a finished program—not just
> to keep things going, I ask the American people for a man-
> date to begin. This Nation—this generation—in this hour,
> has man's first chance to build the Great Society—a place
> where the meaning of man's life matches the marvels of
> man's labor.[33]

Primaries and Conventions

While Johnson had no serious rivals to the Democratic nomination, Barry Goldwater had to survive a bitter battle with Republican
moderates, chiefly New York Governor Nelson A. Rockefeller.[34] The
Goldwater path to the nomination was another symptom of the feud
within the Republican Party that pitted northeastern liberals against
western and southern conservatives. The party's recent nominees—
Wendell Willkie, Thomas Dewey, and even Dwight Eisenhower—
had been the choice of northeastern party elites. Conservatives in
the party argued that there was a "silent conservative vote" waiting
to be tapped if the party would just nominate the right candidate.
When Goldwater captured the nomination, he and his supporters
were uncompromising in the party platform and in their convention
rhetoric. Goldwater selected a vice presidential running mate, Con-
gressman William E. Miller of New York, who held views similar to
his own. The Republican convention, platform, and nominee were
clearly more conservative than they had been in 1960. Moderate
Republicans, the "Eisenhower" Republicans of the previous decade,
were isolated from their nominee.

The General Election Campaign

Both major party candidates, but Goldwater in particular, readily
labeled the election as a "choice, not an echo." Goldwater put himself squarely in opposition to the Democratic policies of the past
thirty years, promising to stop the trend of national policymaking
since the time of the Great Depression and the Second World War.[35]

In his convention speech, he defended himself against accusations that he was too conservative by making the famous remark that "extremism in defense of liberty is no vice; moderation in the pursuit of justice is no virtue."

Goldwater argued for limited government, states' rights over civil rights, and tougher action against communism and the Soviet Union. He questioned the financing of the Social Security system. As a senator, he had voted against the Civil Rights Act of 1964, arguing that its public accommodations and equal employment provisions were unconstitutional. He opposed racial discrimination but argued that efforts to combat the problem should rely on the "hearts of people" rather than on legislation. In international relations, he proposed that the United States seek "total victory" over international communism. He wanted to include nuclear weapons as part of the conventional arsenal of weapons under NATO command. He tried to appeal to the "silent conservative" in all voters with the campaign slogan, "In Your Heart You Know He's Right."

Lyndon Johnson, on the other hand, repeatedly stressed "national unity" and a moderate government that would work to make all Americans better off. The Democratic convention and platform were fashioned to appeal to moderates offended by extremism of all kinds, from the left (Communists) and the right (the Klan and the John Birch Society). Through his Great Society program, Johnson envisioned new federal programs in education, medical care, and urban renewal. He vowed to further his efforts to end poverty, illiteracy, and discrimination. In foreign affairs, Johnson argued that he would continue to pursue peace in the world, while Goldwater would be reckless and run the risk of starting a nuclear war. Though his reputation was that of a moderate, Johnson bolstered his image with the left wing of his party by picking the liberal senator Hubert Humphrey of Minnesota as his running mate. The Democratic retort to the Goldwater campaign was, "In Your Guts You Know He's Nuts."

Johnson clearly endorsed the expansions of federal government responsibility since the New Deal:

> If you will give us the mandate, if you, by your vote, will give us your approval, we will go back to that Capital City on the Potomac and we will take the programs that were started by Franklin Delano Roosevelt and carried on by

Harry S. Truman, and advanced by John Fitzgerald Kennedy, and we will build a greater America.[36]

The Democrats portrayed Goldwater as an extremist who would dismantle domestic programs and destabilize international relations. Liberal Republicans never rallied around Goldwater, as he refused to compromise on his conservative policies and philosophy. The projected outcome of the election—a landslide win for Johnson—was treated by many to be a foregone conclusion. In mid-October, Goldwater led in only three states, for a total of twenty-seven electoral college votes.[37] Polls in October reported 64 percent of the electorate for Johnson, 29 percent for Goldwater, and 7 percent undecided.[38] Though it seemed Johnson would win by a substantial margin, analysts did not think that the Republican Party would suffer major losses in the congressional races.[39]

The Election Outcome

When it was over, Johnson won 61.4 percent of the popular vote to Goldwater's 38.6 percent, the most resounding victory of any presidential candidate in history. He won 486 of the 535 electoral college votes and carried every state except for five southern states and Goldwater's home state of Arizona. The Republican Party lost 38 seats in the House, reducing them to 140 seats, less than half of the Democrats' 295 and their lowest number since 1936. The Democrats gained 2 seats in the Senate, for a total of 68 seats to the Republicans' 32. The Democrats had not enjoyed such a large majority since the administrations of Franklin Roosevelt. Given the magnitude of Johnson's victory, it was apparent that many voters had split their tickets, voting for Johnson while supporting Republican candidates for senator and governor.[40] Nevertheless, the Democratic sweep at the national level boosted Democratic gains in state legislatures across the country.[41]

Interpretations of Victory

Johnson interpreted his victory as a "command" to build on the principles and policies of the Kennedy–Johnson administrations.[42] He was widely perceived to have strong popular support for his Great Society agenda because he had centered his campaign on these issues and had been rewarded with an electoral victory of historic proportions. The voters were presented with a clear choice, since the candidates had emphasized their differences. Analysts concluded that voters had rejected Goldwater's assault on big government and the social and welfare programs of the previous thirty years. A review of the voting patterns of key demographic groups bolstered claims that a majority of voters favored Johnson's views on welfare and civil rights; because of Johnson's stance on these issues, he won by overwhelming margins among ethnic minorities and the poor. By contrast:

> The average Goldwater voter was white. In the cities and towns he was a young man on the rise professionally and financially. On the farms he was distinctly southern. Among the aged, he was financially independent, reasonably secure without the help of Social Security. And among low-income persons, he was a rarity. . . . There were two groups on Tuesday—the white Goldwater South and everybody else.[43]

Martin Luther King said that the landslide should convince the president that he has a "definite mandate from the American public" to seek passage of civil rights legislation.[44]

Congress was also predicted to be favorable to Johnson's legislative program. The Democratic gains in the House meant "he has all but broken the conservative Southern Democratic and Republican coalition that hampered passage of Administration measures."[45] Liberal Democrats talked about overturning the power structure of the House of Representatives by changing the procedure for making committee assignments and punishing conservative Democrats who refused to support Johnson's program.[46] The Democratic leadership seemed persuaded that the election was a signal about popular support for legislation such as Medicare, since polls showed that Medicare was a significant factor in Johnson's victory.[47] Wilbur Mills, chairman of the Ways and Means Committee, "conceded that before the election members of congress may not have been in step with the people's thinking on Medicare; but after Johnson campaigned on the issue and won by an unprecedented margin, they 'realized that people were for it for the first time.'"[48]

In the Republican camp, the election was widely regarded as having put to rest the "conservative Republican charge [that] the GOP has lost the presidency six out of the last eight times because it has put up progressive candidates."[49] Immediately after the election, moderate Republicans fought with Goldwater supporters for control of the party.[50] Moderates organized conferences of leading Republican officeholders to "rebuild" the party and urged that the Goldwater-appointed chair of the Republican National Committee be forced to resign. Goldwater maintained that "25 million people" had voted for his philosophy and that he would not compromise on his principles even in the face of Johnson's landslide victory.[51] But the editors of the New York Times expressed a more common sentiment when they wrote, "The Republican party almost destroyed itself in this election."[52]

Johnson's Policy Agenda

In his January State of the Union Address, Johnson spent most of his speech outlining his vision of the "Great Society." He mentioned general directives and specific programs in the areas of health, education, and urban development. He emphasized creating equal opportunity and an improved quality of life for all Americans. Regarding U.S.-Soviet relations, he declared his intention to "seek peaceful understandings that can lessen the danger to freedom. Last fall I asked the American people to choose that course. I will carry forward their command."[53]

The 89th Congress was one of the most productive ever in terms of the quantity and scope of new laws.[54] By early April, the House and Senate had passed major legislation providing federal aid to elementary and secondary schools. In July, the administration's Medicare bill, which provided a health insurance system for the elderly, became law. A cabinet-level Department of Housing and Urban Development was created. The Voting Rights Act was passed, outlawing the use of literacy tests and other devices that had repeatedly denied voting rights to African American citizens throughout the United States, particularly in the South. Overall, 68.9 percent of the massive volume of legislation that Johnson requested was approved by Congress, the highest rate of presidential success since 1953.[55]

THE ELECTION OF 1980

In 1980, Ronald Reagan claimed a mandate to get government "off the backs" of American citizens.[56] During the election campaign, he attacked President Carter's economic record and argued for less government regulation, spending, and taxation. When he won, the common wisdom of journalists and politicians was that Americans were asking for significant changes in economic policy. Reagan falls somewhere between Eisenhower and Johnson in terms of the amount of political capital he possessed at the start of his term. His margin of victory was by no means as big as Johnson's, but it was substantial, and it was unexpected. With the Republican takeover of the Senate, it looked as if he might also have congressional support for his legislative agenda.

Primaries and Conventions
The Democratic Party

From mid to late 1979, incumbent Jimmy Carter's public approval rating as measured by Gallup polls was hovering around 30 percent, having steadily declined throughout the year.[57] Polls in mid to late 1979 also revealed that a race between Carter and Reagan would be very competitive.[58] Sensing Carter's vulnerability, Senator Ted Kennedy announced his candidacy for the Democratic nomination on November 7, 1979, and California governor Jerry Brown announced his candidacy on November 8.[59] Between the Iowa caucuses and the New Hampshire primary, President Carter announced that he would need to stay in the White House rather than campaign actively in order to deal with the hostage crisis in Iran.[60] During the primary season, this "Rose Garden" strategy worked to Carter's advantage by denying his opponents public exchanges with the president that might have increased their stature as candidates.[61] The Carter campaign ran ads emphasizing his personal qualities ("Husband, Father, President . . .") rather than the issues. He made phone calls to party leaders in competitive states and (in the tradition of incumbents) distributed federal grants and projects to shore up support in key states.[62] He welcomed interest group leaders and activists to the White House.

Though Carter's popularity fell throughout the primary season, he steadily accumulated delegates from states in all regions of the country.[63] By the last primary, Carter had received 50 percent of all votes cast, while Kennedy had received 38 percent. Even so, Kennedy stayed in the race until the convention in mid-August. At the convention, Kennedy and disaffected members of Congress tried to change party rules in order to release delegates from their candidate pledges so that they would be free to abandon the increasingly unpopular incumbent.[64] The move was defeated, but it signified the lack of support for Carter within his own party.[65]

In his acceptance speech, Carter emphasized the issues and themes that would be at the center of his fall campaign. He spoke of the importance of trust and experience and argued that Reagan and the Republican Party's assessment of the country and their plans for the future were based upon fantasy. He emphasized his administration's energy policy, employment and job training programs, investment in infrastructure, and care of the poor and the elderly. He contrasted his party's commitment to underprivileged groups to what he characterized as the Republican Party's irresponsibility and indifference.

The Republican Party

Republican Party candidates declared their intention to seek the presidency as early as August 1978.[66] At the start of the primary season, seven major candidates vied for the nomination, mostly representing the moderate and conservative wings of the Republican Party. Senator Howard Baker and George Bush presented themselves as party moderates. Representative Phil Crane, Senator Bob Dole, John Connally, and former California governor Ronald Reagan were the conservative candidates. John Anderson, a twenty-year veteran of the House of Representatives, was the only "liberal" in the field. Though the Republican Party had no incumbent, Ronald Reagan was perceived early on as the front-runner. Gallup polls throughout 1979 showed Reagan overwhelmingly preferred by a wide margin over Connally, Baker, and Bush (who were relatively unknown). Only former President Gerald Ford came close to having as much support as Reagan, and he had not declared he was in the race.[67]

Reagan had mounted a strong challenge to incumbent Gerald

Ford for the Republican nomination in 1976 and had networked with party activists and interest groups on behalf of his organization "Citizens for the Republic" ever since. The Republican candidates viewed Reagan as the candidate to beat and devised their strategies with that in mind.[68] Even so, many thought Reagan was too conservative to win the general election. As James Reston wrote, "The Republicans are compassionate people. . . . They know Mr. Carter didn't invent inflation or mean to get into all this trouble at home or abroad, so they are giving Carter, as they gave to Lyndon Johnson in 1964, their favorite candidate, and Carter's favorite opponent— Ronald Reagan. Seldom in the history of American politics has a party out of power shown so much generosity to a President in such deep difficulty."[69]

The field narrowed quickly to Anderson, Bush, and Reagan.[70] George Bush, who had campaigned vigorously in Iowa, beat Reagan in the Iowa caucuses. Bush's momentum was cut short, however, by the New Hampshire primary. In contrast to his strategy in Iowa, Reagan campaigned actively in New Hampshire and beat Bush by a two-to-one margin with 49.6 percent of the vote. While John Anderson had respectable showings in early primaries in Massachusetts, Vermont, and Connecticut, his popular vote totals did not translate into many delegates. He lost to Reagan both in his home state of Illinois (36.7 percent to Reagan's 48.4 percent) and in Wisconsin, states in which he was expected to do well. On April 24, he declared that he would run as an independent candidate. George Bush won only six of thirty-five primaries that he contested, and he withdrew from the race May 26, six weeks before the Republican National Convention.

Reagan had been careful not to isolate the moderate wing of the party during the primaries and in the weeks before the convention.[71] Though there were differences within the party on platform issues (most notably on abortion and the Equal Rights Amendment), the supply-side economic policies and foreign policy provisions of Reagan's campaign were incorporated into the platform with relatively little dissent.[72] Conservative positions clearly dominated the platform, but language was modified so as not to offend moderates, and sections were written to appeal to traditionally Democratic groups such as blue-collar workers. Throughout the convention, in speeches and events, moderate Republican leaders (such as Ford and Henry Kissinger) were given their due respect. The social conservatism of the party was masked by appeals to patriotism and pragmatism.[73] Reagan selected George Bush as his vice presidential running mate.[74]

In his acceptance speech, Reagan attacked Carter for suggesting that the nation was in a "malaise," and he attacked Democrats in general for failed economic and foreign policies.[75] He downplayed his social conservatism and offered details about the economic policies he would pursue if elected.[76] While reassuring his audience that programs such as social security would be preserved, he argued that "our federal government is overgrown and overweight." At several points, he promised that federal spending would be limited and the cost of government would be reduced. In addition, "Everything that can be run more effectively by state and local government we shall turn over to state and local government, along with the funding sources to pay for it." Reagan outlined his plan to reduce income tax rates by 30 percent over three years and to link taxes to his notion of government accountability. Finally, he asked his audience whether they could put up with "four more years" of the current administration.[77]

The General Election Campaign

Campaign strategists on both sides agreed that there were new issues and attitudes developing in the late 1970s that worked to the advantage of Republicans. After the Great Depression, the Republican Party was viewed as the party of Herbert Hoover, the party of recession. But since 1974, the number of voters who viewed the Republican Party as the party of prosperity had been steadily increasing.[78] Between 1959 and 1978, the percentage of Americans who thought that "big government" was the major cause of inflation went from 14 to 51 percent.[79] As Vietnam faded from memory, more and more Americans favored increasing defense spending.[80]

Republicans and Democrats agreed that conservative issues were popular in 1980, though they disagreed about the reasons behind it.[81] Republicans argued that the electorate's preferences were in fact shifting to the right on economic policy and social issues. Democrats countered that short-term problems such as high inflation and the hostage crisis simply made conservative issues more salient. Whether or not preferences were changing in a conservative direction, polls showed convincingly that Americans believed current policies had not worked. In December 1979, 74 percent of voters thought the country had gotten severely off track. On the eve of the election, 56 percent still believed the country was on the wrong track.

Reagan's Campaign Strategy

Ronald Reagan's general election strategy was characterized by several objectives.[82] First, the campaign focused on economic issues. The Republican National Committee had run ads throughout the year, attacking the Democrats for their handling of the economy.[83] According to Bill Brock, chairman of the Republican National Committee: "What we were trying to do from the very front end of the campaign, going back before we had a nominee, before we even had some candidates, was to try to keep the election non-ideological, to keep it focused on the economy because that was our issue."[84] Peter Dailey, deputy director of media for the Reagan–Bush campaign, argued that "one of the most important things we tried to do throughout the campaign was to keep the focus [on the economy]. . . . That was the issue we felt we were strongest in dealing with, and we wanted to stay with it as long and as hard as we could, not be diverted into a separate battle even when the media turned their guns."[85]

The economy was the number one issue in the campaign according to the polls. One out of three voters thought inflation was the most important problem facing the nation. When asked what voters wanted to talk about, Tim Wirth, a Democrat from Colorado, replied, "Inflation, Government spending, inflation, the effect of Government spending on inflation, the effect of printing money on inflation, inflation, Government spending and inflation."[86]

Second, while focusing on the economy, the Republicans also sought to highlight Carter's incompetence and his weak record.[87] As expected, economic issues worked to the president's disadvantage. Of those who considered the economy the most important problem, 47 percent felt the Republican Party more capable than the Democratic Party at making things better; only 33 percent felt the Democrats were better able to handle economic problems.[88] A huge budget deficit and rising consumer prices obviously did not work in Carter's favor.[89] The Reagan campaign ran several negative ads attacking Carter's economic policies and devoted a thirty-minute televised ad to the economy the week before the election.[90]

The specific demographic groups targeted for conversion to the Reagan side were blue-collar workers, Catholics, and southerners. Reagan's stand against abortion and his general social conservatism made him attractive to both Catholics and southerners. Throughout his political career, Ronald Reagan had run well among blue-collar, union voters.[91] He liked to remind people that he was a former union president, having once headed the Screen Actors Guild. In general, the slumping economy worked to his advantage. By mid-October, Reagan led Carter by eighteen points among those voters who thought that unemployment was the most serious economic problem and by twelve points among the larger group of voters who thought that inflation was the most serious economic problem.[92]

Third, the Reagan campaign focused on the issue of leadership. Voters said that strong leadership was the most important quality they sought in a president.[93] Polls showed consistently that Reagan was viewed as decisive and strong, someone who could get things done. In a mid-October *New York Times*/CBS poll, 62 percent of probable voters described Ronald Reagan as a "strong leader"; only 34 percent were willing to describe Jimmy Carter as such.[94] A Gallup poll in this period found that 43 percent of voters felt that "forceful and decisive" better described Reagan than Carter; only 24 percent said these terms described Carter better than Reagan.[95] Voters believed that Ronald Reagan had a definite vision of the country's future.

As the hostage crisis wore on, Reagan was able to turn the issue against Carter. He called the situation "a humiliation and a disgrace." Voters feared Reagan would get them into a war, but they also felt he would see to it that America was respected in the rest of the world.[96] To counter Reagan's hawkish reputation, the Reagan campaign ran several ads early on that showed him sitting in an easy chair, talking in measured tones about the economy and world peace.[97] He gave a thirty-minute televised commercial on foreign policy on October 19 in which he noted, "I have known four wars in my lifetime, and I don't want to see a fifth."[98] Reagan's campaign tried to minimize any boost that a preelection release of the Iranian hostages would give President Carter by coining the phrase "October Surprise" and mentioning the possibility to the press frequently, in the hope that the event would seem conveniently orchestrated if in fact it did occur.[99]

Carter's Campaign Strategy

The major objective of the Carter campaign was to deflect attention from the president's record in office and instead to emphasize his honesty and integrity. Its goal was to "make people make a choice between two candidates—two personalities—and, to the extent that we could, between two parties."[100] References to Carter's time in office were largely restricted to discussing the immense responsibilities of the office. Early television ads emphasized the difficulties of the presidency and showed Carter hard at work at night. Polls showed that Carter was viewed as being more honest and fair and as having the higher ethical standards of the two candidates.[101] Voters also felt Carter understood the problems and demands of the presidency better than did Governor Reagan. In addition, polls indicated that voters agreed with the notion that Carter had learned a great deal in his first term and would be a better president in a second term.[102]

Among those voters who felt foreign policy was the most important problem facing the country, the Democratic Party was slightly more likely to be seen as the party most capable of dealing with this issue.[103] Polls consistently showed that voters believed Jimmy Carter was best able to keep the country out of war. Carter emphasized the issue of war and peace and implied that Reagan was trigger-happy and would get the nation involved in a nuclear war. The Carter campaign portrayed Reagan as risky, dangerous, and beyond the mainstream of American political beliefs. They ran negative "man in the street" ads in which Californians spoke about their former governor, saying things like, "I think it's a big risk to have Reagan as president. Reagan scares me. He really scares me."[104] Another ad featured Carter speaking on nuclear arms control: "We are not dealing with just another shoot-out at O.K. Corral. We are dealing with the most important issue facing human beings on this planet."[105] As Patrick Caddell put it: "It was our job to deny Reagan the ability to pass that acceptability threshold and create enough doubt so that at the end of the campaign, we would be in a situation where the edge that normally comes to an incumbent late in a campaign would benefit us."[106]

Unfortunately, Carter's negative attacks on Reagan backfired. The more he attacked Reagan personally, the more he compromised his image as a decent and moral candidate. In early October, for example, in a commentary that drew a great deal of criticism, Carter alleged that Reagan would divide the country along racial, religious, and sectional lines. He said, "You'll determine whether or not this America will be unified or, if I lose the election, whether Americans might be separated, black from white, Jew from Christian, North from South, rural from urban."[107] Reagan responded by taking the high road: "I was greatly saddened myself that the President would stoop so low."[108] The Reagan campaign painted Carter as desperate, vicious, and unpresidential.[109]

The Candidacy of John Anderson

The third candidate in the race, John Anderson, joined forces with his vice presidential candidate Patrick Lucey, a Democrat and former Wisconsin governor, in a "National Unity Campaign." Anderson shed his Republican partisanship to run as an independent candidate, making no attempt to form a third party. He hoped to replace President Carter as Ronald Reagan's main opponent. Eventually, he was on the ballot in all fifty states. However, his task was difficult if not impossible, given the funding inequities between his campaign and those of the major parties. While Carter and Reagan were each guaranteed $29.4 million in federal funding (and the parties were given $4.6 million), Anderson could not collect matching funds until *after* the election, and then only if he garnered at least 5 percent of the popular vote. His campaign efforts were mostly directed at getting on the ballot in all fifty states and raising enough money to keep his campaign afloat.[110]

In addition to his financial concerns, Anderson had two objectives. First, he had to get the two major candidates to address his ideas and treat him as a worthy opponent. He criticized both candidates in his efforts to force them to engage with him. He attacked Carter's economic record and accused him of incompetence, and he criticized Reagan's policies and divisive themes. Second, and related, he had to convince voters that a vote for Anderson was not a wasted vote. He argued that "polls have been wrong" and urged voters to vote their consciences. He appealed to voters who rejected both major candidates and tried to persuade voters on the basis of his policy positions.

Anderson argued that neither Carter nor Reagan would be able to work with Congress. In fact, he said he didn't think it would make a difference which of his opponents won. "We really won't see a lot of programs, and we'll just kind of muddle through."[111] On August 30, he released a 317-page campaign platform that was fiscally conservative and socially liberal. He favored tax incentives but opposed a tax cut for individuals. He called for a fifty cents per gallon excise tax on gasoline. Like Carter, he supported ratification of the SALT II treaty, opposed constitutional amendments banning abortion, and favored ratification of the Equal Rights Amendment. Like Reagan, he opposed a comprehensive national health care plan.

The Presidential Debate

The one and only televised debate between Carter and Reagan on October 28, one week before the election, involved no major surprises.[112] The League of Women Voters had instituted a rule that any candidate with at least a 15 percent rating in the polls should be included in the debates. Anderson narrowly met that criterion in September (when Carter refused to participate in a three-way debate) but failed to meet it in late October.[113]

During the debate, President Carter stressed nuclear arms control as the most important issue of the campaign, while Ronald Reagan stressed the country's economic position ("Are you better off than you were four years ago?"). Carter cast himself as a mainstream Democrat and tried to keep Reagan on the defensive with respect to his issue positions. Reagan accused the president of misrepresenting his record ("There you go again"). Debates tend to be the vehicle of challengers as opposed to incumbents, because they put the challenger on a par with the president and often resolve doubts about whether the challenger has the stature to be president. The 1980 Carter–Reagan debate was no exception. Reagan appeared competent, reasonable, and reassuring.[114] Immediately after the debate, Reagan moved into a five percentage point lead in the polls, and assessments of his character improved.[115]

The Congressional Races

Democratic control of the House and Senate was not thought to be in peril. As late as October 26, an article in the *New York Times* stated:

> Republicans expect to gain some Congressional seats Nov. 4, but not enough to jeopardize the Democratic Party's 26 year control of the House and Senate. Despite the most sophisticated, highly coordinated challenge in years by the Republican Party, the vast majority of Democratic Congressional candidates appear to be holding their own.[116]

The article reported that "analysts from both parties" predicted the Democrats would lose 3 to 6 Senate seats and 15 to 25 House seats.[117] Republicans would need to gain 10 Senate seats and 59 House seats in order to control both chambers of Congress. At the same time, the volatility of the electorate was noted: "Virtually all analysts are hedging their projections, given the closeness of many races, the rapid and frequent unpredictable shifts in public mood, and widespread unhappiness with the choices in the Presidential race."[118] The vulnerable members of Congress included several members of the "Watergate class" of 1974 who won in the aftermath of the Nixon resignation; six Democrats tainted by the "Abscam" scandal; long-term Democrats perceived to be out of touch with their districts; and finally, six senators targeted for defeat by the National Conservative Political Action Committee (NCPAC). Senate Minority Leader Howard Baker estimated that Republicans had a "fifty-fifty" chance of gaining control of the Senate.[119]

Carter was viewed as a liability to most of the Democrats running in congressional races. Democratic members of the House and Senate had been the greatest supporters of Kennedy's "open convention" movement. Due to Carter's low approval ratings, most Democrats kept their distance. Many believed that the presence of John Anderson on the ballot would bring out voters who would vote Democratic at the congressional level. Activists complained about the lack of a unifying positive theme for the party.

The Republican Party, on the other hand, tried to join the presidential and congressional races in the minds of the voters, spending $5 million on their "Vote Republican—for a Change" campaign. Republicans worked to get voters to recognize that the Democrats were the party that had controlled Congress for the past twenty-five years. In 1979 only 68 percent of all voters knew the Democrats controlled Congress; by June of 1980, 80 percent knew.[120] Republicans running for Congress viewed Reagan positively, and he cultivated his ties with both candidates and Republicans in office. He gave a press conference on the economy in July after which he was praised by congressional Republicans; in September he met with them to sign a "Capitol Compact" of general policy directives.

Final Projections

Both the Carter and Reagan camps agreed that the campaign was marked by extreme volatility in the electorate. The number of undecided voters was the highest it had ever been at all stages of the campaign, right up to the last week.[121] Polls in mid-October revealed that 36 percent of voters were not strongly committed to any candidate and might change their minds before election day.[122] The large number of uncommitted voters and the closeness of the race led both candidates to pursue more national strategies.[123] The final polls gave Reagan a slight lead, though this was always within the margin of error.[124] Reagan was thought to have 235 firm votes out of the 270 required for an electoral college victory; Carter was thought to have 145.[125] Experts predicted that turnout would be lower in 1980 than in 1976, somewhere between 52 and 54 percent of all eligible voters.[126]

Days before the election, a columnist lamented: "Thus, without the kind of overriding mandate from the electorate that now seems improbable, it would be surprising if any of the contenders enters the White House next January with the kind of special momentum that would help him alter the limiting realities and fulfill more than a modicum of his promises."[127] The feeling was echoed in the last edition of the *Congressional Quarterly Weekly Report* before the election: "The 1980 presidential campaign will probably end November 4 like the one four years ago—with the nation spending a long evening in front of the television set."[128]

The Election Outcome

The magnitude of the Republican Party victory exceeded the expectations of most politicians and observers.[129] Reagan won 50.8 percent of the popular vote. Jimmy Carter ran almost ten points behind, with 41 percent of the popular vote. Reagan won 489 of the 538 electoral college votes, while Carter won only 49 electoral college votes. John Anderson won 6.6 percent of the popular vote and no electoral college votes. Carter carried only Georgia, Maryland, Rhode Island, Minnesota, Hawaii, West Virginia, and the District of Columbia. The victory was so decisive that NBC officially declared Reagan the winner at 8:15 P.M. EST, and Carter conceded at 9:45 P.M. EST, before the West Coast polls closed. Turnout was 54 percent, down slightly from the 1976 level of 54.3 percent.

The magnitude of Reagan's victory was not only much larger than expected, it was matched by Republican gains at the congressional level. Republicans gained thirty-three seats in the House of Representatives, returning their numbers in that chamber to the level before Watergate and the 1974 election. Past Republican presidents who had won impressive victories, such as Eisenhower and Nixon, did not have such impressive gains in the House.[130] Democrats still controlled the House, with 243 seats to the Republicans' 192. However, several prominent Democrats lost their bids for reelection: Al Ullman (OR), Chairman of the Ways and Means Committee; Harold Johnson (CA) Chairman of the Public Works and Transportation Committee; and John Brademas (IN), majority whip.[131] The chairmen of the Merchant Marine and Fisheries Committee and the Administration Committee, both of whom had been indicted in the Abscam investigation, were also defeated.

Twenty-four Democratic and 10 Republican Senate seats were contested in the election. The Republicans held all 10 of their seats and won 12 of the Democratic seats. Their net gain of 12 seats gave them a 53 to 47 majority in the Senate, which they now controlled for the first time since 1954. The elections left in their wake the largest number of Republican senators since the 71st Congress (1929–1930) and ended the longest one-party domination of the Senate in U.S. history. In addition, the Republicans gained Senate seats in all regions of the country.[132] Four of the six liberal senators targeted by the National Conservative Political Action Committee (NCPAC) were defeated: Birch Bayh (IN), Frank Church (ID), John Culver (IA), and George McGovern (SD). As in the House of Representatives, a number of prominent committee chairmen were defeated, including Warren Magnuson (D–WA) of the Appropriations Committee and Herman Talmadge (D–GA) of the Agriculture Committee.

Commentators focused on regional and demographic patterns of support for the candidates and on exit polls.[133] Extensive coverage was devoted to the fact that Carter's vote share declined among all parts of the old New Deal/Democratic coalition, except among blacks. Carter won 10 percent more Catholic votes than Ford in 1976 (54 to 44 percent) and 10 percent less than Reagan in 1980 (51 to 40 percent).[134] Carter's margins among "Jews, liberals, and low income voters" were "well below the percentages that Democrats usually get."[135] Teachers voted for Reagan. Carter did only slightly better than Reagan among voters in union households. Whereas Carter had the support of 77 percent of self-identified Democrats in 1976, he won the support of only 66 percent in 1980. His loss of southern support was also deemed significant.[136] In 1976, Carter won all of the southern states except Virginia.[137] In 1980, he lost all of them with the exception of his home state of Georgia. He also managed to lose Pennsylvania, Massachusetts, and New York, three states that had voted Democratic fairly consistently in the recent past.

The flip side, of course, was that Reagan appeared to have a broad coalition of support. He did gather support from some traditionally Democratic groups such as blue-collar workers, conservative Democrats, and Catholics. He won by a wide margin among whites, men, Protestants (especially born-again Christians), the wealthy, and white-collar and professional workers. Reagan had the usual Republican support of the business community.

The message behind the Anderson vote was difficult to decipher. His supporters were mostly independents; partisans who voted for Anderson were about evenly split between Democrats and Republicans. If Anderson had not been in the race, it seems that his supporters would have divided their vote equally between the major party candidates. And even if they had all voted for Carter, Reagan would still have won the election.

Exit polls revealed that the most frequently cited reasons for voting for Reagan were a desire for change and dissatisfaction with economic conditions, especially inflation.[138] More than two-thirds of voters cited economic problems such as unemployment, taxes, and inflation as a key reason for their vote.[139] Exit polls showed that foreign policy and social issues were viewed as being much less important. One in five registered voters changed his or her mind about whom to vote for or whether to vote in the last four days before the election.[140] About a third of those who switched from Carter to Reagan in the final days cited the economy as the reason for their switch; 23 percent cited the hostage crisis.[141] According to polls, low turnout (especially in states like New York and Massachusetts) hurt Carter.[142]

Interpretations of Victory

If the immediate reaction to the outcome was to express surprise, the second reaction was to attach significance. The *New York Times* headline two days after the election read "Reagan Buoyed by National Swing to the Right; Position Bolstered by G.O.P. Senate Control." The emerging consensus was that the victory was a call for policy change. The lesson drawn by defeated Vice President Walter Mondale was typical: "There's no question that the people yesterday decided they wanted a fundamental change in government. I don't know any other explanation for the number of outstanding Senators and Congressmen who lost."[143] The few who disagreed cited low turnout ("Reagan was elected by only a quarter of eligible voters") and close margins in some of the large states.

Reagan's election was hailed as a national triumph for several reasons. First, both parties, but especially the Republicans, had run "national" campaigns. Second, Reagan and other candidates of the

Republican Party were victorious in all regions of the country. Republicans won four of the thirteen contested governorships.[144] They increased their share of the 5,900 state legislative seats by more than 200 seats, for a total of 39 percent of those offices nationwide. They won control of five additional state legislative chambers.[145] Third, the Reagan campaign focused almost exclusively on the Carter record and on the state of the national economy. The economy was a "unifying theme with no divisive component" that Republicans at all levels had been able to run on.[146] Finally, the Republicans downplayed the role of constituencies like the New Right.[147]

Republicans attributed their victory primarily to economic issues. As one of Reagan's pollsters put it: "We felt that if this election did come down to the issue of the economic cluster, if people asked themselves if there was better hope to reduce inflation with a Reagan presidency, we would win it. And that's exactly what happened in the last four or five days of this campaign."[148] The Democrats agreed: "If the test came down to whether people felt better, whether we had performed satisfactorily for the last four years, we knew we were gone from the beginning, or words to that effect."[149] Editorials proclaimed, "Mr. Reagan has a mandate for dramatic economic innovation."[150]

In his first news conference, on the Thursday after the Tuesday election, Reagan pledged to act immediately on his economic program. "I expect to move as swiftly as possible. I think this is the most important thing, I think it was the issue of the campaign; I think it is what the American people told us with their votes they wanted. And so we'll move instantly on that."[151] When asked about the party platform, he stated:

> I ran on the platform; the people voted for me on the platform; I do believe in that platform and I think it would be very cynical and callous of me now to suggest that I'm going to turn away from it. Evidently, those people who voted for me—of the other party or of independents—must have agreed with the platform also.[152]

Vice President Elect George Bush noted, "We didn't imagine a sweep like this. It will make it easier for Governor Reagan to put in his programs to help people."[153] Reagan's aides claimed, "There will be a willingness on the part of Congress to pass some kind of new economic package. . . . I think the huge support the Governor got provides a mandate for change."[154]

For some people, the message of the election was the rejection of Jimmy Carter more than a preference for Reagan's economic agenda. Carter's own advisors, in a postmortem discussion, provided several reasons for the president's failure, from the hostage situation to the debate.[155] They acknowledged that the troubled economy was the biggest factor in the election but felt this did not imply that voters agreed wholeheartedly with the specifics of Reagan's policy agenda.[156] John Anderson agreed:

> I do believe that it was essentially a negative kind of vote that was cast by the American voters, that they were not really trading in one set of policies for a new set of policies. The centerpiece of the Reagan economic program is certainly the Kemp–Roth bill, and the last survey I saw indicated that as of the present time, a majority of the American people still think that would be inflationary.[157]

Journalists and politicians recognized that the new Congress would be more conservative than the old one on economic, social, and military issues.[158] Senate committees would have new and more conservative leaders, along with extensive staff turnover.[159] Within days after the election, the possibility of a coalition of conservative House Democrats and House Republicans was being discussed.[160]

Representatives and senators were thought to have been swept in on Reagan's coattails. "Riding Ronald Reagan's coattails and a tide of conservatism, Republicans gained 12 seats, for a total of 53 in the new Senate."[161] Polls showed that as Carter lost ground to Reagan in the final days before the election, Democrats in Congress also lost ground to their challengers.[162] The same groups that defected from Carter to Reagan defected from the Democrats to the Republicans in Congress. Low turnout hurt Democratic senators in key states, as well as President Carter.[163] The Democrats conceded that the Republicans had been successful at blaming Congress, along with the president, for the nation's economic problems.[164]

The Democrats reacted to the outcome with caution but were willing to give Reagan a chance. Speaker of the House Tip O'Neill commented that "the people of America have spoken, and America comes first, party comes second. We will cooperate as much as we can."[165] A representative said, "I think for a while there's going to be a lot of shadow-boxing and everybody is going to hold his fire. . . . The liberals are just going to pull in their horns and see how things go."[166] House Majority Leader Jim Wright (D–TX) expressed caution:

> We must demonstrate our capacity to cooperate with the president and the Senate. . . . We will not be obstructionist because we recognize the mandate for change. But if the Republicans try to undermine Social Security or retreat on the minimum wage or on basic human rights, then we would have to stand as a roadblock against these movements.[167]

Prominent Democrats began a reappraisal of their issue positions. John White, the Democratic national chairman said, "The thing that I get is that everybody thinks we ought to reassess some of the positions that we've taken."[168] The defeat of a number of prominent liberals and "close calls" for others struck fear in the hearts of many Democrats, who immediately started talking about revising the party's issue positions in a conservative direction. Defeated Senator Frank Church observed, "The conservatives are in charge now. This is what they wanted, and the people have given it to them."[169] Representative James Jones (D–OK) commented, "If we ignore the mandate of the election, we will become a minority party."[170]

Republicans in Congress were both motivated and optimistic. Representative Guy Vander Jagt of Michigan, who had been chairman of the Republican Congressional Campaign Committee, stressed his party's incentive. "We're very aware of the fact that we won, we won big, and now we've got to produce." Since Reagan had met with Republican congressional leaders before the election and issued a five-point "Capitol Compact" that included making cuts in government spending and reducing individual income taxes, his party was ready to move forward with his agenda. Republican governors submitted proposals to Reagan shortly after the election, asking for more state authority on a wide variety of issues.[171]

Reagan's Policy Agenda

President Reagan and his advisors focused on his economic proposals almost exclusively immediately after his inauguration on January 20.[172] Reagan gave a nationally televised address on economic issues on February 5. His televised address before a joint session of Congress on February 18 focused almost entirely on the economy, rather than being a general "state of the union" address. His top legislative priorities were the passage of his budget and tax policies. He proposed massive, across-the-board spending cuts (except for defense) and a 30 percent cut in individual income tax rates (over three years).

The Reagan White House made a concerted effort to keep the election results in the minds of legislators. In the message accompanying the details of his budget plan, he warned Congress to adopt his program or risk angering voters:

> When considering the economic recovery package, I urge the Members of Congress to remember that last November the American people's message was loud and clear. The mandate for change, expressed by the American people, was not my mandate; it was our mandate. Together we must remember that our primary responsibility is to the Nation as a whole and that there is nothing more important than putting America's economic house in order.[173]

White House memoranda in the early months articulated "the importance of preserving the appearance of the president's strength through association with an election mandate, public support, and a string of legislative victories."[174] On a trip to the South in June, Reagan told Democrats that he "could not in good conscience campaign against any of you Democrats who have helped me."[175]

In addition to concentrating his staff's efforts and reminding legislators of the potential for voter retribution, the Reagan team put all of the budget cuts in one package, a "reconciliation bill." Instead of voting on individual spending cuts, members of Congress were forced to vote on all of them at once in a single, up-or-down vote. As *Congressional Quarterly* reported, "The administration billed it as a vote on the Reagan economic program—a program that was the mandate of the 1980 election." Reagan appealed to members of Congress once again:

> More important, let us never forget the mandate of November. The people of this Nation have asked for action—and they deserve it now, not somewhere down in a misty future. Therefore, I'm asking Congress today to live up to its original commitment and deliver to my desk before the August recess, not one but two bills—a spending bill and a tax bill. Only then can we say as elected representatives that we truly deserve a rest.[176]

In late July, the Senate passed the conference bill version of Reagan's program.[177] In the House, conservative (mostly southern) Democrats joined Republicans to pass the budget resolution.[178] Days later, Congress passed one of the largest tax reduction bills in history.[179] The plan cut individual income taxes by 25 percent over three years and also contained business tax cuts intended to spur investment and growth. Though he made some concessions, Reagan boasted that he had received "95 percent" of what he sought. Polls showed a surge in Republican partisan identification and a growing perception that the Republican Party was best at handling economic issues.[180]

*

Reagan's impressive victory, and the lessons about public opinion that politicians learned from it, paved the way for Reagan to ask for major changes in economic policy. Like the aftermath of any election, winners and losers offered different interpretations. Politicians appealed to standard pieces of evidence to make their arguments about the election. Reagan's big electoral college victory and the unexpected gains by Republicans in Congress made the landslide status of the election compelling. The Republicans had worked to frame the election around economic policy, and the behavior of defecting Democratic voters and the electorate in general supported the view that economic discontent was behind the landslide.

In 1952, 1964, and 1980, politicians and journalists simplified the logic of the election and zeroed in on a policy-oriented explanation for the outcome. This was facilitated by the fact that the campaigns themselves focused on the issues—Ike's dramatic promise to go to Korea in 1952, Goldwater versus the New Deal in 1964, and the Republican Party focus on the economy in 1980. In every case, the winner emerged with a landslide victory that bolstered his claim to having *national* electoral support. Eisenhower won a landslide in the electoral college, picking up states in the previously Democratic south. Johnson won one of the greatest popular and electoral college victories in history, in all regions of the country. Reagan had a surprisingly large electoral college victory and plurality over Carter plus Republican Party gains in Congress throughout the country. In every case, members of Congress, including members of the opposition, recognized the new president's strong popular support. These presidents had every incentive to ask for a change in that national agenda. As it turns out, they got what they wanted.

Mandates and Incumbency

The cases in this chapter raise the question of mandates and incumbency. After presidents claim mandates, they often try to reaffirm their mandate throughout their term and in any campaign for reelection. A president who wins crucial legislative votes on the mandate policy, whose party is not too deeply hurt at midterm elections, or who wins reelection claims to reduce the uncertainty about approval with his original policy mandate. How could a president who was completely wrong about his ability to mobilize voters on the basis of policy be elected to a second term? How could he have gotten his key policy proposals passed if he did not have a mandate?

Reelection has the potential to reduce the ambiguity of policy signals from the electorate, since incumbents campaign on their record of policy accomplishments. In 1932, Franklin Roosevelt had campaigned to use the federal government to do something about the Great Depression. The people, he said "have registered a mandate that they want direct, vigorous action."[181] After his 1936 landslide, he was able to articulate his policy instructions more carefully:

> I believe the country has this last week given a mandate in unmistakable terms to its legislators and executives to proceed along these lines until working people throughout the Nation and in every State are assured decent working conditions, including safe and healthful places of work; adequate care and support when incapacitated by reason of accident, industrial disease, unemployment, or old age; reasonably short working hours; adequate annual incomes; proper housing; and elimination of child labor.[182]

After his reelection in 1984, Reagan stated that "we must never again abuse the trust of the working men and women, by sending their earnings on a futile chase after the spiraling demands of a bloated Federal Establishment. You elected us in 1980 to end this prescription for disaster, and I don't believe you reelected us in 1984 to reverse course."[183]

Presidents are highly aware of the capacity of an election to send a signal. Indeed, presidents frustrated with Congress sometimes explicitly ask voters to send a message. Campaigning in 1972, President Nixon told his audience:

> We are seeking in this election something that no President has had since 1956, with the exception of President Johnson in '64 after his landslide, and that is a majority, because there was not a majority even in 1960 and of course there was not in 1968 because of third-party candidates. I think what we need now is a clear majority, a clear majority of the American people. That means a clear mandate, a mandate for what I have described as change that works, for progress. Because, when I see what has happened to, for example, revenue sharing, government reorganization, our health plan, our welfare reform, and all of our programs— there are 12 different bills on the environment that are still stuck in the mud of Senate and House controversy—when I see that, I think that the country needs to speak out.[184]

Nixon argued that he was running "on the issues" and that he and his opponent, George McGovern, were presenting voters with a clear choice. The message from the nation would be more clear if his victory was not viewed as a strictly partisan affair:

> If we can get a new majority at the Presidential level in this campaign, which we are going to seek by crossing the country and crossing all the lines of various age groups and religious groups and ethnic groups, et cetera, then we could have a legislative record in the first 6 months of the next Congress which could equal in excitement, in reform, the 100 days of 1933.

After his landslide in 1972, Nixon did declare a mandate.[185]

Lyndon Johnson clearly looked to the 1964 election for a political opportunity to pass stalled legislation. When asked about his failure to get the Medicare and Social Security bills that he wanted, Johnson replied:

> I did everything that I could to get it accepted in the Senate and the House. I had many, many conferences with many, many people. But they felt that they couldn't get agreement. . . . I think Senator Gore very properly presented the situation when he said that it is now a matter that the people of this country can pass judgment on. I hope that we get a mandate in November.[186]

Gerald Ford, who attained his position without the benefit of popular election, pursued a mandate in the election of 1976:

> Our victory . . . will be a clear signal to our own citizens, to our allies, and to our adversaries. . . . It will be a mandate to continue the policies of economic strength and growth, of limited government, of decision-making at the local and State level, of fiscal restraint and tax relief, which so many millions and millions of Americans are demanding and to which our party has always been committed.[187]

Ford repeatedly used the phrase "Give me your mandate" in his stump speeches.[188]

Presidents may invoke their victory to remind Congress of their ability to mobilize voters. They even try to influence midterm elections. Before the 1954 midterm elections, Eisenhower harked back to his 1952 victory to encourage voters to cast their ballots for Republican candidates for Congress: "On you today—as politicians in the finest meaning of the term—and on your leaders—rests the responsibility of justifying now and for history the mandate of November, 1952."[189] Johnson did the same thing in 1966 when he said, "It was 2 years ago that the American people gave us one of the biggest mandates in electoral history. Now we are asking them to renew and to continue that mandate in the congressional elections of 1966."[190] In 1982, Ronald Reagan told his supporters, "If we do our job well, the voters will be in a mood to reconfirm the mandate they gave us in 1980."[191]

Mandates as a Dynamic Political Process

Presidents try to renew or build mandates because they are more than simple assessments of the preferences of voters. Mandate claims reflect political opportunities signaled by elections and are capable of being accentuated by savvy bargaining skills or deflated by scandal. Successful outcomes such as the end of a war or a booming economy may be taken as proof that the policy was in fact right for the times and may build even more popular support for a president's agenda. Politicians and voters may update or change their preferences and political calculations.

Lyndon Johnson explained his rush of legislative activity following his landslide victory:

> I was just elected President by the biggest popular margin in the history of the country—16 million votes. Just by the way people naturally think and because Barry Goldwater had simply scared the hell out of them, I've already lost about three of those sixteen. After a fight with Congress or something else, I'll lose another couple of million. I could be down to 8 million in a couple of months.[192]

Even a landslide victory is no guarantee that the political landscape will not change. Presidents do not simply invoke mandate rhetoric and get their way; they set their agenda and fight to make the most of their political opportunity. Success is never easy.

In the next chapter, I describe two additional elections after which presidents declared mandates. In direct contrast to the cases in this chapter, these presidents did not have stunning popular victories. Third-party challengers kept the campaigns focused on the issues but prevented the winners from drawing large majorities. These presidents faced their own party in Congress at a time in which party leaders had a heightened sense of party accountability. They had an incentive to declare a mandate, knowing that they would most likely receive substantially less than they asked for.

| # Bargained Mandates: 1948 and 1992

In recent years, several presidential candidates have attempted to invoke the legacy of Harry Truman. The underdogs of the presidential race, whether incumbents or challengers, use the imagery of the candidate who surprised the pollsters and the pundits to win the presidency in 1948. In 1992, both Bill Clinton and George Bush tried to claim the mantle of Harry Truman during the general election campaign.[1] In his speeches, President Bush argued that he was on a "similar mission," to do battle with an uncooperative Congress, take his case to the people, and confound the experts who predicted his defeat. The day before the election, Bush told a crowd in Pennsylvania, "We are going to pull off one of the biggest surprises in political history. Discard the pundits! Discard the pollsters! Discard the rhetoric out of Governor Clinton! Vote for me and we will lead this country to new heights!"[2]

Clinton argued that *he* was the successor to Truman because he cared about the hopes and dreams of the middle class. In the end, Clinton turned out to be more like Harry Truman than any recent president, though not for the reasons that he thought. Clinton is the president who faced a postelection environment that was most similar to Truman's. Bill Clinton was also elected in a highly charged three-way race with less than 50 percent of the popular vote, and like Truman, he had an opportunity to work with a Congress controlled by his fellow partisans. In 1948, the Democratic Party seemed united by the fact that they had regained control of both chambers of congress with Truman's election. In Clinton's case, the Democratic Party seemed united by calls to end the gridlock of divided government during the Bush presidency. Like Truman, Clinton's mandate claim was based as much on the prospect of a congenial congressional environment as on the power of the policy signal sent by voters. Both Truman and Clinton had victories that paid homage to their personal will and endurance.

No one questioned the salience of policy issues in Truman's and Clinton's election campaigns, but their slim victories created doubt about whether they could mobilize a *majority* of voters behind their initiatives. Both Truman and Clinton represent the type of president identified by my model who will seek major policy changes only if his party's strength in the House and the Senate adequately compensates for the narrow margin of his electoral victory. When such presidents claim a mandate, they do so because they are confident that Congress is in tune with their preferences, even if there is uncertainty about the state of public opinion. I refer to these victories as "bargained" mandates to note their reliance on Congress in the face of ambiguous popular support. Though they do not have "popular" mandates, these presidents can see that by placing a new initiative on the agenda, they are likely to move policy in the direction of their preferences. At worst, their efforts will leave the status quo unchanged.

THE ELECTION OF 1948

In 1948, Democratic incumbent Harry S. Truman beat Republican Thomas E. Dewey in one of the greatest political upsets of the century.[3] Truman fended off challenges from the left wing of his party, led by former Vice President Henry Wallace, and from the right wing of his party, led by States' Rights candidate Strom Thurmond. Politicians and pundits forecast a Dewey victory throughout the campaign, until the morning after the election, when Truman's victory was finally assured. While he claimed a mandate, Truman's victory had different underpinnings than the landslide elections presented in the last chapter.

Nominations and Conventions
The Democratic Party

Though Truman was the incumbent president, by virtue of Roosevelt's death in office, his nomination was by no means assured in 1948. Truman had fired Secretary of Commerce (and former Vice President) Henry A. Wallace over his public opposition to Truman's foreign policy. Wallace subsequently became a candidate for the presidency under the banner of the group Progressive Citizens of America, an alliance of liberals and communists. Truman was also attacked from the right by southern Democrats, particularly on the issue of civil rights. A group of southern governors joined forces in early 1948, seeking the withdrawal of civil rights legislation before Congress, the weakening of civil rights planks in the Democratic platform, and the nomination of a presidential candidate who would oppose such legislation.

By April 1948, only 36 percent of voters approved of the way Truman was handling his job, and prominent Democrats discussed alternative candidates, including Dwight Eisenhower. By the July convention, efforts to replace Truman had failed, and he won the nomination without the votes of the southern states. Delegates from Mississippi and Alabama left the convention floor after passage of a liberal civil rights plank. In his acceptance speech, Truman called for the continuation of New Deal policies and coalitions, such as the alliance between farmers and labor. He chose Senate minority leader Alben Barkley of Kentucky as his vice presidential running mate. He called for a special session of the Republican dominated 80th Congress later that month. Forty-seven percent of Democratic party identifiers polled after the convention would have preferred a different nominee.[4]

Two disgruntled factions of the Democratic Party ran their own candidates. On the right, a group of southern politicians intent on preserving the "southern way of life" nominated Strom Thurmond, governor of South Carolina, and Fielding Wright, governor of Mississippi, to run as candidates for president and vice president under the banner of the "States' Rights Party." Their goal was to win the 127 electoral votes in the South in order to throw the election into the House of Representatives, where southerners could influence the final outcome. The Thurmond–Wright ticket managed to get on the ballot in thirteen southern states.[5]

The Democratic Party also splintered on the left. The Progressives held a convention, where Henry Wallace and his running mate, Senator Glen Taylor of Idaho, were nominated unanimously. The Progressives were primarily interested in issues of foreign policy.

They opposed the Marshall Plan and Truman Doctrine, the draft, military expansion, and the arms race. Wallace was eventually on the ballot in forty-five of the forty-eight states.

The Republican Party

Thomas Dewey, governor of New York and the 1944 Republican nominee, was the early front-runner in a crowded field of Republican Party candidates. However, former Minnesota governor Harold Stassen, Senator Robert Taft of Ohio, California governor Earl Warren, and General Douglas MacArthur all had substantial support within the party and were viable candidates against Truman, according to public opinion polls. Though Dewey led after the primaries, the outcome of the convention was still uncertain. After the second ballot at the convention did not produce a winner, Dewey's opponents finally withdrew. Dewey was nominated unanimously on the third ballot, and he chose Earl Warren as his vice presidential running mate. The party platform reflected the views of the Dewey campaign but promoted a more liberal agenda than was favored by the Republicans who controlled the 80th Congress.[6]

The General Election Campaign

In his campaign, Harry Truman proclaimed the Democratic Party to be the party of the common man. He told voters, "We don't restrict our sympathies to the people who make $100,000 a year. . . . You can vote for a Federal housing program, a Federal aid to education program, a Federal health program, by marking your ballot for the Democratic candidates."[7] He made targeted appeals to farmers, workers, and African Americans, without worrying about alienating southerners or other Democrats in the process. He vowed to repeal the Taft-Hartley Act, passed by the Democrats and Republicans in Congress who overrode his veto in June 1947. The act limited the power of labor by outlawing industry-wide strikes and closed-shop rules, prohibiting political contributions from unions, and requiring labor leaders to take a loyalty oath. Polls showed that 48 percent of voters wanted either repeal or major changes in the Taft-Hartley Act.[8]

In his campaign speeches, Truman instructed voters about the policy consequences of their choices and asked them to renew the mandate of the Democratic Party:

> When you come right down to the analysis of our Government, our Government is the people, and when the people exercise their right to vote on Election Day they control that Government. When they don't exercise that right then you get—then you get an 80th Congress. So, two thirds of the people of the United States entitled to vote in 1946, stayed at home. They didn't have energy enough to go and look after their political interests on election day—and they got the 80th Congress. Don't do that again.[9]

"They made their great mistake," Truman argued, "when they decided that the election of 1946 was a mandate—a mandate, mind you—to destroy the New Deal."[10] According to Truman, the Republican Congress was but an aberration in the Democratic Party's representation of the people. "The party of progressive liberalism in the United States, the party that carries on the traditions of Jefferson and Jackson, the party that has four times in succession received the people's mandate—is the Democratic Party. This year its mandate must again be considered by the people for renewal."[11] Truman reinforced his populist appeals with a casual grassroots campaign style that contrasted him to the aloof and polished Dewey. He traveled throughout the country by train, giving speeches to groups ranging in number from a handful to thousands.

In July, Truman called a special session of Congress and asked for legislation that he knew the Republicans in control would not grant. For the rest of the campaign, he attacked them for refusing to support his legislative agenda: "The record of that Eightieth Congress is a sad tale of the sellout of the people's interest to put more and more power into the hands of fewer and fewer men. The Republican Congress, acting for big business, has already begun its attack to break the strength of labor unions by voting the vicious Taft-Hartley law."[12] Truman labeled the Republican members "gluttons of privilege" who were captive to the interests of lobbyists. In his view, it was the Republicans' neglect of the common worker and its favoritism toward business that made the country vulnerable to communism:

The real threat of communism in this country grows out of the Republican policies of the 80th Congress—policies which threaten to put an end to American prosperity. The real threat of communism in this country grows out of the submission of the Republican Party to the dictates of big business, and its determination to destroy the hard-won rights of American labor.[13]

Republicans in Congress labeled Truman's call for a special session a "political maneuver" and vowed to do nothing; they would wait to act with a Republican president in the 81st Congress.[14] Truman received nothing from the session except for minor bills, such as funding for the construction of the United Nations headquarters in New York. At the same time, however, Truman had framed his election as a contest between himself and conservative Republicans in Congress rather than as a contest between himself and the more moderate Dewey.

Dewey led Truman in the polls from the start of the campaign. His strategy was simply to maintain his lead. A *Saturday Evening Post* writer commented that Dewey "talks not like a man who wants to be President, but like a man who already is the President in everything but name, and who merely is awaiting the inaugural date before taking over."[15] Dewey gave speeches that included only vague references to the issues.[16] He did not respond to Truman's personal or political attacks and tried to avoid even mentioning Truman by name, perhaps because he had been routed at the polls in the 1944 election after having attacked Franklin Roosevelt. The policies that he advocated were strikingly similar to policies that President Truman had proposed and that had been rejected by the Republican Congress.[17] He followed the administration's line on foreign policy; he ignored issues like civil rights and communism to avoid controversy.[18] Republican Party elites did not criticize Dewey for his aloof campaign style but praised him for his statesmanship. After all, the outcome seemed a foregone conclusion.

Gallup polls showed Dewey about ten points ahead in August. By October, the margin had narrowed, but Dewey was still ahead by about five points. Only President Truman and a small handful of close friends believed Truman would win in November.[19] Truman commented, "There will be more red-faced pollsters on November 3 than there were in 1936 when they had to fold the Literary Digest. . . . You can throw the Gallup poll into the ash can."[20] He charged that the poll results were designed to "lull the voters into sleeping on Election Day." Pollsters responded: "Mr. Truman would love us if we could show him out in front. Nobody wants to be shown behind. Either he is wrong or we are. The people will know in another week."[21] Elmo Roper announced in early September that he had stopped polling owing to the certainty of Dewey's victory.

Though Truman's speeches were colorful, the campaign was marked by apathy among voters, who regarded the outcome as a foregone conclusion.[22] Sunday before the election, the newspapers predicted that Dewey would win by a large margin in the electoral college.[23] The *New York Times* predicted 345 of the 531 electoral college votes for Dewey (twenty-nine states), 105 for Truman (eleven states), 38 for Thurmond (four states), 0 for Wallace, and only 43 votes (from four states) uncertain.[24] Pollsters predicted a small popular vote margin for Dewey. Republicans were expected to lose seats yet retain their control over the House of Representatives. Control of the Senate was less certain, with many commentators predicting a tie between the two major parties (and future vice president Earl Warren casting tie-breaking votes). Little change was expected in the party balance of governorships and other state-level offices.

The Election Outcome

The most surprising election outcome of the century was not confirmed until around 8:30 A.M. the morning after the election. Truman beat Dewey by 49.5 percent to 45.1 percent in the popular vote and won twenty-eight states for a total of 303 electoral college votes. Dewey won sixteen states for a total of 189 electoral votes, and the States' Rights ticket won four southern states for a total of 39 electoral votes.[25] Truman had very slim margins of victory in big states such as Ohio, Illinois, and California. He managed to win without carrying four major industrial states: New York, Pennsylvania, Michigan, and New Jersey. Wallace won no states but did obstruct Truman from winning in New York and Michigan. The 51 percent turnout of all eligible voters was the lowest turnout rate since 1924.

Not only did Truman win, the Democrats gained control of both chambers of Congress. The *New York Times* reported, "The Democrats swept all of Congress yesterday, recapturing the supposedly impregnable Republican House by a landslide and seizing firm control of the Senate in one of the great political revolutions of American history."[26] Democrats gained seventy-five seats in the House of Representatives and nine seats in the Senate. In the 80th Congress, Republicans controlled the House 246 to 188 and the Senate 51 to 45. After the election, Democrats controlled the House 263 to 171 and the Senate 54 to 42. The Republicans also lost eight governorships.

Interpretations of Victory

Truman was called a courageous "miracle man," and the pollsters were indeed red-faced.[27] Truman was reported to have said that "labor did it," while Dewey linked the outcome to his loss of the farm vote.[28] Truman's victory was attributed to holdover New Deal sentiment, evidenced in part by his support among workers and farmers.[29] He was also an incumbent in a time of relative prosperity. Finally, many credited Truman for his populist campaign tactics—his plain speaking and cross-country train tour. His "upset" victory was compared with the "freak Hayes victory in 1876 and the Wilson victory in 1916."[30]

The sentiment was that the "man in the street" and the "little people" had spoken and defied the experts with their verdict. Their message was a vote of confidence in Truman. "Truman won because this is still a land which loves a scrapper."[31] "Even when all the factors making up the surprising victory are accounted for and duly classified, one will stand out: the indomitable will of President Truman."[32] Truman was not credited with carrying the members of his party to victory. Rather, it appeared to be the other way around. Conservative Republicans argued that Dewey lost because he offered a "pale version of the New Deal" instead of a clear conservative alternative.[33] They attacked his campaign as "smug, arrogant, stupid, and supercilious."[34]

Truman's attacks upon the Republican-dominated 80th Congress, particularly with respect to labor issues, were thought to have been successful. More than fifty House Republicans who had backed the Taft-Hartley Act were defeated. Labor leaders were quick to label the election a mandate to Congress to repeal Taft-Hartley.[35] Although labor was given a great deal of credit for Truman's victory, congressional opposition to repeal was forecast: "There is hardly any reasonable explanation for the Truman victory save that the political forces of organized labor were stronger than anyone believed possible, and what the labor bosses want is repeal of the Taft-Hartley Act. With the complexion of Congress what it appears likely to be, repeal could hardly carry."[36] Journalists and politicians were skeptical that southern Democrats, particularly those in the Senate, would follow the party line in support of Truman's policies.[37] Opposition on civil rights legislation was certain. There was some discussion of whether or not Democrats who were openly States' Rights supporters or who had been hostile to Truman should be able to hold powerful committee positions.[38] Journalists repeatedly raised Truman's dismal record with the Democratic 79th Congress early in his first term as president.

Truman's Policy Agenda

President Truman did put repeal of the Taft-Hartley Act at the top of his agenda. Within days after the election, Truman began arranging a series of conferences between representatives of labor and management aimed at repealing or substantially modifying the labor law.[39] Early in his Inaugural Address, Truman pronounced the general principles behind his support of labor and civil rights legislation: "We believe that all men have a right to equal justice under law and equal opportunity to share in the common good. We believe that all men have the right to freedom of thought and expression. We believe that all men are created equal because they are created in the image of God. From this faith we will not be moved."[40]

Though the new Congress was not expected to go along with total repeal, there was a sense that conflict would lead to some significant changes. Ultimately, a coalition of Republicans and southern Democrats emerged and hindered Truman's domestic agenda. Yet a year after the election, Truman still maintained that the election had carried a policy message: "The Democratic Platform sets out what the campaign was fixed on. When the Democrats win an election they have authority—call it a mandate, if you want to—from the people to carry out that Democratic Platform. That's all I am trying to do."[41]

THE ELECTION OF 1992

In 1992, incumbent president George Bush was defeated in a three-way race, only two years after soaring to an 89 percent approval rating in the aftermath of the Persian Gulf War.[42] Democratic party nominee Bill Clinton, the governor of Arkansas, was elected with only 43 percent of the popular vote. Businessman and independent candidate H. Ross Perot garnered 19 percent of the popular vote. After twelve years of Republican control of the presidency, the Democrats in the House and the Senate faced a president of their own party. The election was treated as a call for change, but Clinton's ability to mobilize popular support was in doubt.

Primaries and Conventions
The Republican Party

George Bush had won a solid victory over Michael Dukakis in 1988. Though his victory was attributed to negative campaigning, riding the coattails of former President Reagan, and the poor quality of his opponent's campaign, Bush nonetheless won with 53.4 percent of the popular vote and 78 percent of the states in the electoral college. His largely uneventful first two years in office were marked by a major faux pas in June of 1990. Bush agreed to a tax increase as part of budget negotiations with a Democratically controlled Congress, thus breaking his 1988 campaign pledge of "Read my lips: No new taxes." Fallout from this decision within the most conservative ranks of the Republican Party was mounting when Bush led a military campaign to reverse the Iraqi invasion of Kuwait.

Bush's postwar approval ratings soared, and criticism of his presidency within the Republican Party was temporarily stalled. Less than a year later, however, an economic recession and Bush's inactivity and disinterest in domestic politics led Patrick Buchanan to announce his own bid for the Republican nomination. Buchanan, a conservative journalist and political commentator, attacked Bush for breaking his anti-tax pledge, being soft on moral issues, and ignoring the plight of workers hurt by the economy. In New Hampshire, where 82 percent of the voters ranked the economy as the top issue of the campaign, Buchanan won 37 percent of the vote to Bush's 53 percent. Buchanan continued to challenge Bush right up to the Republican convention, though the strength of his opposition diminished as the primary season progressed.[43]

As the Republican convention opened, Bush was running seventeen points behind Bill Clinton in the polls. Moreover, 92 percent of Americans felt the country needed real change at the same time that 81 percent said that electing George Bush would mean things would stay the same.[44] The Republicans had to finesse the perceived economic downturn and reconcile incumbency with the possibility of change. They contrasted their fiscal conservatism to the Democratic Party's big spending plans. The Republican Party platform contained a statement that called Bush's support of the 1990 tax increase a mistake. In his acceptance speech, Bush himself admitted that it had been a mistake to go along with the Democratic Congress on the tax increase, but he tried to reassure voters that he had learned his lesson: "Who do you trust in this election? The candidate who raised taxes one time and regrets it, or the other candidate who raised taxes and fees 128 times and enjoyed it every time?"[45] He blamed the current state of the economy on the Democratic Congress and promised an across-the-board tax cut and new faces in his cabinet if elected.

Perhaps to draw attention away from the slumping economy, several Republicans ignored economic issues and chose instead to emphasize differences between the candidates and political parties on social and moral issues. For these Republicans, the most important stakes in the election were cultural. None of them argued the case more forcefully than Patrick Buchanan, who had been invited to speak on the first night of the convention:

> The agenda Clinton & Clinton would impose on America—abortion on demand, a litmus test for the Supreme Court, homosexual rights, discrimination against religious schools, women in combat—that's change all right. But it is not the kind of change America wants. It's not the kind of change America needs. And it is not the kind of

change we can tolerate in a nation we still call God's country. . . . My friends, this election is about much more than who gets what. It is about who we are. It is about what we believe. It is about where we stand as Americans. There is a religious war going on in our country for the soul of America. It is a cultural war, as critical to the kind of nation we will one day be as was the Cold War itself. An in that struggle for the soul of America, Clinton & Clinton are on the other side.[46]

Barbara Bush, Marilyn Quayle (wife of the vice president), and televangelist Pat Robertson gave speeches on a convention night devoted to "family values." Vice President Dan Quayle painted the choice as follows: "It's not just a choice between being conservative and liberal; it is a difference between fighting for what's right and refusing to see what's wrong."[47] Bill Clinton was attacked as a draft-dodging, womanizing symbol of the 1960s "counterculture." Hillary Clinton was attacked as a "radical feminist."

Several Republican members of Congress were openly critical of the convention; they feared that the party had appeared too nasty and exclusionary to win broad support in the general election.[48] Bush's control over the convention proceedings was questioned. For instance, the Republican Party platform incorporated a plank that reaffirmed the party's opposition to legalized abortion and advocated a constitutional amendment to outlaw it. Yet the week before the convention, President Bush said he would support a daughter who sought an abortion after urging her not to, and Barbara Bush said that abortion was a "personal decision" that should be "left out of, in my opinion, platforms and conventions."[49] Nonetheless, Bush's postconvention bounce in the polls cut Clinton's preconvention lead in half, from 19 percent to 9 percent, and made the race competitive once again.[50]

The Democratic Party

By the time of the New Hampshire primary, the Democratic Party had five major candidates for the nomination: former California governor Jerry Brown, governor Bill Clinton of Arkansas, Senator Tom Harkin of Iowa, Senator Bob Kerry of Nebraska, and former

Senator Paul Tsongas of Massachusetts.[51] Better-known candidates such as Jesse Jackson, Mario Cuomo, and Richard Gephardt had declined to enter the race, deterred perhaps by Bush's apparent invincibility in the wake of the Persian Gulf War.

The Iowa caucuses were won by favorite son Tom Harkin (with "uncommitted" running second). Since the caucuses were largely uncontested and were won by the home-state candidate, they were not expected to generate any momentum for Harkin in future primaries. The New Hampshire primary, however, was memorable for the Democrats, and for the political career of Bill Clinton. It was here that his reputation as the "Comeback Kid" was first popularized across the nation. A few weeks before the primary, the tabloids printed a story alleging that Clinton had a twelve-year affair with a lounge singer named Gennifer Flowers while he was the governor of Arkansas. In response to this accusation, Bill and Hillary Clinton appeared on the television new program *60 Minutes* on Super Bowl Sunday. Bill admitted to having caused "pain" in their marriage, but the Clintons maintained that their marriage was strong. They also insisted that their private life should be kept private and that the election should be fought over the issues rather than the personal lives of the candidates. Shortly after the Flowers incident, the *Wall Street Journal* ran a story alleging that Clinton had evaded the draft during the Vietnam War. Once again, Clinton's record was scrutinized, and he was forced to defend himself.

Although these controversial issues undoubtedly damaged Clinton's standing and raised doubts about his ability to be elected, he still managed to finish a strong second in New Hampshire, with 25 percent of the vote, compared to 33 percent for the winner, Paul Tsongas. The other candidates trailed far behind. Paul Tsongas, the new front-runner, moved on to primaries outside of New England, where he continued to promote his message that harsh economic realities called for harsh economic policies ("I'm no Santa Claus").[52] Kerry and Harkin withdrew from the race. Despite finishing second, the Clinton campaign spread the word that their candidate was the real winner because he had done far better than expected for someone who had been under such personal attacks. The turning point of the nomination race was the set of mostly southern primaries that were at stake on Super Tuesday. Confounding those who had counted him out, Clinton swept the southern states by large margins. After Clinton went on to win handily in midwestern states like Illinois and Michigan, Tsongas "suspended" his campaign and officially withdrew in early April. Only Jerry Brown persisted right up to the convention, winning two states (Colorado and Connecticut) and coming close to Clinton in large states like Wisconsin and his home state of California.

At the convention, Clinton won the Democratic nomination on the first ballot, with the support of 78 percent of all delegates.[53] He had announced his choice of Senator Albert Gore Jr. of Tennessee as his running mate the week before the convention. Bucking tradition, Clinton picked a running mate who did not bring geographical, generational, or ideological balance to the ticket. Instead, Gore's presence helped the Clinton campaign emphasize that they were the ticket for change, a new way of running and organizing government. Gore's policy expertise on the environment and emerging technology bolstered their claim to have the ability to face new issues. Gore also complemented Clinton on character issues; unlike Clinton, Gore was widely perceived as extremely trustworthy and honest, and he had served in Vietnam.

From the beginning of his acceptance speech, Clinton emphasized his identification with the middle class: "And so, in the name of all the people who do the work, pay the taxes, raise the kids, and play by the rules—the hardworking Americans who make up our forgotten middle class, I accept your nomination for the Presidency of the United States of America."[54] He used his family story to further identify himself with the aspirations of the middle class, and he attacked the "privileged, private interests" that had taken over government.[55] Like many earlier speakers at the convention, Clinton pounded home the theme that the Bush administration had ignored the failing economy, because it was out of touch with the problems of ordinary Americans.

Clinton argued, "We have got to go beyond the braindead politics in Washington, and give our people the kind of Government they deserve: a Government that works for them. George Bush, if you won't use your power to help people, step aside, I will."[56] He promised to create jobs, balance the budget, streamline the bureau-cracy, and provide cost-effective and universal health care. At the same time that he proposed recapturing and using government, he emphasized moderation. He took great pains to distinguish his agenda from the "big government" solutions of the past: "The choice we offer is not conservative or liberal, Democratic or Republican." The "New Covenant" would provide incentives and opportunities and yet demand responsibility. The rich would have to pay their share, and the poor would receive no handouts (ending "welfare as we know it").

The convention presented a unified Democratic Party and a call for change after twelve years of Republican presidential leadership. The major speakers focused on solutions to the nation's economic problems and offered almost no dissent from the official Clinton cam-paign agenda. The "values" that the party emphasized were fairness, opportunity, responsibility, and community. At the end of the con-vention, Clinton and Gore began a series of bus trips, in which they traveled through towns large and small to meet and greet voters. The bus trips were meant to emphasize the empathy and responsiveness of the Clinton/Gore team.

H. Ross Perot

The third major candidate for the presidency was Texas business-man and billionaire H. Ross Perot. Two days after the New Hamp-shire primary, Perot announced his candidacy for the presidency dur-ing an appearance on a television talk show. He argued that he was the only real alternative for change and that he would break the "gridlock" that kept politicians from reducing the federal deficit and fixing the economy. He entered no Democratic or Republican pri-maries and won no delegates to the major party conventions. Instead, he rallied his supporters to get his name on the ballot for the Novem-ber election. Perot claimed that he would not be beholden to PAC money or lobbyists because he would pay for most of his campaign expenses out of his own pocket.

Perot argued that it was possible to cut taxes and reduce the deficit at the same time. Without offering many details, he charged that he would cut wasteful spending. He opposed NAFTA because he believed it would lead to a major loss of industrial jobs to Mexico. Saying, "I don't want to live in a country that can't make its own television sets," he argued that government should intervene to make American industries more competitive.[57] On social issues, he took a mix of Democratic and Republican positions: He favored a woman's right to an abortion at the same time that he opposed gun control legislation. He wanted to bar foreign lobbyists and eliminate PAC money in political campaigns. He exhorted voters to support his candidacy as a way to shake up the system and protest "politics as usual" in Washington.

Perot's vote share in polls during the primary season rose steadily from the time of his declaration in February. His support peaked in mid-June, when polls revealed that in a hypothetical three-way race, Perot was clearly preferred to Clinton and within two percentage points of George Bush.[58] His strength in the polls began to fade, however, when concerns were raised about his abrasive personality, and when major members of his campaign team resigned. He officially withdrew from the race during the Democratic convention in July, saying that the Democratic Party had sufficiently "revitalized itself" in response to the concerns of Perot voters. He argued that this revitalization meant that he would no longer be able to win the election outright. Instead, according to Perot, if he stayed in the race, the election would be decided in the House of Representatives, where he would not have a chance of being selected. All of this, he claimed, would be too "disruptive to the country."[59] Though he withdrew from the race, he urged his supporters to continue to file their petitions to get his name on the general election ballot, so that "everybody running for president will know the names and addresses of all the people who are not happy with the way things are today."[60] Pundits speculated for weeks on the true reasons behind Perot's withdrawal, from his unwillingness to undergo press scrutiny of his business dealings and personal life to his inability to run a professional political campaign.[61]

The General Election Campaign

Perot reentered the race on October 1, a mere thirty-three days before the election. He chose as his vice presidential running mate a sixty-eight-year-old political novice named James B. Stockdale, a former P.O.W. and retired vice admiral in the Navy. At his press conference, Perot described government as a "mess" and said that "nobody takes responsibility." He accused the major parties of avoiding to address the major problems facing the nation.[62] He went on national television in a series of thirty-minute "infomercials" in which he addressed issues like the federal budget deficit and his own personal fitness for the office of the presidency. Throughout the month of October, he outspent both of his rivals on advertising on the major television networks. His media campaign culminated with two hours of paid prime-time television on election eve.[63] He published a 118-page book entitled *United We Stand* that laid out his economic plan in broad terms; more importantly, it sounded the alarm about an impending economic crisis and urged its readers to demand greater accountability from elected politicians.[64] It was a call for the end of "politics as usual" dominated by special interests and gridlock, and for the beginning of a government that would take the issues seriously, develop pragmatic policies, and be responsive to the people.

The Clinton campaign also emphasized the themes of change and responsiveness to the electorate: "Bill Clinton and Al Gore have a bold new plan to change America—to get our economy back on track. They'll stop the broken promises, stop the blame, and make government work for people. And the American people know it. It's time to hope again."[65] Clinton's economic strategy, "Putting People First," centered on the creation of jobs and the reduction of the deficit but also included health care reform and welfare reform. The mantra of the campaign was posted at campaign headquarters: "Change vs. more of the same. The economy, stupid. Don't forget health care." Clinton used new media venues to spread the word about his policies; his willingness to reach out to people on late-night and daytime talk shows, radio shows, and MTV reinforced the notion that he was more in touch with voters than was George Bush.

Though the issues of jobs and the economy dominated the campaign advertisements of both Perot and Clinton, their issue campaigns were by no means identical. Perot's campaign advertisements focused on the budget deficit, while Clinton's largely ignored it. Perot made almost no mention of families or values.[66] Clinton's ad campaign highlighted health care, education, and welfare reform, which he linked to economic vitality. Clinton made little or no mention of foreign policy or values. George Bush, on the other hand, stressed foreign policy and tax relief. His campaign sought to shift attention from the economy, first by denying that the problems were severe and then by ignoring the issue altogether. He avoided economic issues for good reason: from the New Hampshire primary through the general election campaign, roughly 75 percent of voters disapproved of the way President Bush was handling the economy.[67] Unfortunately for Bush, the economy and jobs were overwhelmingly identified as the key issues throughout the campaign for all types of voters; the budget deficit and health care were also consistently raised as policy concerns.[68] The Bush campaign's attempts to hold the election on other terms reinforced the notion that he was out of touch with the needs of ordinary voters.

The second presidential debate symbolized the course of the fall campaign.[69] At the suggestion of the Clinton campaign, it was fashioned after a "town hall meeting." An audience of undecided voters asked questions of the three presidential candidates, with time allowed for follow-up questions and interaction with the audience. The candidates were able to sit or move about the stage as they responded to questions. The format itself, and the positive public reaction to it, highlighted the themes of populism and candidate accountability that recurred throughout the campaign. Early on, the audience requested that the candidates talk about the issues rather than attack each other's character. A journalist described the implications for President Bush: "The President, cut off on character and foreign policy issues for the most part and boxed into a situation where he was forced to confront his weakest issue, the economy, seemed uncomfortable and sometimes grew testy. By 9:50 P.M. he was checking his watch to see how much longer this infrastructure quizzing would go on."[70] Bill Clinton, on the other hand, "had the empathy and confidence of a television evangelist."[71] He appeared much more at ease than the other candidates, and his answers highlighted his ability to empathize with voters. Bush was unable to field a question about how economic circumstances had affected him personally, thus giving the impression that he could not sympathize with the economic hardships of voters. Perot continued to offer snappy one-liners and plain talk about how he would end gridlock in Washington. As a newspaper headline declared, "Bush Didn't Score the Needed Knockout; Clinton Achieved Goal; Perot Provided Humor."[72]

Days before the election, Bill Clinton claimed, "This year, when the history of this election is written, it will not be about politics and manipulation. It will be about how the American people took charge of their future again."[73] He and Perot continued to emphasize economic issues, while Bush emphasized the issues of character and trust. Gallup polls taken the weekend before the election showed Clinton barely ahead with 41 percent of likely voters to Bush's 39 percent.[74] Perot had the support of 14 percent of likely voters. Clinton's big lead in California, his support in large industrial states, and close contests in the South gave him the edge in electoral college vote projections.[75] A Bush victory would have required too many undecided and close contests to go his way. Still, polls showed that many voters were undecided, and Perot voters were viewed as somewhat unpredictable. The number of open seats in Congress guaranteed that an unusually large number of new members would be elected, but the partisan content of the surge was expected to be mixed.[76]

The Election Outcome

In the end, Bill Clinton won the race with 43 percent of the popular vote to George Bush's 37.4 percent. With almost 19 percent of the vote, Ross Perot attained the second largest vote total for any third-party or independent candidate in U.S. history.[77] Clinton won 370 electoral votes to Bush's 168. Though Perot won over 20 percent of the popular vote in thirty-one states, he did not win any electoral college votes. As expected, Clinton had his strongest showing in the northeast and in midwestern industrial states, but he also won states in all other regions of the country: in the Mountain West (Nevada, Colorado, New Mexico, Montana), the South (Louisiana, Georgia, Tennessee, Arkansas, Kentucky), and on the West Coast (California, Oregon, Washington). New Hampshire, Vermont, New Jersey, and California went Democratic for the first time since 1964. Clinton came close to winning in both Texas and Florida. Though his

popular vote percentage was not large, analysts referred to his "crushing coast-to-coast electoral [college] victory."[78]

The Democratic Party retained control of both the House and
the Senate, though they lost 10 seats in the House and achieved no
net gain in the Senate. With a total of 57 Senate seats, the Democrats would still be short of the 60 needed to end a filibuster. While
the Democrat's ability to retain control of Congress was no surprise,
the composition of the new Congress suggested that voters were calling for change. Most incumbents had managed to retain their seats
(only 27 of 376 lost), but there had been an unusually large number
of open-seat races. The House had 110 new members, the most new
members since the entering freshman class of 1948. The number of
women in the House doubled, going from twenty-four to forty-
eight.[79] The number of African Americans in the House increased
by thirteen for a total of thirty-nine representatives, including the
first African Americans to be elected in this century from the states
of North Carolina, South Carolina, Virginia, Alabama, and Florida.
Carol Moseley-Braun of Illinois was the first African American
woman ever elected to the U.S. Senate. The number of Hispanic
legislators in the House increased by six. House Speaker Tom Foley
(D–WA) said the new Congress was in tune with "the message of
change and movement."[80] State legislatures also experienced high
turnover, with one out of every three or four state legislative seats
going to a newcomer.[81] Fourteen states passed some version of term
limit legislation.[82]

Interpretations of Victory

Headlines after the election were clear: "The Economy Falters,
A President Falls: Voters Lost Faith and Chose Change"; "Unrespon-
sive to Economic Anxiety, Bush Pays the Price."[83] Exit polls showed
that Clinton managed to rally the Democratic Party base in addition
to wooing back Democrats who had defected in the past to Ronald
Reagan.[84] He made significant gains among young voters and subur-
ban voters. As one analyst put it, Clinton's electoral coalition was
"more Western, more female, more single, more moderate, and more
white than past Democratic mosaics."[85] Ross Perot appeared to have
drawn support equally from Democratic and Republican Party identi-

fiers.[86] The top issues for his supporters were the budget deficit and jobs.[87] Polls also showed that seven out of ten voters thought the economy was doing "not so good" or "poor," and these voters overwhelmingly endorsed Clinton.[88] Jobs and the economy were cited by four out of ten voters as the issue that mattered most to them when making their decision.[89] Only eight out of every hundred voters mentioned foreign policy as their main concern.[90] There was a dramatic shift in the number of voters who thought that the Democrats were better than the Republicans at dealing with the economy.

Voter turnout of 55 percent of the eligible electorate was the highest it had been since 1968.[91] The turnout rate, combined with the performance of Perot and the populist themes sounded in the campaign, was used as further evidence that the election was truly a message from the people.[92] A *Chicago Tribune* reporter wrote that "the size of the Democratic victory, coupled with Perot's protest showing, will undoubtedly be interpreted as a mandate for change, one every bit as strong as the one Ronald Reagan claimed 12 years ago when he won by a landslide over incumbent Jimmy Carter."[93]

Still, there was controversy over whether the election was an indictment of George Bush and proof of the effectiveness of slick campaigning more than it was a call for Clinton's specific policies. Vice President Quayle's explanation was that "Bill Clinton ran a much better campaign and the economy wasn't good."[94] Senate minority leader Bob Dole dismissed the idea that Clinton had a mandate. Since Republicans held 43 percent of the seats in the Senate, Dole argued, "if he has a mandate, then I have a mandate."[95] Like many other Republicans, Dole counted the Perot votes and Bush votes together as votes against Clinton and his policy program. While Republicans acknowledged the call for change, they were hesitant to credit Clinton's victory to his specific policy positions. Within the party, Republicans tried to sort out factional differences and lay blame for their loss. Republican politicians and strategists immediately tried to recast their party as one of inclusion and tolerance.[96]

The day after the election, Clinton promised to "focus like a laser beam on this economy." In his first press conference, a little over a week after the election, Clinton was asked whether or not he had a mandate:

> I think that the clear mandate of this election, by the way, from the American people was an end of politics as usual, and an end to the gridlock in Washington, an end to finger-pointing and blame. I think there is no question that there is a mandate in this election. In terms of whether I got a mandate or not, you know, having a 100 vote electoral majority more than you need is not too bad. There are only a couple of Democrats in this century who've gotten a bigger percentage vote. But arguably, the greatest president we ever had, Abraham Lincoln, was elected with under 40 percent of the vote.[97]

On the economy, Clinton said he thought that voters "expect aggressive and prompt action, and I'm going to give it to them."

Since "gridlock in Washington" had been a major campaign theme and a source of public discontent, politicians and voters linked the congressional outcomes to the presidential race. Six in ten voters said that it was better for the country if both the president and Congress are controlled by the same political party, up from 35 percent three years before.[98] To prove that President Bush was to blame for past gridlock, the Democratic leadership planned to organize committees and work with Clinton to pass legislation. John Dingell (D–MI), House Energy and Commerce Committee chairman, said, "Like everybody else, I'm very happy with the election result and the fact that the gridlock has been broken. Back home there's a sense of optimism. People think we've got somebody in there who cares about their problems and that government is going to do something. We can't squander that."[99] Leon Panetta (D–CA), then chairman of the House Budget Committee, put it this way: "I think this is the change and Democrats in Congress know it. We either work to get something done or both the President and Congress will be in trouble. No more excuses."[100] Republicans also helped to unify the Democrats by reminding them that they would be held accountable for any further gridlock. Bob Dole noted, "The excuses for gridlock and bad legislation are over. . . . If they fail they are the problem, they are the gridlock. Blaming George Bush won't work anymore."[101]

Right after the election, a Gallup poll of one hundred returning and forty-nine incoming members of the House and Senate revealed that 77 percent rated jobs as the single most critical issue facing the new Congress, followed by the budget deficit (69 percent) and health care (65 percent).[102] No other issue on a list of eighteen possibilities that included term limits, welfare, taxes, and trade was considered critical by more than 26 percent of those surveyed. Freshmen Democrats and House Democratic leaders voiced their willingness to work with Clinton to produce major legislative changes. House Speaker Foley said, "I can't quite recall—except the enthusiasm of the early Johnson or Kennedy years—anything that matches the sense that this group and the Congress now has."[103] Representative Dick Gephardt (D–MO) was optimistic about the prospect of early legislative success: "Bill Clinton is a moderate Democrat. He will offer proposals that may well attract the support of some moderate Republicans."[104] The attitude of freshman Corinne Brown (D–FL) was fairly representative: "I'm a tugboat, not a showboat. I'm here to work."[105]

Clinton's early discussions with the Democratic Party leadership in Congress regarding his legislative agenda centered on an economic stimulus package. Clinton emphasized that the Democrats in Congress shared responsibility for governing and that together with the new administration, they could prove to voters that government could be productive again.[106] He noted that "they ran on a promise of quick action."[107] Clinton presided over a two-day conference on the economy in Little Rock in mid-December in which he and his newly named advisors exchanged ideas with prominent economists, business executives, and labor leaders on how best to encourage economic growth and reduce the deficit.

While the Democrats voiced optimism about the Clinton White House, more skeptical analysts wondered if Clinton would suffer the same fate as Jimmy Carter. In 1976, the unity of the Democratic Party had quickly disintegrated into conflict, leaving Carter with a very brief honeymoon. There were early indications that Clinton's support was softer in the Senate than it was in the House.[108] Not only were senior Democrats like Robert Byrd (D–WV) lukewarm toward Clinton, but Bob Dole seemed intent on rallying the Republicans in opposition to the Clinton administration.

Clinton's Policy Agenda

In his Inaugural Address, Clinton referred often to the theme of change and renewal, which he claimed was the message of the election:

> The American people have summoned the change we celebrate today. You have raised your voices in an unmistakable chorus. You have cast your votes in historic numbers. And you have changed the face of Congress, the presidency, and the political process itself. Yes, you, my fellow Americans have forced the spring. Now we must do the work the season demands.[109]

Economic issues were clearly at the top of his agenda.[110] His first televised address from the oval office in mid-February was an appeal to the American people to support his package of tax increases and spending cuts. Two days later, he appeared before a joint session of Congress to unveil additional details of his economic plan.

Clinton's success in Congress was mixed. His budget plan eventually passed by a narrow margin, while other elements of his program were defeated. In early January, the Bush administration revealed that deficit projections were even worse than previously thought. Democrats in Congress immediately voiced doubts about the feasibility of the middle-class tax cut that had been one of Clinton's campaign pledges, so it was abandoned.[111] Clinton's request for $31 billion in spending to stimulate the economy also came under fire. Democrats such as Senator David Boren (D–OK) voiced concerns about the tradeoff between new spending and deficit reduction: "If the first thing they see us do is pass a stimulus package, it's going to destroy our credibility. A lot of us will be extremely uncomfortable with voting more money for anything before we lock in deficit reduction."[112] The $31 billion proposal was thus whittled down to $16.3 billion, and even that failed to win approval by the Senate in late April. In August, Clinton's budget deficit reduction plan passed the House by two votes and the Senate by Vice President Al Gore's tie-breaking vote.

Clinton's early victories were clouded by a series of missteps in the early months of his administration. He clashed with congressional and military leaders over his decision to drop the ban on gays in the military. He chose and then abandoned his first two choices for attorney general (Zoe Baird and Lani Guinier) after their nominations met opposition. Although Clinton achieved a high legislative success rate, he relied on different coalitions for different votes; some called him a master politician, while others said he governed only by reacting to crises. He developed a reputation for trading important concessions for votes as the floor votes neared. In some cases, he lobbied House members to go out on a limb for provisions that he later abandoned in the Senate. Even so, he continued to hark back to his understanding of the meaning of the election:

> As you and I learned from the elections last year, the American people want their political system and their Government to end gridlock, to face problems, and to make progress. They're tired of a process that's been too divided by partisanship or dominated by special interests or driven by short-term advantage of politicians instead of the long-term interests of people. They sent us to the statehouse and to the White House to change America. And they want action now. That is our mandate, and we must never forget it."[113]

Clinton had an 86.4 percent overall success rate in his first year, second only to Dwight Eisenhower and Lyndon Johnson.[114] He got many of the economic policies that he wanted, but only after making substantial compromises. His administration could tout several accomplishments: family leave, motor voter registration, the Brady bill, and NAFTA. Party unity hit a record high in both the House and Senate, with 65.5 percent and 67.1 percent, respectively, of all floor votes having a majority of one party voting against a majority of the other party.[115] A conservative coalition of Republicans and southern Democrats seldom materialized, and when it did it was more likely to be banding together to support Clinton's position than to oppose it.[116]

The 1994 Midterm Elections

The presidency of Bill Clinton provides the perfect opportunity to discuss the signaling capacity of midterm congressional elections.

When presidential and congressional elections take place at the same time, there is a tendency to use the congressional elections as evidence for or against the president's mandate. While this also happens during midterm elections—especially when presidents ask that midterm elections be a referendum on their agendas—it is also possible for midterm elections to be used by party leaders to send a policy message that goes beyond simple approval or disapproval of the president. This was precisely the strategy of the Republican Party leadership in 1994.

Before the 1994 midterm elections, analysts thought that Republican Party control of the Senate was within reach.[117] Control of the House was less certain. Bill Clinton was in trouble, with an approval rating of only 41 percent. His health care plan had met with disastrous defeat, and he continued to be dogged by allegations about the Whitewater land deal. In March 1994, surveys showed that only 18 percent of citizens expressed "a great deal" of confidence in Congress, which had been controlled by Democrats since 1986.[118] Ross Perot urged his supporters to vote Republican because the Clinton administration had not delivered on the change it had promised. Most Democrats tried to loosen their ties to the Clinton administration and to run on local issues.

The Republicans, on the other hand, gambled with a nationally coordinated strategy. They ran against Bill Clinton, using television advertisements that portrayed their Democratic opponents as puppets of Clinton, with their faces morphing into Clinton's face. More than 350 GOP incumbents and challengers signed a ten-point "Contract with America" and promised that these items would be put at the top of the legislative agenda in the first 100 days of a Republican-led Congress. Some of the items had proved popular in the 1992 election cycle, particularly among Perot voters: the promise of a balanced budget amendment and presidential line-item veto, a middle-class tax cut, and term limits for members of Congress. Other items were consistent with long-standing themes of the Republican Party: capital gains tax cuts, welfare reform, limiting appeals in death penalty cases, and restricting United Nations authority over U.S. troops. The party leadership and a group of candidates held a public presentation of the contract on the Capitol steps in late September. Republican leaders, particularly Newt Gingrich, presented the contract on various news programs, and the party ran television and print advertisements promoting the contract. Individual candidates were free to accentuate whichever items they felt were especially appealing to their constituencies.

The strategy appeared to work, as Republicans gained 53 seats in the House, breaking the Democrats' forty-year reign over the lower chamber, the longest in American history. They also won control of the Senate with a net gain of 8 seats, for a 53 to 45 majority.[119] The Republicans were victorious in races across the entire nation. Not a single incumbent Republican governor, senator, or representative failed to win reelection. The Republicans would send seventy-four freshmen to the House and eleven to the Senate. For the first time since 1862, the sitting Speaker of the House, Tom Foley (D–WA), was defeated. Prominent, liberal Democratic incumbent governors Mario Cuomo of New York and Ann Richards of Texas were defeated. Thirty-five Democratic incumbents lost in the House; two were defeated in the Senate. Only 39 percent of registered voters turned out to vote. Former Perot voters supported the Republican candidates by overwhelming margins.[120]

The magnitude of the Republican victory and the takeover of the House came as a surprise to most, even to the Republican leadership. Republicans were quick to label their sweep a victory for their policy agenda. Newt Gingrich argued that it was "clearly a historic election, which clearly had a mandate. And that's outside the Washington elite's view, and they don't want to believe that, because it's not the mandate they wanted."[121] He disagreed with those who said the result was simply a triumph of southern Christian religious groups: "In Washington State we went from 7–1 Democrat to 6–1 Republican. You can hardly argue that it's that Southern fundamentalism swept through Washington State."[122]

President Clinton, in his first press conference after the election, said:

> I agree with much of what the electorate said yesterday. . . .
> Though we have made progress, not enough people have felt more prosperous and more secure, or believe we are meeting their desires for fundamental change in the role of

government in their lives. With the Democrats in control
of both the White House and the Congress, we were held
accountable yesterday.[123]

Clinton did not interpret the election as a vote to reverse legislation
like the Brady bill or the military assault weapons ban. Rather, he
said, voters were dissatisfied with the pace of change and wanted to
send a message. "We all work for them," he said, "every one of us.
And their will, their voice was heard. We got the message."[124]

One might dismiss Republican mandate claims, given the low
turnout and polls showing that voters had little knowledge of the
Contract with America. Nevertheless, specific items on the platform—for instance deficit reduction, the middle-class tax cut, and
term limits—had strong popular support, as evidenced in both public
opinion polls and in the popularity of Ross Perot. Aversion to gridlock had been one of the major themes of the 1992 election, and
polls showed that some voters thought that unified government had
not delivered on its promise of change.

It was shrewd for the Republican leadership to try to set the legislative agenda by organizing their campaign around the Contract with
America. They were rewarded at the polls with an unexpected landslide victory that gave them control of both the House and the Senate. They had majority support for some elements of the contract
and could do no worse than the status quo by introducing the others.
President Clinton said that he agreed with some parts of the contract, such as the line-item veto, and he pledged cooperation in general. With a slim margin in the House (231 to 203), the party leadership changed the rules for committee assignments and jurisdiction,
to enhance party discipline and streamline the legislative process.
Republicans in 1994 had reason to be optimistic.

Like the president, party leaders in Congress will claim a mandate
only when they have a favorable political opportunity. Their opportunity depends upon voters, the preferences of members of the opposing party, party discipline within and across chambers, and the popularity and preferences of the president. Are their claims about the
public plausible? Will the president go along, or can they override
a potential veto? Will enough members of the opposing party join

them in their efforts? Does their party have an opportunity to make a change or at least shift the status quo in their direction?

The 1994 elections illustrate that midterm elections also have the capacity to send a message. In the nineteenth century, midterm elections were likely to result in divided government until voters could also change the party controlling the presidency two years later. Divided government therefore occurred only in the two-year segments between midterms and the following presidential election. Midterm elections were often interpreted substantively, while the presidential election was seen as a confirmation of what had occurred two years earlier. In the twentieth century, midterm elections have not functioned in this way because they have become predictable, thus rendering them much less informative. In the post-Roosevelt era prior to 1994, the president's party had always lost seats in the midterm election, but not control of the House. The 1994 outcome was therefore a dramatic departure, and analysts thought it contained important clues about public preferences. By the same token, when President Clinton broke the pattern of midterm losses in 1998, that outcome was viewed as surprising enough to warrant explanation. In that case, the outcome was interpreted as a public statement against his impeachment.

*

Both Truman and Clinton relied on grassroots campaign styles that reinforced their identification with voters and their role as advocates of change against the status quo in Washington. Truman's feat was managing to do this as the incumbent president. Both were admired for their personal will power and stamina during the campaign. One was a "miracle man," the other a "comeback kid." The Democrats' recapture of both chambers of Congress in 1948 and their mantra to end gridlock in 1992 led to optimistic forecasts of congressional action on the major issues of the day. Truman and Clinton set the agenda according to their reading of the election. Third-party challenges heightened discussion of major policy issues at the same time that they foreshadowed difficulty in the coalition building to come. Unfortunately for both presidents, some members of their party in Congress had the same policy preferences as the third-party challengers in the election. Southern Democrats in the late 1940s shared the States' Rights ticket's opposition to civil rights legislation. Southern Democrats in the early 1990s shared Ross Perot's concern about reducing the federal budget deficit. Truman's and Clinton's policy successes came with great effort if at all.

While Truman and Clinton did not have the stunning popular victories of the other mandate-claiming presidents, they did have an incentive to ask for a major policy change. The gamble looked like it was worth it. In the next chapter, I describe three elections in which both popular and congressional support appeared lacking for any major changes in public policy. The outcomes were close, and the signal noisy. Interpreters leaned not toward a policy explanation but toward matters of practical political strategy or normal partisan tides in the electorate. Even the victors seemed uncertain about their policy agenda.

SEVEN | **Victories but Not Mandates:**
1960, 1976, and 1988

In the aftermath of the elections of 1960, 1976, and 1988, there was no reason to hold out hope for bold policy initiatives from the new administration. Not only did these elections suggest little impetus from the public for change, but the new Congresses they produced would make it difficult for the president to pass his programs. Unlike Eisenhower, Reagan, and Johnson, Presidents Kennedy, Carter, and Bush did not have landslide victories, nor did their victories come on the heels of campaigns focused on policy or the ideological differences between themselves and their opponents. They did not enter office accompanied by strong ideological support in Congress. Unlike Truman and Clinton, they did not have the appearance of at least moderate support from the electorate and the Congress. Presidents Kennedy, Carter, and Bush did not ask for a major policy change because they would most likely have been unsuccessful. They would have to be content with incremental changes to the national policy agenda.

Once again, I describe the campaign, outcome, postelection interpretations, and analysis of popular and legislative coalitions. Unlike elections after which presidents claim mandates, these campaigns were not highly polarized or focused on the issues. The outcomes were not dramatic or surprising. Explanations for victory centered more on matters of strategy and the normal party balance in the electorate than on policy changes demanded by voters. Though two of the three presidents belonged to the party in control of both chambers of Congress, each was expected to encounter legislative resistance. Immediately after the election, their agenda was unclear.

THE ELECTION OF 1960

In 1960, Democratic senator John F. Kennedy defeated Republican vice president Richard M. Nixon by little over 100,000 votes nationwide, the smallest plurality in the history of U.S. elections.[1] Kennedy was the first (and only) Catholic to be elected president and the first Democratic nominee from New England in over 100 years. At age forty-three, he was the youngest man ever elected to the office. Throughout his time as president, Kennedy remained keenly aware of the narrowness of his victory. He did not ask for major policy changes, and the legislation he requested encountered a great deal of resistance in Congress.

Primaries and Conventions
The Democratic Party

Kennedy gained national exposure in 1956 as a potential nominee for vice president alongside presidential nominee Adlai Stevenson. In 1960, Kennedy and three other senators—Lyndon Johnson of Texas, Hubert Humphrey of Minnesota, and Stuart Symington of Missouri—actively sought the Democratic presidential nomination. Kennedy won all of the primaries that he entered, often by very large margins. His primary victories lay to rest reservations about his age and religion. Of the other major candidates, only Humphrey received a substantial number of primary votes, but he withdrew from the race in mid-May. While Symington and Johnson did not do well in the primaries, they each hoped to be the choice of a deadlocked convention, as did Adlai Stevenson. After a struggle, Kennedy won on the first ballot and picked first runner-up Johnson as his vice presidential running mate. In his acceptance speech, Kennedy spoke of the need for new and creative leadership to confront the "New Frontier" of challenges of the 1960s. Vice President Richard Nixon was called an unsuitable successor to Eisenhower; Kennedy warned that Nixon would preside over an era of "creeping mediocrity."

The Republican Party

That the Republican nomination would be Vice President Richard Nixon's was hardly in doubt. His only significant rival, New York governor Nelson A. Rockefeller, withdrew from the race in December 1959. Nixon swept the Republican primaries in a series of uneventful contests. At the convention, he chose UN Ambassador Henry Cabot Lodge as his running mate, in large part because Nixon intended foreign policy to be the centerpiece of his campaign. In his speech, Nixon emphasized the unity of his party and his ticket and disparaged the factionalism that had been displayed at the Democratic convention. He pledged to run a national campaign and to visit all fifty states. Like Kennedy, he did not mention specific policy positions but instead spoke abstractly of America's role in the world and of "working for the victory of freedom."

The General Election Campaign

Both candidates put foreign policy at the center of their campaigns. Yet detailed discussion of foreign policy was hampered at the height of the Cold War. The Democrats did not have access to intelligence reports, and Nixon could not reveal any secret plans for action. Kennedy voiced alarm about a growing "missile gap" with the Soviet Union; Nixon expressed the same concern but did not speak with any precision about the size of the gap. Kennedy decried the Communist takeover in Cuba; Nixon decried the same event but could not go further and reveal secret plans for action. Rather than debate major directions in U.S. foreign policy or concrete plans for dealing with conflict in a particular location, Nixon and Kennedy offered only general statements. They debated the pace of action to fight communism in Cuba and whether or not the U.S. had lost influence and prestige around the world. Both candidates favored increased defense spending, and Kennedy also favored a reorganization of the four armed services.

On the domestic front, the nation entered a recession, which Nixon denied as he defended the record of the Eisenhower administration. Both candidates and parties claimed to be advocates of civil rights for African Americans, though Kennedy distinguished himself by calling Coretta Scott King to offer his support after Martin Luther King was jailed in Atlanta for participating in a sit-in. Neither candidate proposed spending cuts; indeed, both raised the possibility of higher taxes. During the first debate, Nixon went so far as to say,

"I can subscribe completely to the spirit that Senator Kennedy has expressed tonight."[2] With Democrats in the majority in the electorate, Nixon had every incentive to portray the parties as similar in their goals and different only in their methods. President Eisenhower waited until the last two weeks before the election to campaign on Nixon's behalf and was not thought to be a major factor in the election. Kennedy was pleased that he did not have to attack a popular incumbent president; Nixon needed Ike's support but also wanted to assert his independence.

Because it was difficult to separate the candidates on the basis of their policy positions, there was much discussion during the campaign of the candidates' personalities and character. Nixon tried to persuade voters that Kennedy's youth and inexperience would be a major liability when dealing with the Soviet Union and the Communist threat around the world. He suggested that Kennedy's wealth and privilege made him insensitive to the concerns of average Americans. Both candidates were generally silent about Kennedy's Catholicism. Kennedy addressed the issue of his religion in an appearance before a minister's association in September, where he affirmed that he believed in "an America that is officially neither Catholic, Protestant, nor Jewish . . . where there is no Catholic vote, no anti-Catholic vote . . . and where religious liberty is so indivisible that an act against one church is treated as an act against all."[3] His speech was well received by the group, and neither he nor Nixon raised the issue again. Kennedy argued that he had the energy and imagination to make the country better and that Nixon, from the party of Hoover and Dewey, would only make things worse.

Television played a much larger role than ever before. The campaigns ran short television advertisements, and the candidates participated in telethons and interviews at television stations throughout the nation. For the first time, the presidential candidates met in televised debates. Nixon and Kennedy appeared in four televised debates in late September and October. On balance, the debates were thought to help Kennedy because they gave him exposure, and his confident performance helped him counter Nixon's argument that he was too inexperienced to be president. Kennedy's healthy and youthful appearance, in contrast to Nixon's pale and sickly demeanor, also suggested that Kennedy had the vitality to "get the country moving again."

Most of the final polls gave Kennedy the edge in electoral college votes (though not a firm majority), but the popular vote was too close to call.[4] The day before the election, polls reported that Kennedy was leading in nineteen states for a total of 244 electoral college votes, while Nixon was leading in sixteen states for a total of 109 electoral college votes.[5] Fifteen states, including California, Illinois, Pennsylvania, and Texas, with a total of 184 electoral college votes, were too close to call. Most nationwide polls had Kennedy one to four points ahead, within the margin of error.[6] Though Kennedy was ahead, pollsters were uncertain about the effect of Kennedy's religion, particularly in the South.[7] The possibility of neither candidate winning an electoral majority was discussed.[8]

No one predicted that the partisan makeup of Congress would change. Democrats were expected to maintain control of the Senate, though the Republicans were expected to pick up one or two seats.[9] In the House, Republicans were expected to pick up several seats but not to threaten Democratic control of that chamber.[10] No changes were anticipated in Democratic Party dominance at the state level.[11]

The Election Outcome

The outcome of the presidential race was so close that Richard Nixon did not concede until noon EST the day after the election. The *New York Times* proclaimed Kennedy the "apparent victor" the morning after the election. Kennedy won 49.72 percent of the popular vote, while Nixon won 49.55 percent. Kennedy's plurality was roughly 114,000 votes out of 68 million votes cast. His plurality was as low as 8,000 votes in Illinois and only 115 votes in Hawaii.

Analysts made much of the close margin of victory: "Senator Kennedy of Massachusetts finally won the 1960 Presidential election from Vice President Nixon by the astonishing margin of less than two votes per voting precinct."[12] Article after article referred to past close elections like 1948, 1916, 1884, and 1880.[13] In eight states (including California, Illinois, and Texas), a shift of less than 1 percent in the popular vote would have switched the state's electoral votes.[14]

Kennedy won twenty-two and a half states for a total of 303 electoral college votes, while Nixon won twenty-six states for a total of 219 votes.[15] A conservative Democrat, Senator Harry F. Byrd of West Virginia, received 15 electoral college votes from delegates in Alabama, Mississippi, and Oklahoma. Kennedy won a majority of northeastern states, southern states (including Texas), and large mid-western states (Illinois, Michigan, and Minnesota). Nixon won most of the western states (including California) along with a handful of midwestern and border states.[16] Sixty-three percent of the eligible voters turned out to vote, the highest turnout since 1908.

The Democrats retained control over both chambers of Congress, though they lost seats. In the House, Republicans gained 20 seats, so that the new party balance was 263 Democrats to 174 Republicans. In the Senate, Democrats lost 2 seats, leaving a total of 64 Democrats to 36 Republicans.[17] There were few new faces. Postelection analysis revealed that Kennedy ran about seven percentage points behind local Democratic candidates throughout the nation.[18] There were no surprises at the state level, with the Democrats picking up one governorship.

Interpretations of Victory

Kennedy's win was explained in large part as a triumph of his political party.[19] Nixon's personal campaign manager commented, "One of the things he did very well was to keep emphasizing that 'I am the Democratic candidate.'"[20] Kennedy relied heavily on organized labor and on Democratic machine politicians such as Chicago's Mayor Daley. Lyndon Johnson helped him carry the traditionally Democratic South. In addition, Kennedy received the overwhelming support of black and Hispanic voters. While some observers suspected his margin might have been larger had he not been a Catholic, there was little evidence that his religious affiliation hurt him. The exposure he gained in the televised debates was also thought to be crucial to his successful campaign.

In the week after the election, aides for both candidates explained the outcome as a strategic failure on the part of the Nixon campaign. Kennedy aides said, "Mr. Nixon's biggest blunder was the failure to concentrate on the industrial northern states."[21] Nixon aides said, "The Republicans were beaten by the big city machines in the North . . . plus the power of the labor unions . . . plus Johnson's effectiveness in the South."[22] The close victory meant that the campaign could "cite any of several factors—the Catholic vote, the Negro vote, Vice President Elect Johnson's role in holding most of the South, the TV debates—and say 'But for this, Nixon would be President.'"[23]

While his victory was heralded as an end to divided government, there was little or no mention that Kennedy's victory meant that voters wanted major policy changes:

> The pace rather than the direction of policy by the central government was in dispute. . . . Neither party asked the electorate to repeal the social programs introduced by Presidents Roosevelt and Truman and expanded by President Eisenhower. Nor was either party questioning America's economic or military efforts as a leading member of the non-Communist nations.[24]

Kennedy was expected to bring a change in tone and emphasis rather than a change in substance and policy. Editorial writers around the country agreed: "There is no sweeping mandate to be read into the results."[25] "The American people, taken together, want to stay middle of the road."[26] "The American people have shown faith in President-elect Kennedy to make a change for the better. At the same time, they have told him that a radical shaking is not desired."[27]

The new House of Representatives was expected to be more conservative, given the addition of twenty new Republicans to the coalition of Republicans and southern Democrats.[28] "The liberal legislative program to be submitted early next year . . . may consequently face handicaps in the new Congress."[29] While the Senate was viewed as "predominantly liberal," conservatives dominated the committee and leadership structure.[30] Lyndon Johnson's move to the vice presidency meant Kennedy would face a new Senate majority leader. Since Kennedy ran behind most local Democratic candidates outside of New England, he was not credited with having coattails.[31]

Kennedy's Policy Agenda

In his first press conference, Kennedy said that he was going to do his best to meet his responsibilities and to implement the political views expressed in his campaign.[32] When asked if the outcome was a repudiation of the Republican administration, Kennedy replied, "No, I think it is a victory for the Democrats, but I don't think we can certainly call the result a repudiation of anyone. But I do think that at least the responsibility has been given to us by a majority of citizens. The margin is narrow but the responsibility is clear."[33] Kennedy said he was "hopeful" that he and the new Congress would be able to work together.

Before the election, Kennedy alluded to Roosevelt's first 100 days when he discussed his intention to move quickly in his first months in office. His first task was to confront a House Rules Committee dominated by a conservative coalition of Republicans and southern Democrats. The Rules Committee had the power to prevent legislation from getting to the floor for a vote. He narrowly succeeded in enlarging the committee in order to give his administration's supporters a narrow majority. His legislation made it to the floor, but most of it did not pass. Overall, he was successful on only 48.4 percent of his legislative requests in his first year.[34]

Kennedy was most successful in the area of defense, where he asked for increased funding for defense and space programs.[35] He also won approval for bills extending unemployment benefits during the recession, increasing the minimum wage, improving social security benefits, and increasing aid to economically depressed areas. He was least successful with respect to aid to education, medical care for the elderly, and tax reform. Despite the Democratic platform, Kennedy did not propose new civil rights legislation in his first year. Though he asked for increases in spending, he did not offer radically different programs or ideas. Unified government did not lead to major policy changes.

THE ELECTION OF 1976

In 1976, Democrat Jimmy Carter, a former governor of Georgia, won a close race against Republican incumbent president Gerald Ford.[36] Carter was the first southerner to be elected president in over 100 years. Ford was the first incumbent to lose reelection since Herbert Hoover. As in the race between Kennedy and Nixon, the candidates in 1976 did not accentuate their ideological differences. Instead, the Watergate scandal had heightened concern over government ethics. Both candidates emphasized their personal integrity and their ability to steer the country through a time of healing in the aftermath of President Nixon's resignation.

Primaries and Conventions
The Democratic Party

Carter captured his party's nomination by the end of the primary season, but the fight had not been easy.[37] Favorite-son candidates proliferated—in West Virginia, Illinois, Texas, and California. Carter's resources were stretched thin because he was the only candidate trying to run in all of the primary states. An even greater impediment to Carter was that the Democratic Party leadership did not accept him until the end of the primary season; a "stop Carter" faction, consisting mostly of liberals within the party, was determined to find an alternative. They did not seem eager to acknowledge Carter's victories, and they encouraged speculation that Hubert Humphrey might emerge from a brokered convention as the party's nominee.[38]

By the end of the primary season, however, Carter had the delegates he needed to win the nomination. At the convention he won the nomination with over 2,000 votes; his closest competitors, Morris Udall and Jerry Brown, had about 300 votes each. Carter chose liberal Minnesota senator Walter Mondale as his running mate in an effort to join forces with the wing of the party he had defeated in the primaries. His convention speech played up his outsider, populist status. He emphasized that government should be "honest" and "efficient," and he discussed broad principles as opposed to specific issues.

The Republican Party

Gerald Ford's bid to secure the Republican nomination ran into trouble within his own party, as he had to fend off a strong challenge from conservative Republicans rallying around Ronald Reagan. Ford's slim victory over Reagan in New Hampshire (49.4 percent to 48 percent) was followed by wins in northeastern and industrial midwestern states but losses in the West and the South. Even after the primary season ended in early June, his quest for the nomination was not over; the delegate count was so close that the results of uncommitted and caucus delegates were crucial. At the August convention, Ford won the nomination on the first ballot, 1,187 votes to Reagan's 1,070 votes. To appease the right wing of the party, he abandoned incumbent vice president Nelson Rockefeller and instead picked Senator Bob Dole of Kansas as his vice presidential running mate. In his acceptance speech, Ford blamed the Democratic Congress for the nation's problems and challenged Carter to what would be the first presidential debates since the Nixon–Kennedy series in 1960.

The General Election Campaign

Carter ran as an outsider, claiming that he would restore public trust in government and enact reforms to make government more efficient. He also promised to undertake tax reform and enact comprehensive energy and health care policies. Ford, on the other hand, stressed that America was at peace at home and abroad. He claimed that as president, he had presided over both the healing of America after Watergate and the economic recovery.

Ford and Carter were perceived to differ mainly in the details rather than in the general direction of their policies.[39] One journalist wrote, "Mr. Ford is supposed to be . . . the more conservative candidate, but Mr. Carter is giving him a good run for his money."[40] Ford promised a balanced budget by 1978, Carter by 1980. Ford promised to cut taxes, while Carter called for a reform of the tax system that did not rule out a tax cut. Carter said he could trim $5 to $7 billion in waste from the defense budget outlined by President Ford.

Throughout the campaign, journalists, voters, and politicians voiced their concern about the apathy, pettiness, and lack of focus on the issues in the campaign.[41] John Chancellor's assessment was typical: "I've been covering politics for more than 20 years, and I don't think I've ever seen a pettier campaign, an emptier campaign, a campaign so lacking in a discussion of real issues. I don't recall a campaign so dependent on slips of the tongue, misinterpreted remarks, and accidents."[42] Though they complained, journalists spent a great deal of time discussing such matters as Carter's interview in *Playboy* magazine, Ford's statement that the Soviet Union did not dominate Eastern Europe, and vice presidential nominee Bob Dole's suggestion that all twentieth-century wars had been "Democratic wars."

Immediately after the Democratic convention, Carter led Ford in the polls by thirty-three percentage points. After the Republican convention, Carter led by about ten points. In mid-October, Carter led by only six percentage points. Ford never led in the polls for the duration of the campaign. But at the very end, only days before the election, the race tightened and was too close to call. Most of the final polls had Carter ahead by one percentage point, well within the margin of error.[43] The final predictions of electoral college votes gave Carter twenty states with 222 electoral college votes, while Ford appeared to have twenty-one states with 198 electoral college votes.[44] Nine states with a total of 118 delegates were too close to call. For weeks, the closeness of the popular and electoral college votes led journalists to compare the election to the 1960 and 1968 races.[45] The possibility of incongruent electoral college and popular vote outcomes was raised.[46] The Democratic Party's dominance of both the House and Senate was not expected to change.[47]

The Election Outcome

The outcome was close, as anticipated. Carter won twenty-four states for a total of 297 electoral college votes, while Ford won twenty-seven states for a total of 241 electoral college votes.[48] Carter won the popular vote 50.1 to 48 percent. Turnout was 53.3 percent, down from 55.4 percent in 1972. The party lineup in Congress hardly changed. The partisan split in the Senate would remain the same as before—62 Democrats and 38 Republicans. However, though the party balance remained the same, eighteen new senators were elected. In the House of Representatives, Democrats gained one seat for a total of 292 Democrats to 143 Republicans.

Interpretations of Victory

Journalists were quick to label Carter's election "a victory, but not a mandate."[49] Analysis of the election focused on three elements: the closeness of the race, the traditional breakdown of sectional and group bases of candidate support, and the short coattails of the new president. First, commentators emphasized how easily Ford could have been the victor in the electoral college.[50] If he had switched 5,000 votes in both Ohio and Hawaii, he would have won the electoral college vote. Carter's margin of victory was less than five percentage points in half of the states, and less than two percentage points in thirteen states wielding a total of 174 electoral college votes. As one commentator remarked, Carter's electoral college majority "was the most fragile since Woodrow Wilson, an earlier moralizer, won the White House 60 years ago, and his popular vote was no more substantial than that by which Harry S. Truman achieved an upset three decades ago."[51] In addition to election statistics, reporters analyzed the mind-set of voters: "The fact that so many voters had difficulty deciding has obvious bearing on the question of whether the victor can now claim a mandate."[52]

Second, as journalists noted, the outcome looked a lot like 1960, when the pattern of victory also broke along the parties' traditional regional and group lines.[53] Carter, the Democrat, won the South, a majority in the northeastern states, and enough of the Midwest to forge a victory. Ford, the Republican, won all of the western states and several midwestern states. Carter's victory was explained by his ability to maintain the loyalty of Democratic Party identifiers, especially labor union and minority voters, who overwhelmingly preferred Carter to Ford.[54] Eighty percent of all self-identified Democrats voted for Carter. Eighty-nine percent of all self-identified Republicans voted for Ford. Independents split about evenly between the two candidates. Carter also had strong support from younger voters and earned twice as many southern votes as McGovern did in 1972. Carter won these voters in part by being ambiguous about his policy positions and by highlighting his honesty, trustworthiness, and outsider status. In his own analysis of the outcome, Carter credited his victory to the exposure he gained in the televised debates, because he felt they allayed voters' fears about his ability to be president.[55]

Finally, hardly anyone argued that the new and incumbent members of Congress owed their victory to Carter.[56] One article noted, "He was elected by an eyelash, and his presence at the head of the ticket seems to have been hardly a factor in the election of a heavily Democratic Congress, meaning that there are few in Congress who owe him a political debt."[57] *Congressional Quarterly* editor Rhodes Cook stated, "There were no coattails to speak of in the 1976 presidential election."[58] Forecasts made during the transition period about the likely relationship between Carter and Congress were mixed.[59] While some Democrats were enthusiastic and reported an "awfully good mood and atmosphere" of cooperation, others, such as the chairman of the Ways and Means Committee, voiced concern over some of Carter's economic policies. Congressional Republicans either spoke of offering their own proposals or denounced Carter's honeymoon as "short or non-existent." Journalists compared the 1976 election with the 1960 election, noting that the congressional power structure (particularly in the House) had changed since then and would work to Carter's disadvantage.[60]

Jimmy Carter was one of the few candidates in American history to defeat a sitting president. Still, in his first news conference, he denied that the election was a "strong negative reaction to President Ford or his administration."[61] When asked if the closeness of the election was a message from the people, Carter put his election in the context of past elections: "I think that the outcome is fairly typical. I think that in 1948, 1960, 1968 for instance, in all these instances, the victor got less than 50 percent of the votes and approximately 300 Electoral College votes." Nonetheless, Carter said that he did not feel cautious about carrying out his campaign commitments because "the fact that the Congress is likely to be willing to cooperate—at least for the early stages of my campaign—will much more than compensate for the closeness of the election." Throughout his news conference, he referred to his "broad-based" and "adequate" support. At the end, Carter was asked whether he had a timetable or "first 100 days" plan. He replied, "Whether we'll move first, though, on health care or welfare reform, or Government reorganization or energy policy or tax reform or those sequence of major proposals, will have to be evolved in the weeks to come. I do not know the sequence yet."[62] *Congressional Quarterly* reported, "As in 1961, the nation will be inaugurating a president who campaigned on the promise of an aggressive and imaginative new government, but who has offered few specifics about what he will do."[63]

Carter's Policy Agenda

By February, little over a month after his inauguration, Carter was having trouble with Congress. House and Senate Democrats were voicing their independence and their equal status with the president. By April, journalists were writing, "In the 100 days since his inauguration, Carter has shown that the marriage between a Democratic Congress and the first Democratic president since 1969 is not one made in heaven."[64] He angered members of Congress by attacking traditional pork barrel legislation, proposing to eliminate funding for eighteen water projects.

Overall, however, in his first year Congress supported Carter on 75 percent of the votes on which he stated a clear position. In this regard, Carter fared slightly better than Nixon, but worse than fellow Democrats Johnson and Kennedy.[65] Carter was not opposed on defense issues, where he asked for no major changes. He sought and received a renewal of presidential authority to reorganize the executive branch. In April, he presented a comprehensive energy conservation plan as the centerpiece of his legislative agenda. By the end of the first congressional session, the bill had not passed, though he did get approval for a cabinet-level Department of Energy. In the postVietnam and Watergate era, he had to deal with a newly assertive Congress without the benefit of strong popular momentum.[66]

THE ELECTION OF 1988

In 1988, George Bush became the first sitting vice president since Martin Van Buren (1836) to make a successful bid for the presidency.[67] For the first time since 1968, no incumbent president ran for either party, though Ronald Reagan was certainly a presence in the fall campaign. Bush won a landslide victory over Democratic candidate Michael Dukakis, but the campaign was condemned as one of the most negative in recent history. The attribution of Bush's victory to negative campaigning, coupled with the Democratic Party's lock on Congress, meant that the new administration was not in a position to ask for major policy changes.

Primaries and Conventions
The Republican Party

As vice president, George Bush had a distinct advantage in the race for his party's nomination. He was well known and had the most legitimate claim to be Ronald Reagan's heir. He was recognized, experienced, and well financed. Still, several prominent Republicans ran for the nomination, including Representative Jack Kemp of New York, Senator Bob Dole of Kansas, Governor Pierre DuPont of Delaware, the television evangelist Reverend Pat Robertson, and former secretary of state Alexander Haig. Both Dole and Robertson beat Bush in the Iowa caucuses, but neither could keep the momentum going in later contests. Bush won in New Hampshire and then won every other primary contest he entered, except for South Dakota. He swept the southern states on Super Tuesday. Kemp, DuPont, and Haig withdrew early in the season, and Dole withdrew in late March after Super Tuesday. Robertson waited until late May to withdraw, though he never posed a significant challenge to Bush.

The Republican Party platform restated the conservative principles of the Reagan era. For his vice presidential running mate, Bush chose Senator Dan Quayle of Indiana. Quayle's appeal was limited to conservatives within the party; he was unknown to the electorate and did not help to expand Bush's electoral base. In his convention speech, Bush expressed his desire to continue with the policies of the "Reagan–Bush" administration, while also promising a "kinder, gentler" approach. He made a firm promise on taxes ("Read my lips. No new taxes."). He attacked Dukakis's record in the state of Massachusetts. He and other Republicans united in pressing the ideological differences between the parties. They attacked "liberalism" and spoke of their allegiance to the family, religion, and patriotism. Bush closed his speech by reciting the pledge of allegiance.

The Democratic Party

In the Democratic Party the field was wide open. Several prominent politicians withdrew or refused to run before the season started.[68] By the beginning of the primary season, there were six candidates: Arizona governor Bruce Babbitt, Massachusetts governor Michael Dukakis, Senator Al Gore from Tennessee, Representative

Richard Gephardt from Missouri, the Reverend Jesse Jackson, and Senator Paul Simon from Illinois. Babbitt did not win any primaries, and Simon won only his home state of Illinois. Gephardt won in the Iowa caucuses but then only in South Dakota and his home state of Missouri. Thus by the March 8 Super Tuesday contests, the race had narrowed to Dukakis, Gore, and Jackson. By May, it became apparent that Dukakis would win the nomination, but Jackson stayed in the race until the end.

At the Democratic convention, Dukakis chose Senator Lloyd Bentsen of Texas as his running mate. Bentsen was viewed as a moderate and appealed to centrist members of the party and the electorate. Jackson, denied the vice presidency, was influential in changing party rules and in drafting the party platform. The platform was relatively brief, emphasizing party unity and general goals rather than specific policies. When Dukakis spoke at the convention, he stressed broad themes such as economic opportunity and honesty among public officials. He asserted one of his major campaign slogans: "This election is not about ideology, it's about competence."

The General Election Campaign

After the Democratic convention, Dukakis led Bush by about seventeen percentage points in the polls. His popularity was short-lived. Bush managed to capture the agenda of the campaign. In television ads, interviews, and debates, Bush accentuated topics like crime, the pledge of allegiance, and the environment. Independent organizations working for the Republican ticket ran the now infamous "Willie Horton" television ad about a black convicted killer who, on a weekend furlough program at a Massachusetts prison, raped a white woman and stabbed her fiancé. Bush questioned Dukakis's patriotism when he attacked him for vetoing a bill requiring teachers to lead students in reciting the pledge of allegiance at the start of each school day. The Bush campaign ran ads of Boston harbor overflowing with waste. They emphasized Dukakis as a "card-carrying member of the ACLU."

The Dukakis campaign failed to respond to Bush's attacks. As Dukakis staff members later recalled, they could not believe voters would take any of it seriously.[69] Dukakis himself was adamant about stressing positive messages and achievements. Since he had declared that the election was about competence rather than ideology, he did not respond to Bush's attacks linking him with the "L-word"— liberalism. By not counterattacking, Dukakis came across as unemotional and technocratic.

In the final weeks before the election, however, the Dukakis campaign became more aggressive. Dukakis acknowledged his liberalism and went on the trail with the populist message of "I'm on your side."[70] Like every other underdog presidential candidate, he urged crowds to remember Harry Truman's 1948 upset. While Dukakis did pick up some support, it was not enough. The Bush campaign was boosted the weekend before the election with news that the unemployment rate was down to its lowest level since 1974.[71]

The final polls put Bush ahead in the popular vote by 48 percent to 40 percent.[72] Late-deciding voters leaned toward Dukakis, polls found, in part because they were more likely to blame Bush for negative campaigning.[73] Sixty-two percent of voters said the campaign was more negative than any in the past. Turnout was expected to be disappointing due to unfavorable perceptions of the candidates and the campaigns.[74] A majority of newspapers declined to endorse either candidate; indeed, together the candidates received the fewest endorsements of any set of candidates since endorsement surveys began in 1932.[75] The final estimate of the electoral college vote was 306 votes for Bush from states leaning toward or certain to support him, and 137 votes for Dukakis; states that were too close to call held the remaining 95 votes.[76]

Democrats were expected to retain control of both chambers of Congress.[77] Democratic control of the House of Representatives was not in question because the Democratic majority in the 100th Congress—255 to 177—was so large. In Senate races, both Republican challengers and incumbents seemed to be in trouble, so the 54 to 46 advantage of the Democrats was safe. Democrats were expected to gain a small number of governorships.

The Election Outcome

Bush's victory was so decisive that CBS declared him the winner at around 9:15 P.M. EST. He beat Dukakis 53.4 to 45.6 percent in the popular vote and 426 to 112 in the electoral college.[78] Bush won forty states, in all regions of the country. He won all of the southern states and all of the western states except for Washington and Oregon. Dukakis won ten states plus the District of Columbia.[79] Only 51 percent of all eligible voters turned out to vote, the lowest turnout since 1924. Democrats gained one seat in the Senate and five seats in the House of Representatives, strengthening their majorities.[80] Not since 1960 had the party of a president-elect failed to pick up any seats in the House.

Interpretations of Victory

Bush's victory was explained by three key factors.[81] First, he was the candidate of the incumbent party at a time of relative peace and prosperity. Second, he was strongly identified with Ronald Reagan. Polls showed that voters who approved of Reagan overwhelmingly supported Bush.[82] Finally, his relentless negative attacks on Michael Dukakis worked. The issues his supporters named most frequently were crime, strong national defense, and low taxes. The Dukakis camp conceded that it waited too long to respond to the attacks of the Bush campaign.[83] Their own theme, that Dukakis was on the side of the middle class, barely managed to get through to voters by the time of the election.

While Bush had substantial electoral support, he was hindered by the type of campaign he had run. Right before the election, Lloyd Bentsen voiced the opinion, "I don't see how a President has any kind of mandate if he wins by negative advertising, by a concentration on negative advertising."[84] James Baker, the Bush campaign manager, responded, "It is only in these waning days that our opponents have tried to undercut any possible mandate by raising the charge of negative campaigning. Before they just disagreed with us."[85] The Bentsen view, however, predominated after the election.

Among politicians, the most frequently offered explanation for Bush's victory centered on the superiority of Bush campaign tactics as opposed to issues, ideology, national conditions, or the personal characteristics of the candidates.[86] Liberals and Democrats promoted this view of the election, but so did moderates and Republican campaign consultants.[87]

Forecasts about congressional cooperation with a Bush agenda were decidedly pessimistic. Members of his own party, such as Senate minority leader Bob Dole, acknowledged, "This situation is going to spell trouble right from day one for George Bush."[88] Democrats in Congress were not ready to forgive Bush for his nasty campaign tactics. The lack of substance in Bush's campaign and the fact that voters had voted for a Democratic Congress contributed to a consensus among observers that the support of the people was not clearly behind any Bush policy. Michael Dukakis's reaction was typical:

> I don't see a mandate. Not when the House of Representatives has increased its Democratic members and the Senate has increased its Democratic members. Although they may have expressed a desire to have some continuity in the presidency, I don't think you can look at those results on the Congressional side and not conclude that they're also expressing some very strong, progressive feelings about what this country has to do, and they want a government in Washington which is on their side when it comes to dealing with these problems.[89]

House majority leader Tom Foley concurred: "To pick up seats in a year like this is a very clear signal of a deliberate judgment on the part of the American people to keep Democrats in Congress."[90]

Bush's Policy Agenda

In his first press conference after the election, Bush was asked if he considered his victory a mandate. He replied:

> Well, I don't know whether I want to use the word 'mandate.' . . . I do feel that the vote was convincing enough, and the margin great enough, and the number of states carried big enough, that it gives a certain confidence to the Executive branch of government that I hope will carry over and influence the Congress, with whom I am pledged to work.[91]

Bush revealed that he would use the transition period to establish his policy priorities and to come up with a game plan for his first 100 days. Politicians and observers were still uncertain about what would happen when Bush was no longer in the shadow of Ronald Reagan. Would he revert to his more moderate past?[92] His advisors ranged from conservatives such as John Sununu of New Hampshire to moderates like Jim Baker, whom he nominated to be secretary of state. Though he picked Dan Quayle to be his vice president, he rarely appeared with him during the campaign.

The 1989 congressional session was viewed as "groping for direction," with no clear policy agenda.[93] Senate minority leader Bob Dole commented, "There hasn't been any demand, any mandate in the Congress and the executive branch for major changes. We've done some sort of nibbling around the edges."[94] Bush did not request major policy changes, and much of the session was devoted to internal politics, such as the resignation of House Speaker Jim Wright. Bush's first-year success rate in Congress on those policies on which his administration took a clear stand was only 63 percent, the worst record of any postwar president except Gerald Ford.[95]

*

It is not surprising that none of the three elections discussed in this chapter was thought to be about policy. In 1960 and 1976, the candidates debated the pace rather than the direction of change. The victors won by extremely thin margins and drew their electoral support from their traditional constituencies. Presidents Kennedy and Carter declined to label their victories as a repudiation of previous Republican regimes. In 1988, Bush's victory was described as a triumph of negative campaigning. Several factors rendered his election relatively uninformative about voters' policy preferences: Issues were an afterthought in the campaigns; polls failed to show public support for specific policy changes; and there were no significant deviations from traditional voting patterns. Bush's own mixed political past as a sometimes moderate and sometimes conservative confounded forecasts of his future behavior.

Kennedy, Carter, and Bush entered office without optimism about their prospects in Congress. For Kennedy and Carter, party control of Congress did not change; party gains were small and anticipated. Yet though the Democrats were in control, there was little feeling of shared fate and ideological closeness. In 1988, the Republicans remained a minority party and actually lost a small number of seats in both chambers. Under divided government, Bush had even less incentive to propose major policy changes. Unfortunately for Bush, his electoral landslide was compromised by the nature of his campaign, so it did not provide him with leverage against Congress.

Immediately after their election, presidents who claim mandates reiterate the policy goals they championed in their election campaigns. They focus "like a laser beam" on these issues in their public statements and early meetings with fellow partisans in Congress. In contrast, Presidents Kennedy, Carter, and Bush proceeded with caution. They did not immediately enunciate their policy agenda for their first 100 days in office.

We should not expect every election to produce shifts in policy. The preferences of the electorate, of members of Congress, and of the president could all be close to the status quo, and the election might be an affirmation of existing policies. The elections in this chapter, however, were not "mandates for the status quo" because the candidates did not campaign for the status quo and did not win by opposing change. Rather, these elections failed to convey a signal for change, and they failed to produce a Congress that would make it easy for the new president to pass his agenda. The status quo resulted by default rather than by design.

EIGHT | Conclusion

Political representation through elections takes place in an environment of uncertainty, inferences, forecasts, and strategy. We send the president a signal in the course of the campaign and election; he sends one back after he evaluates the prospects for policy change. Every presidential election results in a new set of politicians in office, a new signal about public preferences and issue salience, and the potential for a new policy agenda. Presidents claim mandates when the policy signal is strong and the preferences of politicians are sufficiently aligned to facilitate policy change.

Throughout the book, I have compared presidents who declared mandates with those who did not. All presidents who declare mandates must win an election that can be viewed as a policy signal. This signal is strongest for those who win landslides and upset the received wisdom about groups of voters and their party loyalties. But it is also possible for the election to send a strong signal when significant third-party challengers make issues salient. The winner's margin of victory will be smaller due to the third party, but the priorities of the electorate may still be clear. When presidents in these races are fortunate enough to face their own party in control of Congress, they have an incentive to declare a mandate. For some presidents, neither the interpretation of the election nor the congressional environment provides an incentive to make major changes in the national policy agenda. They do not claim mandates.

Though elections are highly idiosyncratic events, postelection agenda setting is predictable because politicians have norms for deciphering which elections contain the most information about voter preferences on matters of public policy. Politicians share the information that forms their explanations for victory or defeat. They have an incentive to be accurate because they care about their reputation and they care about being reelected. The competition serves to keep the victors honest. Though a wide variety of explanations may be offered, only one or two stand the test of time and gather support from politicians across the political spectrum. The focus of electoral interpretation tends to be the unusual or surprising aspects of the outcome, whether this concerns shifting coalitions, regional anomalies, or gains in Congress. Politicians use various decision heuristics to sharpen their explanations and compare the current outcome with past election outcomes. They try to find the simplest explanation that can explain the most deviations from the normal or expected vote. They ask whether a policy explanation is sustainable given the quality of the campaign, the ideology of the presidential candidates, public opinion polls, and patterns of wins and losses for the parties nationwide. Landslides, particularly if surprising, increase confidence in policy-oriented explanations.

Presidents are careful in their use of mandate rhetoric because they know that it would be unwise to make bold claims and ask for a policy change that has little hope of passage. A president will claim a mandate only if he thinks that he and his party can mobilize a majority of voters behind his point of view. The less certain a president is about mobilizing voters, the more he needs to consider the preferences and partisanship of members of Congress. As long as he thinks he can shift the status quo toward his preferred policy position, the president will place a major policy change on the agenda. On the other hand, without a policy-oriented explanation for victory and strong congressional support, a president has no incentive to claim a mandate.

PRESIDENTIAL MANDATES AND POLITICAL REPRESENTATION

Our understanding of presidential mandates is informed by how we view political representation and the role of elections in democracy. Previous empirical studies have been grounded in two theoretical debates. First is the debate about the proper role of an elected official: Should a legislator be bound by the preferences of constituents or be free to use his or her own judgment? Second is the debate about the proper role of elections: Are elections mechanisms of accountability or signals about popular policy preferences? The latter possibility is sometimes posed as a crude distinction between Madison and Rousseau: voting as mere control of officials versus voting as embodying the will of the people in some form.[1] In empirical work, this is the distinction between retrospective and prospective explanations of voting behavior, whether voters reject the record of the incumbent party or advocate the policy platform of the winner.

In the context of these debates, presidents who claim mandates are declaring themselves to be delegates of the people, bound by their policy preferences. Moreover, presidential mandate claims imply that elections allow voters to send affirmative policy messages, which means widespread prospective issue voting on the part of the electorate. Since mandate rhetoric states that the voters have issued a command, it is only natural to examine public preferences and check the president's claim for accuracy in order to gauge the quality of political representation. Individual-level survey data appear to be the key to finding out whether the president is truly a delegate and whether there is a coherent voice of the people.

This kind of empirical analysis is clearly relevant to evaluating how well a president represents his constituents. With survey data, elections can be placed along a continuum according to the extent of policy-oriented voting in the electorate. We find more evidence of policy voting in some elections (1980 and 1964) than others (1976 or 1960). However, researchers must make several crucial and somewhat arbitrary decisions in order to certify the empirical existence of mandates.[2] First we have to decide how to measure policy opinions and prospective policy-oriented voting. Should we use self-described political ideology? A single policy question? A series of policy questions? If the latter, would we ask about general policy directions (whether the respondent favors tax cuts) or particular policy initiatives (whether the respondent favors a 30 percent reduction in personal income taxes over the next three years)? Second, we have to decide how much policy-oriented voting needs to take place before we consider an election a mandate. Do we need a simple majority of voters to agree with the president's position? Must they say that they voted on that basis only? What about the opinions of those who did not turn out to vote? These questions would remain even if we had better information about public preferences than exists in the typical public opinion poll.

When we understand mandates from the point of view of political elites, it becomes clear that this focus on voter preferences ignores several features of elections that shape the process of political representation. First, election outcomes are always viewed with uncertainty because politicians never have complete information about the preferences of their constituents. Constituencies are large—whether we are considering the entire nation, states, or House districts. Politicians have to make extrapolations about the population based on smaller samples of voters. Electoral turnout may be low, and the nonresponse rate of polls high; inferences have to be made about latent constituencies. Politicians attempt to forecast future political participation as well as understand what has recently occurred. It is impossible to evaluate the responsiveness of politicians without knowing how they make inferences about their constituents and how they deal with these information problems.

Second, though analytically distinct, retrospective and prospective voting are difficult to disentangle in the minds of politicians. Elected officials try to figure out policy preferences and salience at the time of the election; they look for a command or signal from voters regarding what to do. But they also forecast which policy agenda would result in the most favorable conditions for their reelection in the future. Politicians know that they will be held accountable for their actions; they try to figure out the instruction of the voters because they anticipate the retrospective judgments of voters in the next election. Therefore, regardless of the normative and empirical debates in political science, politicians believe that elections hold them accountable and send policy messages. This function of elections is difficult to tease apart empirically by looking at the actions of politicians, for the simple reason that they generate the same first-best agenda-setting actions by the government.[3]

Third, public opinion may not be well formed, but it instructs nonetheless. Presidential elections are not single-issue referendums, nor are they uninformative.[4] Elections are the creation, recreation, and interpretation of publics; they provide information about the changing boundaries of public opinion rather than a point estimate of the majority will. As Bruce Ackerman has written, "'The People' is not the name of a superhuman being, but the name of an extended process of interaction between political elites and ordinary citizens."[5] Representation emerges over time through recurring elections and agenda-setting processes.[6] Because presidential elections are repeated events, both politicians and citizens can learn and send signals about their understanding of one another. If this is the way that elections function in democracy, then public opinion at one point in time is not the last word on the quality of political representation.

When the president claims a mandate, he does not know with certainty the detailed policy preferences of a majority of voters, nor does he believe in a general will. Rather, his performance in the election makes him think he can mobilize a majority of voters in the future. Organizing, debating, campaigning, fundraising, and voting have fashioned a majority in support of him and his agenda. This support is enough to provide him with an incentive to try to change policy directions. If he is wrong, he and his party risk the wrath of voters in the future. Thus it would be a mistake to treat mandates as though the presidential election is a tool of direct democracy. Mandates in a representative democracy are a function of inferences, institutional procedures, and the incentives offered to politicians within the system.

PRESIDENTIAL MANDATES AND PRESIDENTIAL POWER

Our understanding of presidential mandates also has implications for our understanding of presidential power. President-elect Kennedy, tired of questions about his narrow margin of victory, joked with reporters, "Mandate, schmandate, the mandate is that I'm here and you're not."[7] If elections mean nothing except that the president has won the right to take office, then mandate claims are rather uninteresting. Throughout the book, I have argued that mandate claims are informative, for they do not occur randomly and they reflect variation in political opportunities. The empirical evidence suggests that mandate claims can be predicted by public and congressional support for a president and his policy agenda.

A more serious concern is that presidents could use the rhetoric of mandates to implement policies at odds with the interests of the American people.[8] Woodrow Wilson hit upon this dilemma when he said, "Leadership, for the statesman, is interpretation. . . . If he fairly hit the popular thought, when we have missed it, are we to say that he is a demagogue?"[9] The president is the only elected representative of the entire nation. Perhaps he could identify himself with the will of the people and use the power of his office to further his own personal agenda.

I find no evidence that presidents claim mandates that tyrannize or utterly neglect the public. Presidents are held accountable by competitive elections and by the fact that their claims are grounded in commonly shared evidence about the public. The president, his partisans, and his opponents all have strong incentives to pay attention to public preferences, or they will fail to be reelected. In an atmosphere of political competition, mandate claims are sure to be contested.

The use of mandate rhetoric within the American political system does not automatically legitimize any policy action and silence opponents. Throughout American history, specific edicts and claims have always been contested, even in the case of divine or royal mandates. King George and his ministers mandated taxes that the American colonists thought illegitimate. Even in cases when the authority of the entity issuing a mandate was not questioned, the precise interpretation of the command could be contested. When the Continental Congress gave delegates to a constitutional convention a mandate to *revise* the Articles of Confederation, did this mean the Articles could be abandoned altogether? While the legitimacy of the president's authority stems from the consent of voters, this does not mean that he will dictate the interpretation of his victory. Political forces are too entrenched for a president to achieve policy success while misreading the political environment.[10]

ELECTORAL REFORM

Though my theory of presidential mandates is optimistic about the limits of presidential power, it also suggests that we take a close look at the quality of campaigns and elections. If elections are signals, representation turns on the following issues: How well do politicians make inferences? How good is their information? Who are they listening to? Electoral participation is biased toward the wealthier and better-educated segments of society. Politicians might make forecasts based less on the average voter than on the interest groups that mobilize voters. If the media focus on the horse race during the campaign rather than on the issues, the end result will be a noisier policy message than if the media had focused on the issues. If the candidates simply bought votes, then the result would be a reflection of their war chest rather than a signal about policy preferences.

The signal from the election will be clearer with better-informed voters, issue-oriented campaigns, and higher turnout—recurring themes in the literature on electoral reform. Presidents themselves have argued for ways to increase responsiveness through elections. Franklin Roosevelt urged employers to give their workers time off to vote because "it is important that the mandate of the election should be as representative of the whole people as possible, irrespective of whom they vote for."[11] Calvin Coolidge argued for responsible parties in office to enhance the signals from the electorate over repeated elections. He said that "unless those who are elected under the same party designation . . . cooperate with each other in the support of the broad general principles, of the party platform, the election is merely a mockery, no decision is made at the polls, and there is no representation of the popular will."[12] Prominent scholars of elections, such as Stanley Kelley, have suggested reducing the indeterminacy of the interpretation of elections by thoroughly investigating survey data and by taking a stab at imposing criteria for the existence of presidential electoral mandates.[13]

We should not assume that better signals from the electorate would end up being repeated calls for policy change. After Kennedy's election, former president Harry Truman remarked, "There is something to be said for the narrow margin of victory in a presidential election. It makes the new President realize in a very dramatic and material way that there is more than one side to a question."[14] There may be times when the status quo is exactly what a majority of voters want. There may also be times when it makes little sense to speak of a coherent national majority at all. Whatever the case, we are better off if elections are conducted in a way that maximizes their ability to inform politicians of the wishes of their constituents.

*

Over thirty years ago, V. O. Key made the "perverse and unorthodox argument . . . that voters are not fools."[15] Looking at aggregate groups of voters, particularly those who switched party affiliation across repeated elections, Key found that party defections were correlated with policy views and with assessments of governmental performance. His data and his analysis bear a striking resemblance to the ways that politicians make interpretations about the electorate. Indeed, the argument of this book is that politicians also believe that voters are not fools. They pay attention to voters and adjust their policy behavior accordingly. They recognize that policy behavior today shapes voter reactions tomorrow.

By taking a different approach to electoral mandates, I have tried to reorient the way that we think about the link between voters and public policy. Instead of asking whether mandates exist independent of the subjective evaluations of politicians, I have argued that it is necessary to understand when and why American presidents claim mandates in practice. It is meaningful to say that the president has a mandate, but politicians' criteria for a mandate are different than scholars' criteria. Politicians interact with voters throughout the campaign, and they have a personal and historical context with which to view the results. After election, they must work with one another. The evaluation of public preferences and priorities is essential to their assessment of political opportunity, but their vantage point provides them with more varied sources of information and with the need to anticipate the reactions of their opposition.

We need not choose between a populist view in which elections translate voter preferences into policy and an elitist view in which politicians compete in elections for the privilege of furthering their own personal interests. Yet we should keep both views of elections in mind. We should encourage politicians to pay attention to the public, and we should understand how they perceive us. We should work on sending a better message. Though we should not fear presidents who invoke the name of the people, we should continue to hold them accountable for their interpretations of voters. In this sense, presidential mandates will be what the people make them.

Notes

CHAPTER ONE

1. See for example Robert Dahl, "The Myth of the Presidential Mandate," *Political Science Quarterly* 105 (1990): 355–372; Stanley Kelley, *Interpreting Elections* (Princeton: Princeton University Press, 1983); George C. Edwards III, *At the Margins* (New Haven: Yale University Press, 1989).

2. Quoted by Cecil Emden, *The People and the Constitution*, 2d ed. (London: Oxford University Press, 1956), 220.

3. Dahl, "Myth"; Richard Ellis and Stephen Kirk, "Presidential Mandates in the Nineteenth Century: Conceptual Change and Institutional Development," *Studies In American Political Development* 9, no. 1 (1995): 117–186.

4. Candidate Bill Clinton, televised presidential debate, ABC, 15 October 1992.

5. Edwards, *At the Margins*; Kelley, *Interpreting Elections*. Prior to the advent of election surveys in 1940, Dahl argues, no president could possibly have a "valid reconstruction of the policy views of the electorate" to support his claim. Dahl, "Myth," 363.

6. See, for example, Kelley, *Interpreting Elections*, and George C. Edwards III, *The Public Presidency: The Pursuit of Popular Support* (New York: St. Martin's Press, 1983), 18. Kelley also discusses such factors as the importance of whether voters are strongly or weakly committed to the candidates, whether the issues are transient or enduring, whether the vote represents prospective issue voting rather than the choice of a lesser evil, and the degree of mobilization that would be necessary to reverse the outcome.

7. See Paul Abramson, John Aldrich, and David Rohde, *Change and Continuity in the 1996 Elections* (Washington, D.C.: Congressional Quarterly Press, 1998); Angus Campbell et al., *The American Voter* (New York: John Wiley and Sons, 1960); Warren Miller and J. Merrill Shanks, *The New American Voter* (Cambridge, Mass: Harvard University Press, 1996).

8. V. O. Key, *The Responsible Electorate* (Cambridge, Mass: Harvard University Press, 1966).

9. Bruce Cain, John Ferejohn, and Morris Fiorina, *The Personal Vote* (Cambridge: Harvard University Press, 1987); Richard Fenno, *Homestyle* (Boston: Little, Brown, and Co., 1978); Ben Page, *Choices and Echoes in Presidential Elections* (Chicago: University of Chicago Press, 1978).

10. William Riker, *Liberalism Against Populism* (San Francisco: W. W. Freeman, 1982).

11. See Kenneth Arrow, *Social Choice and Individual Values*, 2d ed. (New Haven: Yale University Press, 1951); Dennis Mueller, *Public Choice II* (Cambridge: Cambridge

University Press, 1979); Peter Ordeshook, *Game Theory and Political Theory* (Cambridge: Cambridge University Press, 1986); Riker, *Liberalism Against Populism*.

12. Dahl, "Myth," 365.

13. Ibid.

14. Ibid., 366.

15. Richard Fenno, *The U.S. Senate* (Washington, D.C.: American Enterprise Institute, 1982); Richard Fenno, "Adjusting to the U. S. Senate," in *Congress and Policy Change*, ed. Gerald Wright et al. (New York: Agathon Press, 1986), 123–147; Marjorie Hershey, "Campaign Learning, Congressional Behavior, and Policy Change," in Wright, *Congress and Policy Change*, 148–172.

16. "The first thing a leader does is to situate himself in a public discourse, and construct a narrative relating what has been done previously to what he proposes to do in the moment at hand. The basic parameters of the politics of leadership are set here, in the president's initial assertions about who he is and where he sees himself fitting into the nation's history." Stephen Skowronek, *The Politics Presidents Make* (Cambridge: Harvard University Press, 1993), 24.

17. There are several advantages to a multimethod approach. Examining a topic using more than one methodology refines theories, solves empirical puzzles, and provides a context in which to view conclusions. The ability of methods to check one another improves model specification, the conceptual and operational definitions of variables, and the evaluation of alternative hypotheses.

CHAPTER TWO

1. Walter Dean Burnham, *Critical Elections and the Mainsprings of American Politics* (New York: Norton, 1970); Angus Campbell et al., *The American Voter* (New York: John Wiley and Sons, 1960); Jerome Clubb, William Flanigan, and Nancy Zingale, *Partisan Realignment: Voters, Parties, and Government in American History* (Boulder, Colo.: Westview Press, 1990); V. O. Key, "A Theory of Critical Elections," *Journal of Politics* 17 (1955): 3–18; V. O. Key, *The Responsible Electorate* (Cambridge, Mass.: Harvard University Press, 1966).

2. David Brady, *Critical Elections and Congressional Policy-Making* (Stanford: Stanford University Press, 1988), 17.

3. Key, *The Responsible Electorate*, 30.

4. Clubb et al., *Partisan Realignment*.

5. Gerald Pomper, "Classification of Presidential Elections," *Journal of Politics* 29 (1967): 535–566. His categories follow the contributions of Campbell et al., *The American Voter*.

6. Raymond Wolfinger, "Dealignment, Realignment, and Mandates in the 1984 Election," in *The American Elections of 1984*, ed. Austin Ranney (Washington: American Enterprise Institute, 1985), 277–296.

7. Stephen Skowronek, *The Politics Presidents Make* (Cambridge: Harvard University Press, 1993).

8. Ronald Reagan is also in this category, and Skowronek assumes that the 1980 election represents a realignment of sorts.

9. Specifically, the periods between 1876–1896 and 1955 to present. See Charles Cameron, *Veto Bargaining* (Cambridge: Cambridge University Press, 2000).

10. See, for example, Richard Fenno, "Adjusting to the U.S. Senate," in *Congress and Policy Change*, ed. Gerald Wright et al. (New York: Agathon Press, 1986), 123–

147; John Mark Hansen, *Gaining Access* (Chicago: University of Chicago Press, 1991); Marjorie Hershey, "Campaign Learning, Congressional Behavior, and Policy Change," in Wright, *Congress and Policy Change*, 148–172; Stanley Kelley, *Interpreting Elections* (Princeton: Princeton University Press, 1983); V. O. Key, *The Responsible Electorate*; John Kingdon, *Candidates for Office* (New York: Random House, 1968); Nelson Polsby and Aaron Wildavsky, *Presidential Elections*, 9th ed. (New Jersey: Chatham House, 1996); Austin Ranney and Willmoore Kendall, *Democracy and the American Party System* (New York: Harcourt, Brace, 1956), 340–341; Kay Schlozman and Sidney Verba, "Sending Them a Message—Getting a Reply," in *Elections in America*, ed. Kay Schlozman (Boston: Allen and Unwin Inc., 1987), 3–25.

11. David Mayhew, *Congress: The Electoral Connection* (New Haven: Yale University Press, 1974), 71.

12. See Jon Bond and Richard Fleisher, *The President in the Legislative Arena* (Chicago: University of Chicago Press, 1990), chap. 8.

13. Skowronek, *The Politics Presidents Make*.

CHAPTER THREE

1. Richard Fenno, *Home Style* (Boston: Little, Brown, and Co., 1978).

2. John Kingdon, *Candidates for Office* (New York: Random House, 1968). Kingdon labels it the "congratulation-rationalization effect." The phenomenon is similar to the "illusion of control" observed among casual gamblers: people view success at the gaming table as a reflection of their skill, but they view losses as rotten luck. Thomas Gilovich, "Biased Evaluation and Persistence in Gambling," *Journal of Personality and Social Psychology* 44 (1983): 1110–1126.

3. Kingdon, *Candidates for Office*.

4. Paul Boller Jr., *Presidential Campaigns* (Oxford: Oxford University Press, 1984), 71.

5. Ibid.

6. Michael Oreskes, "Democrats Begin Quadrennial Debate: How to Win the White House," *New York Times*, 11 November 1988, A22.

7. Ibid.

8. R. Douglas Arnold, *The Logic of Congressional Action* (New Haven: Yale University Press, 1990); V. O. Key, *Public Opinion and American Democracy* (New York: Alfred Knopf, 1961).

9. Arnold, *The Logic of Congressional Action*, 10.

10. Kay Schlozman and Sidney Verba, "Sending Them a Message—Getting a Reply," in *Elections in America*, ed. Kay Schlozman (Boston: Allen and Unwin Inc., 1987), 3–25.

11. John Mark Hansen, *Gaining Access* (Chicago: University of Chicago Press, 1991), 16, n. 14.

12. Philip Tetlock, "The Impact of Accountability on Judgment and Choice," *Advances in Experimental Social Psychology* 25 (1992): 331–376; Ziva Kunda, "The Case for Motivated Reasoning," *Psychological Bulletin* 108 (1990): 480–498.

13. Kunda, "The Case for Motivated Reasoning"; Tetlock, "The Impact of Accountability."

14. This argument is consistent with findings in the field of social psychology. See, for instance, Kunda, "The Case for Motivated Reasoning"; Tetlock, "The Impact of Accountability"; Tom Pyszczynski and Jeff Greenberg, "Toward an Integration of

Cognitive and Motivational Perspectives on Social Inference," *Advances in Experimental Social Psychology* 20 (1987): 297–340; Arie Kruglanski and Icek Ajzen, "Bias and Error in Human Judgment," *European Journal of Social Psychology* 13 (1983): 1–44; Arie Kruglanski and Tallie Freund, "The Freezing and Unfreezing of Lay Inferences," *Journal of Experimental Social Psychology* 19 (1983): 448–468.

15. Daniel A. Kahneman and Amos Tversky, "The Simulation Heuristic," in *Judgment under Uncertainty*, ed. Daniel Kahneman, Paul Slovic, and Amos Tversky (Cambridge: Cambridge University Press, 1982), 201–208.

16. See C. G. Hempel, *Philosophy of Natural Science* (Englewood, N.J.: Prentice Hall, 1966), 40–46.

17. This is similar to the "hydraulic" model of causality in which the presence of a sufficient cause for an outcome means that alternative factors are ignored or downplayed. Richard Nisbett and Lee Ross, *Human Inference* (Englewood, N.J.: Prentice-Hall, 1980), 127–130. Interestingly, parsimonious explanations on some topics, such as campaign finance, are seldom chosen.

18. Georges Florovsky, "The Study of the Past," in *Ideas of History*, Vol. 2, ed. R. H. Nash (New York: Dutton, 1969), 369; for a discussion of hindsight bias, see Baruch Fischoff, "For Those Condemned to Study the Past: Heuristics and Biases in Hindsight," in Kahneman, *Judgment under Uncertainty*, 335–351; Jonathan Casper, Kennette Benedict, and Jo Perry, "Juror Decision Making, Attitudes, and the Hindsight Bias," *Law and Human Behavior* 13 (1989): 291–310.

19. Jon Hale, "Shaping the Conventional Wisdom," *Political Communication* 10 (1993): 300.

20. In the chapters that follow, the journalists to which I refer are generally those working for major national newspapers like the *New York Times* or the *Washington Post*. Though I do not explicitly discuss journalists' interests or constraints, these certainly shape the reporting of the election story.

21. Patricia Cheng and Laura Novick, "A Probabilistic Contrast Model of Causal Induction," *Journal of Personality and Social Psychology* 58 (1990): 545–567; Patricia Cheng and Laura Novick, "Causes versus Enabling Conditions," *Cognition* 40 (1991): 83–120; Patricia Cheng and Laura Novick, "Covariation in Natural Causal Induction," *Psychological Review* 99 (1992): 365–382; W. Turnbull and B. Slugoski, "Conversational and Linguistic Processes in Causal Attribution," in *Contemporary Science and Natural Explanation*, ed. D. Hilton (New York: New York University Press, 1988), 66–93.

22. Turnbull and Slugoski, "Conversational and Linguistic Processes," 67.

23. William Dray, *Laws and Explanations in History* (Oxford: Oxford University Press, 1957), 157. See also Cheng and Novick, "A Probabilistic Contrast Model," "Causes Versus Enabling Conditions," and "Covariation in Natural Causal Induction"; Germund Hesslow, "The Problem of Causal Selection," in *Contemporary Science and Natural Explanation*, ed. D. Hilton (New York: New York University Press, 1988), 11–32; Turnbull and Slugoski, "Conversational and Linguistic Processes."

24. See Angus Campbell et al., *The American Voter* (New York: John Wiley and Sons, 1960), 531–538; Gerald Pomper, "Classification of Presidential Elections," *Journal of Politics* 29 (1967): 535–566.

25. For the concept of the normal vote in public opinion literature, see Philip Converse, "The Concept of a Normal Vote," in *Elections and the Political Order*, ed. Angus Campbell et al (New York: John Wiley and Sons, Inc., 1966), chap. 1.

26. The tendency to search for causes that resemble effects is described by Nisbett and Ross, *Human Inference*, chap. 6.

27. Cheng and Novick, "Causes versus Enabling Conditions"; Hesslow, "The Problem of Causal Selection"; Denis Hilton, "Logic and Causal Attribution," in *Contemporary Science and Natural Explanation*, ed. Denis Hilton (New York: New York University Press, 1988), 33–65; Turnbull and Slugoski, "Conversational and Linguistic Processes."

28. Thomas Weko and John Aldrich, "The Presidency and the Election Campaign," in *The Presidency and the Political System*, ed. Michael Nelson (Washington, D.C.: Congressional Quarterly Press, 1990), 279.

29. Boller, *Presidential Campaigns*, 157.

30. The British ambassador to Washington, quoted by Arthur Link and William Leary Jr., "Election of 1916" in *History of American Presidential Elections*, Vol. 3, ed. Arthur Schlesinger and Fred Israel (New York: Chelsea House, 1971), 2270.

31. This is similar to the "politics of articulation" in which a president makes the previously established regime or existing orthodoxy more relevant. Stephen Skowronek, *The Politics Presidents Make* (Cambridge: Harvard University Press, 1993).

32. John Stuart Mill, *A System of Logic*, 8th ed. (1843; reprint, London: Longmans, Green, Reader, and Dyer, 1872), chap. 8. Harold Kelley's influential "ANOVA" paradigm is substantially an elaboration of Mill's method: "consistency" information conveys evidence about agreement, "distinctiveness" and "consensus" information conveys evidence about two kinds of difference (intrapersonal and interpersonal). H. H. Kelley, "The Process of Causal Attribution," *American Psychologist* 28 (1973): 107–128.

33. There may be a psychological reason for the greater confidence in causal attributions made to causes that "stimulate" response: the "prejudice that the conditions of a phenomenon must *resemble* the phenomenon" (J. S. Mill, as quoted by Nisbett and Ross, *Human Inference*, 115). The tendency is not necessarily suboptimal, as many psychologists appear to believe. See J. R. Anderson, "Is Human Cognition Adaptive?" *Behavioral and Brain Sciences* 14 (1991): 471–484 and commentary following.

34. Joshua Klayman and Young-Won Ha, "Confirmation, Disconfirmation, and Information in Hypothesis-Testing," *Psychological Review* 94 (1987): 211–228; Richard Skov and Steven Sherman, "Information-Gathering Processes," *Journal of Experimental Social Psychology* 22 (1986): 93–121.

35. Dennis Jennings et al., "Informal Covariation Assessment: Data-Based versus Theory-Based Judgments," in Kahneman, *Judgment under Uncertainty*; Nisbett and Ross, *Human Inference*. This strategy is similar to the assessment of covariation reported in studies of human judgment. In general, people have trouble estimating the relationship between variables because they tend to rely exclusively on the instances of the positive association between the two variables. For example, subjects will say that a symptom is associated with a disease simply because many people with the disease have the symptom. They ignore information about those who have the symptom but not the disease, the disease but not the symptom, and those who have neither the disease nor the symptom. Nisbett and Ross also cite the example that when asked "Does God answer prayers?" some people say yes, "because many times I've asked God for something and he has given it to me" (*Human Inference*, 92). The answer ignores information about the results of other combinations of asking and receiving.

36. James Reston, "Kennedy Is Victor by Close Margin," *New York Times*, 10 November 1960, p. 1; Philip Benjamin, "Other Elections Have Been Closer," *New York Times*, 10 November 1960, p. 36.

37. James Naughton "Survey Shows Union Households Giving Carter 60% of Their Votes," *New York Times*, 3 November 1976, p. 22.

38. Klayman and Ha, "Confirmation, Disconfirmation, and Information in Hypothesis-Testing."

39. Jon Bond and Richard Fleisher, *The President in the Legislative Arena* (Chicago: University of Chicago Press, 1990); Mark Peterson, *Legislating Together* (Cambridge, Mass.: Harvard University Press, 1990).

40. See Gary Jacobson, *The Electoral Origins of Divided Government* (Boulder, Colo.: Westview Press, 1990); David Mayhew, *Divided We Govern* (New Haven: Yale University Press, 1991); Morris Fiorina, *Divided Government*, 2d ed.(Boston: Allyn and Bacon, 1996).

41. This is John Kingdon's distinction between agendas and alternatives in his book *Agendas, Alternatives, and Public Policies* (Boston: Little, Brown, 1984).

CHAPTER FOUR

1. For a discussion of mandate claims in the Jacksonian period, see Robert Dahl, "The Myth of the Presidential Mandate," *Political Science Quarterly* 105 (1990): 355–372, and Richard Ellis and Stephen Kirk, "Presidential Mandates in the Nineteenth Century," *Studies in American Political Development* 9 (1995): 117–186.

2. See Stephen Skowronek, *The Politics Presidents Make* (Cambridge: Harvard University Press, 1993), 53, Table 2; Samuel Kernell, *Going Public*, 3d ed. (Washington, D.C.: Congressional Quarterly Press, 1997).

3. Jeffrey Tulis, *The Rhetorical Presidency* (Princeton: Princeton University Press, 1987); Richard Ellis, ed., *Speaking to the People* (Amherst: University of Massachusetts Press, 1998).

4. Richard Neustadt, "Presidency and Legislation: Planning the President's Program," *American Political Science Review* 49 (1955): 980–1021.

5. Richard Neustadt, *Presidential Power and the Modern Presidents* (New York: John Wiley and Sons, 1960).

6. From *Inaugural Addresses of the Presidents of the United States from George Washington 1789 to George Bush 1989* (Washington, D.C.: U.S. Government Printing Office, 1989). Before the passage of the Twentieth Amendment in 1933, inaugural addresses were delivered on March 4 of the year following the presidential election. After the passage of the Twentieth Amendment (beginning with FDR's second term) addresses were given on January 20 following the election.

7. Plots are formed using lowess-locally weighted scatterplot smoothing. Dickey-Fuller tests indicate that the time-series data used in this chapter are stationary.

8. See Jon Bond and Richard Fleisher, *The President in the Legislative Arena* (Chicago: University of Chicago Press, 1990); Paul Light, *The President's Agenda* (Baltimore: Johns Hopkins University Press, 1991); Mark Peterson, *Legislating Together* (Cambridge, Mass.: Harvard University Press, 1990); Aaron Wildavsky, "The Two Presidencies," *Trans-Action* 4 (1966): 7–14.

9. Though they regard these critical elections as turning points, realignment theo-

rists recognize that change may take place in different regions or groups at different rates. Realignments may also occur over a series of elections rather than in one election.

10. Walter Dean Burnham, *Critical Elections and the Mainsprings of American Politics* (New York: Norton, 1970); V. O. Key, "A Theory of Critical Elections," *Journal of Politics* 17 (1955): 3–18; Joseph A. Schlesinger, *Political Parties and the Winning of Office* (Ann Arbor: University of Michigan Press, 1991); Skowronek, *The Politics Presidents Make*.

11. Assuming that 1980 represents a realignment is controversial. However, this coding better approximates Skowronek's theory of leadership, as well as realignment theory, for later analysis.

12. The majority of presidents in the minority party category are like Wilson or Cleveland, who served as minority presidents in the middle of a partisan era. However, presidents at the very beginning of a realignment era are also classified as minority presidents (Jackson in 1828; Lincoln in 1860; FDR in 1932; Reagan in 1980). Even if these four cases are counted as being in the majority party, the relationship between majority/minority status and mandate claiming is still strong and statistically significant.

13. Bond and Fleisher, *The President in the Legislative Arena;* Peterson, *Legislating Together.*

14. The exception is Zachary Taylor in 1848. For an extended discussion of the pattern and sources of divided government, see Morris Fiorina, *Divided Government,* 2d ed. (Boston: Allyn and Bacon, 1996); David Mayhew, *Divided We Govern* (New Haven: Yale University Press, 1991).

15. This difference is more striking in the nineteenth century (63 percent versus 56 percent).

16. I assume the following party regimes: 1828–1860, Jacksonian/Democratic Party; 1864–1932, Republican Party; 1936–1980, Democratic Party; 1984–present Republican Party.

17. For example, the elections of 1852, 1856, and 1860 are all coded as having a vulnerable partisan regime because a party regime was crumbling and then being rebuilt. By 1864 the newly dominant Republican Party regime is no longer vulnerable and will not be coded as vulnerable until the elections before the 1932 realignment.

18. Phil Duncan and Steve Langdon, "When Congress Had to Choose, It Voted to Back Clinton," *Congressional Quarterly Weekly Report,* 12 December 1993, p. 3428, 3473.

19. See, for example, Bond and Fleisher, *The President in the Legislative Arena,* chap. 3, and Peterson, *Legislating Together,* app. B.

20. Presidential approval at the beginning of a term is not a suitable proxy for the strength of a president's mandate. It is first measured for new presidents at the time of inauguration by asking, "Do you approve or disapprove of the job X is doing as president?" It is unclear what this measure picks up, given that the president has just taken office. It could be approval on any number of issue dimensions or personality or media savvy. The president's behavior during the transition period might affect his initial approval rating, regardless of how he is judged on the issue that forms the basis of his mandate. For instance, Clinton's approval at the start of his first term may have been a function of his stated intention to remove the ban upon gays in

the military as one of his first official duties as president. Average approval ratings for the first year are also problematic, since they may be based upon the state of the economy or foreign policy crises. Finally, the starting and average approval ratings of presidents before the Vietnam/Watergate era are distinctly higher than the ratings of the presidents that follow, making comparison over time difficult. Approval of the way a president is handling the mandate issue in particular would be more relevant. See George C. Edwards III, *Presidential Approval: A Sourcebook* (Baltimore: Johns Hopkins University Press, 1990).

21. Lyn Ragsdale, *Vital Statistics on the Presidency* (Washington, D.C.: Congressional Quarterly Inc., 1996), chap. 8, Table 8.8.

22. Peterson, *Legislating Together*.

23. Ibid., 232.

24. Ibid., 232, 242–247.

25. Ibid.

26. Ibid., 239.

27. Neustadt, *Presidential Power*.

CHAPTER FIVE

1. I use the public papers of the presidents and the *Congressional Quarterly Weekly Report* and yearly *Almanac*.

2. Robert Dahl, "The Myth of the Presidential Mandate," *Political Science Quarterly* 105 (1990): 355–372; Stanley Kelley, *Interpreting Elections* (Princeton: Princeton University Press, 1983).

3. On the election of 1952, see John Robert Greene, *The Crusade* (Lanham, Md.: University Press of America, 1985); Barton Bernstein, "Election of 1952," in *History of American Presidential Elections*, ed. Arthur Schlesinger Jr. and Fred L. Israel, vol. 4 (New York: Chelsea House Publishers, 1971), 3215–3337; Angus Campbell et al., *The Voter Decides* (Evanston, Ill.: Row, Peterson, and Company, 1954); Robert A. Divine, *Foreign Policy and U.S. Presidential Elections, 1952–1960* (New York: New Viewpoints, 1974).

4. Divine, *Foreign Policy and U.S. Presidential Elections*.

5. Eisenhower won 27 percent of all primary votes, against Taft's nearly 36 percent.

6. Clayton Knowles, "Campaign Plans Designed to Put Rivals at Their Best," *New York Times*, 19 October 1952, E1; W. H. Lawrence, "The Nature of Campaigning," *New York Times*, 2 November 1952, 5E.

7. See Kathleen Hall Jamieson, *Packaging the Presidency* (Oxford University Press, 1984).

8. "Four Man Race," *New York Times*, 12 October 1952, sec. 4, p. 1.

9. Elmo Roper, *You and Your Leaders: Their Actions and Your Reactions, 1936–1956* (New York: William Morrow & Co., 1957), 146–147.

10. Ibid., 218.

11. See pre-election polls cited in Campbell et al., *The Voter Decides*, chap. 4.

12. Ibid.; "Observers Find Conduct of War in Korea an Issue of Importance," *New York Times*, 13 October 1952, 17.

13. Bernstein, "Election of 1952," 3260.

14. Ibid. Gallup polls found that Korea ranked as the primary issue among independent voters. When asked which candidate could best handle the situation in Korea,

67 percent responded Eisenhower and only 9 percent Stevenson. Divine, *Foreign Policy and U.S. Presidential Elections*, 70.

15. Leo Egan, "Heavy Registration Has Politicians Guessing," *New York Times*, 12 October 1952, 6E; Cabell Phillips, "Vote May Be Biggest Ever Thanks to Concerted Drive," *New York Times*, 26 October 1952, E5.

16. Speech by Eisenhower, reprinted in *New York Times*, 25 October 1952, 8.

17. James Hagerty, "Election Outcome Highly Uncertain, Survey Indicates," *New York Times*, 3 November 1952, 1.

18. "As the Campaign Reaches its Climax—Minimum Claims of Electoral Support by Rival Parties," *New York Times*, 2 November 1952, sec 4., p. 1.

19. *New York Times*, 5 November 1952, 1.

20. William S. White, "Eisenhower Victory Brings Start of Two-Party System to the South," *New York Times*, 6 November 1952, 1; William S. White, "Outlook for the Democratic Party," *New York Times*, 9 November 1952, E4.

21. Arthur Krock, "Personal Victory," *New York Times*, 6 November 1952, 1.

22. Divine, *Foreign Policy and U.S. Presidential Elections*, 83.

23. Ibid.

24. Ibid.

25. Interior Secretary Oscar Chapman, quoted in Ibid., 83.

26. James Reston, "President Eisenhower May Lack a Working Majority in Congress," *New York Times*, 5 November 1952, 1.

27. Clayton Knowles, "GOP Old Guard Holds Key Roles in Congress," *New York Times*, 9 November 1952, E5.

28. James Reston, "GOP Has 48 Senate Seats," and C. P. Trussell, "Margin in Lower Chamber Is Now Three," *New York Times*, 6 November 1952, 1; Krock, "Personal Victory."

29. Dwight D. Eisenhower, First Inaugural Address, in *Inaugural Addresses of the Presidents* (Washington, D.C.: U.S. Government Printing Office, 1989), 293–299.

30. "Eisenhower's Friendly Congress," *1953 Congressional Quarterly Almanac*, 87.

31. Senator John Sherman Cooper (R–KY), *Face the Nation, 1956* (New York: Holt Information Systems, 1957), 361.

32. For an account of the 1964 election, see Theodore White, *The Making of the President, 1964* (New York: Atheneum Publishers, 1965); Daniel Ogden Jr. and Arthur Peterson, *Electing the President* (San Francisco: Chandler Publishing Co., 1968); John B. Martin, "Election of 1964," in Schlesinger, *History of American Presidential Elections*, 4:3565–3702.

33. *The Public Papers of the Presidents*, Lyndon B. Johnson 1963–1964, p. 1012, item 541, August 27.

34. Johnson was only the second Democratic candidate in history to be nominated by acclamation at the national party convention (FDR in 1936 was the first).

35. See Barry Goldwater, *The Conscience of a Conservative* (Sheperdsville, Ky.: Victor Pub. Co., 1960).

36. Remarks in Peoria at the Convention of the Illinois State Federation of Labor, 7 October 1964.

37. "Democratic Presidential Sweep Likely," *Congressional Quarterly Weekly Report*, 23 October 1964, 2517.

38. Ibid.

39. Ibid.

40. "Johnson Defeats Goldwater by 16 million" *1964 Congressional Quarterly Almanac*, 1007; "Ticket Splitting Offsets Democratic Presidential Landslide," *1964 Congressional Quarterly Almanac*, 1008–1009.

41. Ibid.

42. Text of Johnson's victory speech, *New York Times*, 4 November 1964, 22.

43. Ben A. Franklin, "G.O.P. Seeks Clues to Party Future in Study of Vote," *New York Times*, 8 November 1964, 1.

44. Fred Powledge, "Dr. King to Renew Southern Protests," *New York Times*, 5 November 1964, 1.

45. "Mandate," *New York Times*, 8 November 1964, sec. 4, p. 1.

46. John D. Morris, "Liberals in House Seek Wider Role," *New York Times*, 8 November 1964, 76.

47. Larry Jacobs, *The Health of Nations* (Ithaca: Cornell University Press, 1993), 191–192.

48. Jacobs, *The Health of Nations*, 197; personal interview with Mills. Another member of Congress (Robert Ball) recalled the 1964 election as "giving a specific mandate for a series of liberal legislative proposals," particularly Medicare.

49. James Reston, "What Goldwater Lost," *New York Times*, 4 November 1964, 23.

50. Earl Mazo, "Moderates in GOP Challenge Goldwater Control of Party," *New York Times*, 5 November 1964, 1.

51. Transcript of Goldwater's concession and news conference in Phoenix, Ariz., *New York Times*, 5 November 1964, 21.

52. Editorial, "In the Aftermath," *New York Times*, 5 November 1964, 10E.

53. Text of State of the Union Address, *1965 Congressional Quarterly Almanac*, 1348.

54. "Congress 1965—The Year in Review," *1965 Congressional Quarterly Almanac*, 65–68. According to David Mayhew's study of party control and national lawmaking, this congressional session had one of the highest numbers of important laws passed for the years between 1946 and 1990. David R. Mayhew, *Divided Government* (New Haven: Yale University Press, 1991), 118, Table 5.1.

55. Kennedy's success rates had ranged from 27 percent to 48 percent; "Congress Unusually Cooperative with President's Program," *1965 Congressional Quarterly Almanac*, 97–112.

56. For detailed coverage of the election of 1980 see P. Abramson, J. Aldrich, and D. Rohde, eds., *Change and Continuity in the 1980 Election* (Washington, D.C.: Congressional Quarterly Press, 1981); Gerald Pomper, ed., *The Election of 1980* (Chatham, N.J.: Chatham House, 1981); and Austin Ranney, ed., *The American Elections of 1980* (Washington, D.C.: American Enterprise Institute, 1981).

57. Carter's approval ratings in 1979 were lower than any other president had received with the exception of Harry Truman during the Korean War and Nixon during Watergate. Gerald Pomper, "The Nominating Contests," in Pomper, *The Election of 1980*, 6. Moreover, his 34 percent approval rating among Democrats in the summer of 1979 was "the lowest proportion endorsing a President of their own party since Gallup began using this measure during the second term of Franklin Roosevelt." Everett C. Ladd, "The Brittle Mandate," *Political Science Quarterly* 96 (spring 1981): 6.

58. Abramson et al., *Change and Continuity in the 1980 Election*, 21, fig. 1-2.

59. The visibility of Kennedy kept most other challengers out of the race. Brown,

the forty-one-year-old governor of California, who campaigned to "protect the earth, serve the people, and explore the universe," had run unsuccessfully in the 1976 primaries.

60. "I, as President, have got to maintain the accurate image that we do have a crisis, which I will not ignore until those hostages are released. I want the American people to know it. I want the Iranians to know it. I want the hostages' families and the hostages to know it. I want the world to know that I am not going to resume business-as-usual as a partisan campaigner out on the campaign trail until our hostages are back here—free and at home." Presidential news conference on 13 February 1980, reported in Pomper, *The Election of 1980*, 8.

61. Timothy Schellhardt, "Rose Garden Tactic Keeps Carter Home, Leaves Kennedy Railing Out in the Cold," *Wall Street Journal*, 7 February 1980. His first campaign trip, to Ohio, occurred May 29.

62. For example, New Hampshire received twice as many grants in February (its primary was the 26th) as it had in either December or January. Timothy Clark, "As Long As Carter's Up He'll Get You a Grant," *New York Times*, 21 April 1980, A19. See also Timothy Schellhardt, "Carter, Who Railed Against Pork-Barrel Politics in 1976, Now Exploits Them for Illinois Primary," *Wall Street Journal*, 6 March 1980.

63. By March 22, Carter had one quarter of the delegates needed to win. By April 26 he had slightly over half of the delegates needed to win. By May 24 he had three quarters of the delegates needed to win. Nelson Polsby, "The Democratic Nomination," in Ranney, *The American Elections of 1980*, 48, Table 2-2.

64. By early August, Reagan led Carter by more than fifteen percentage points.

65. For a discussion of the incoherence of Kennedy's request for an open convention, see Nelson Polsby, "The Democratic Nomination," 54–58.

66. Three Republicans announced their candidacy in 1978: Phil Crane (August 2); Harold Stassen (November 9), and Benjamin Fernandez (November 29). In 1979, more prominent Republicans entered the race: John Connally (January 24); George Bush (May 1); Bob Dole (May 14); John Anderson (June 8); Howard Baker (November 1); and Ronald Reagan (November 13).

67. Abramson et al., *Change and Continuity*, 26, fig. 1-4.

68. See the discussion of the Republican campaign managers in Jonathan Moore, ed., *Campaign for President: 1980 In Retrospect* (Cambridge, Mass.: Ballinger Publishing Co., 1981).

69. James Reston, "Carter's Secret Weapon," *New York Times*, 21 March 1980, A27.

70. A peculiar twist in the race occurred March 1 when former President Gerald Ford hinted that he would accept his party's draft, arguing that a conservative Republican such as Reagan could not win a national election. Polls at the time showed that Ford was preferred to Reagan by Republican voters (52 to 27 percent), and that Ford was preferred to Carter by all voters (47 to 42 percent). Hearing no response to his offer from Republican activists, Ford formally announced he would not be a candidate on March 15. Pomper, "The Nominating Contests," 14.

71. Reagan retained moderate Bill Brock as national party chairman and expanded his staff to include supporters of other candidates (most notably Bush's campaign manager, James Baker III).

72. For a detailed discussion of the Republican platform process, see Michael Malbin, "The Conventions, Platforms, and Issue Activists," in Ranney, *The American Elections of 1980*, 101–116.

73. Pomper, "The Nominating Contests," 17–18; Malbin, "The Conventions, Platforms, and Issue Activists," 100; "Reagan: Pragmatism over Ideological Purity," *Congressional Quarterly Weekly Report*, 19 July 1980, 1979–1980.

74. Rumors that former President Gerald Ford was a serious candidate for the vice presidency began to circulate the week of the convention and dominated news coverage. In an interview with Walter Cronkite, Ford discussed the selection process and the possibility of a "co-presidency." There is little evidence that the Reagan–Ford negotiations had a negative effect on Reagan's fall campaign. In hindsight, some Republicans expressed more concern. Bill Casey lamented "the difficulties in public perception that might be created. The one that, in retrospect, strikes me most forcibly is that now there's no question as to what kind of mandate Ronald Reagan has. If we had a Ford–Reagan ticket, there'd be all kinds of discussions about what the mandate meant." In Moore, *Campaign for President*, 150.

75. "They say that the United States has had its day in the sun, that our nation has passed its zenith. They expect you to tell your children that the American people no longer have the will to cope with their problems, that the future will be one of sacrifice and few opportunities. My fellow citizens, I utterly reject that view." It is worth noting that Richard Wirthlin said that the Reagan campaign's first voter preference polls taken in five states in mid-December 1979 had revealed that "there *was* a sense of malaise among many people in America. . . . Nevertheless . . . we could counter it strongly by speaking rather hopefully about an America that can deal with its problems if challenged and led by leaders who were strong." Moore, *Campaign for President*, 39.

76. He did repeatedly refer to God or a divine providence and ended his speech by suggesting a moment of silent prayer.

77. "Can anyone look at the record of this Administration and say, 'Well done'? Can anyone compare the state of our economy when the Carter administration took office with where we are today and say, 'Keep up the good work'? Can anyone look at our reduced standing in the world today and say, 'Let's have four more years of this?'"

78. Nelson Polsby and Aaron Wildavsky, *Presidential Elections*, 10th ed. (New York: Chatham House Publishers, 2000), 166; Polsby, "The Democratic Nomination," 41.

79. Richard Scammon and Ben Wattenberg, "Is It the End of an Era?" *Public Opinion* (October/November 1980): 3–4. This is not to say that American ambivalence about the state has vanished. A majority of voters would also like the services government provides.

80. Ibid., 3.

81. See Richard Wirthlin and Patrick Caddell, "Face Off: A Conversation with the Presidents' Pollsters," *Public Opinion* (December 1981): 2–12.

82. The following relies heavily on the discussion between Caddell and Wirthlin in "Face Off," and Moore, *Campaign for President*.

83. Malbin, "The Conventions, Platforms, and Issue Activists," 100. The Republican National Committee also ran ads asking viewers to "Vote Republican, for a Change."

84. Moore, *Campaign for President*, 196.

85. Ibid., 209.

86. E. J. Dionne, "Fear of War or Weakness Resonating in Campaign," *New York Times*, 24 October 1980, A18.

87. Reagan said of Carter, "In place of competence, he has given us ineptitude. Instead of steadfastness, we have gotten vacillation. While America looks for confidence, he gives us fear. His multitude of promises so richly pledged in 1976 has fallen by the wayside in the shambles of his Administration. You know, he reminds me of someone who can name the 50 parts of an automobile—he just can't drive it or fix it." Douglas Kneeland, "Reagan Steps Up Attack on Carter's Performance," *New York Times*, 31 October 1980, A1.

88. Adam Clymer, "The Issues Take a Big Step Forward in the Campaign," *New York Times*, 27 October 1980, B6.

89. Edward Cowan, "U.S. Budget Deficit of $59 Billion for 1980 Is the Second Biggest Ever," *New York Times*, 30 October 1980, A1; Clyde Farnsworth, "Consumer Prices up by 1% in September and 12.7% in a Year: Reagan Says Latest Figures Show President's 'Utter Failure' to Stem Inflation Pressures," *New York Times*, 25 October 1980, A1.

90. One ad featured an empty podium while a woman's voice said, "The League of Women Voters invited President Carter to join in the 1980 debates. He refused the invitation. Maybe it's because during his administration inflation has gone as high as 18 percent, the number of Americans out of work has reached 8.5 million." Another ad presented charts showing the rise in food, automobile, and clothing prices.

91. Wirthlin and Caddell, "Face Off," 6.

92. A *New York Times*/CBS poll cited by Hedrick Smith, "Poll Shows President Has Pulled to Even Position with Reagan," *New York Times*, 23 October 1980, B14.

93. Fifty-one percent of those polled said the most important quality was "to have strong qualities of leadership." Forty-three percent said "to be honest and fair" was most important. Three percent said "to favor policies you think are good." *New York Times*/CBS poll reported in E. J. Dionne Jr., "Definitions of Character Found Elusive to Voters," *New York Times*, 31 October 1980, A18.

94. Reported in Ibid.

95. Ibid.

96. Dionne, "Fear of War or Weakness."

97. Bernard Weinraub, "TV Battlefield Tests Presidential Strategies," *New York Times*, 8 October 1980, B8.

98. On the eve of the election, surveys revealed that 60 percent of likely voters still agreed that Reagan "shoots from the hip too much without thinking things through." Cambridge Survey Research Poll reported by Patrick Caddell, "The Democratic Strategy and Its Electoral Consequences," in *Party Coalitions in the 1980s*, ed. Seymour M. Lipset (San Francisco: Institute for Contemporary Studies, 1981), 270.

99. They were helped by Carter's prior behavior on the morning of the competitive Wisconsin primary, when he offered false hope about the hostages being released and won the primary. See Howell Raines, "Reagan Aides Seek Way to Defeat Any 'Surprise,'" *New York Times*, 7 October 1980, D21. In this article Richard Wirthlin is quoted as saying, "They've got a narrow window of opportunity for an October surprise. . . . I'm convinced they'll try something probably in the area of foreign affairs. But if it comes after October 20 or 25, it will be taken by the voters as cynical manipulation. They've got to do something within the next two weeks."

100. Wirthlin and Caddell, "Face Off," 10.

101. See polls reported by Dionne, "Definitions of Character Found Elusive to Voters."

102. Caddell, "The Democratic Strategy," 280.

103. Clymer, "The Issues Take a Big Step Forward."

104. "Carter TV Ads Attack Reagan on Record As California Governor," *New York Times*, 1 October 1980, B7.

105. Bernard Wienraub, "Carter and Reagan Go on Attack in Ads," *New York Times*, 19 October 1980, 38.

106. Wirthlin and Caddell, "Face Off," 6.

107. Carter later explained that he sometimes got carried away because the issues are "just burning with fervor in my mind and in my heart." Hedrick Smith, "As Underdog, Carter Pushes to Avoid Going Under for Good," *New York Times*, 12 October 1980, sec. 4, p. 1.

108. Howell Raines, "Reagan Camp Sees Carter As His Own Worst Enemy," *New York Times*, 12 October 1980, p. 32. Part of the problem, according to the Carter staff, was that they could not get the press to cover the surrogates who they wanted to use to make the attacks. Wirthlin and Caddell, "Face Off," 10.

109. George Bush remarked that "the American people will not abide a small, mean-minded do-anything-to-win campaigner in the White House." B. Drummond, "Bush Says Carter Is Mean Minded," *New York Times*, 4 October 1980, 8. By the second week of October 40 percent of people polled said the Carter campaign had been "vicious and mean spirited." "Associated Press-NBC poll Says Reagan Leads Carter," *New York Times*, 14 October 1980, D22.

110. "John Anderson Still Trying to Dump His 'Spoiler' Image," *Congressional Quarterly Weekly Report*, 27 September 1980, 2833–2838.

111. Warren Weaver, "Anderson Sees Drift If Either Rival Wins," *New York Times*, 2 November 1980, 40.

112. The lead article by Hedrick Smith in the *New York Times*, entitled "No Clear Winner Apparent," began, "The Presidential debate produced no knockout blow, no disastrous gaffe, and no immediate, undisputed winner." *New York Times*, 29 October 1980, A1. Aside from President Carter's reference to his daughter Amy as a source of information on nuclear issues and Reagan's statement that "when he was a boy" racism didn't exist, neither candidate made a major error.

113. Anderson protested his exclusion in October on the basis of polls showing substantial support (over 13 percent) in several states despite the fact that national polls had his support at 8 or 9 percent. Warren Weaver Jr., "Anderson, Citing Key State Polls, Protests Exclusion from Debate," *New York Times*, 20 October 1980, D9. Throughout the fall campaign there were the usual debate proposals and refusals and finger-pointing as each campaign flip-flopped on the issue of whether or not a debate was good and/or necessary.

114. Stuart Spencer, a Reagan strategist, said, "Carter must have mentioned 'nuclear' 15 times and the camera turned to this very relaxed, articulate, and smiling person who didn't look very threatening." Howell Raines, "Reagan Stresses Economic Issue Anew," *New York Times*, 30 October 1980, B14. A voter observed that Reagan won because he "did not come off being way off the center of the political spectrum as Carter wanted everybody to believe; that Reagan was going to push the button, that Reagan is going to eliminate Social Security and that all the old people are going

to starve." A different voter said of Reagan, "He is very reassuring, very low-keyed. Perfect for the medium of the television set. He comes across so graceful. Without substance though." "Excerpts from Area Panel's Remarks on the Debate," *New York Times*, 30 October 1980, B20.

115. Caddell, "The Democratic Strategy."

116. "Democrats Expected to Hold Their Majorities in Congress," *New York Times*, 26 October 1980, 40.

117. For similar estimates, see "Modest GOP Congressional Gains Expected," *Congressional Quarterly Weekly Report*, 1 November 1980, 3242.

118. Ibid.

119. Martin Tolchin, "Key Posts in Congress at Stake Today," *New York Times*, 4 November 1980, B4.

120. "Convention Unity, Polls Boost GOP's Congressional Hopes," *Congressional Quarterly Weekly Report*, 19 July 1980, 2009.

121. Everett C. Ladd, "Realignment? No Dealignment? Yes," *Public Opinion* (October/November 1980): 55.

122. Albert Hunt, "The Campaign and the Issues," in Ranney, *The American Elections of 1980*, 166.

123. Robert Teeter noted that "this election is by and large a national election, with each side playing for something that will drive them four or five points nationally rather than trying the close states one by one." Adam Clymer, "Stakes Turn National," *New York Times*, 21 October 1980, D11.

124. For example, the *New York Times*/CBS poll reported Reagan with 44 percent, Carter 43 percent, and Anderson with 8 percent of the votes. Gallup reported Reagan with 46 percent, Carter with 43 percent, and Anderson with 7 percent of the votes. Adam Clymer, "Reagan and Carter Stand Nearly Even in Last Polls," *New York Times*, 3 November 1980, p. A1.

125. Hedrick Smith, "Survey Indicates Reagan Is Holding Lead in Battle for Electoral Votes," *New York Times*, 2 November 1980, A1.

126. See, for example, "Just Over Half the Electorate Expected to Turn Out Nov. 4," *Congressional Quarterly Weekly Report*, 25 November 1980, 3193–3195.

127. Hedrick Smith, "Whoever Wins, Reality Will Haunt the Rhetoric," *New York Times*, 2 November 1980, E4.

128. "Unpredictable Race Nears Finish," *Congressional Quarterly Weekly Report*, 1 November 1980, 3231. In 1976 Carter did not win until the last states were reporting. He won 279 electoral college votes to Gerald Ford's 240, and his popular vote margin was two percentage points.

129. The public opinion polls conducted the weekend before the election had the race too close to call. However, the president's own pollster, Patrick Caddell, and Robert Teeter, the Republican pollster, tracked vote intentions right up to election day and did pick up the swing to Reagan in the final two days.

130. Republicans gained twenty-two House members in 1952, three in 1956, five in 1968, and twelve in 1972. The last major gain for the Republicans occurred when they gained forty-seven seats in the House in the 1966 midterm elections.

131. Several major subcommittee chairmen were also defeated. See Marjorie Hunter, "Democrats Keep Control of the House; 4 Major Committee Chairmen Defeated," *New York Times*, 6 November 1980, A29.

132. Republicans gained seats in Montana, Nebraska, Louisiana, Arkansas, Ohio,

Michigan, Kentucky, West Virginia, New Jersey, Massachusetts, Rhode Island, and Hawaii.

133. Adam Clymer, "Displeasure with Carter Turned Many to Reagan," *New York Times,* 9 November 1980, 28.

134. "How Different Groups Voted for the President," *New York Times,* 9 November 1980, 28.

135. Clymer, "The Collapse of a Coalition," *New York Times,* 5 November 1980, A1.

136. See, for example, John Herbers, "Southern States Decisively Reject Bid of President, Their Native Son," *New York Times,* 5 November 1980, A23. The article discusses the unpopular nature of some of his policies (such as his national energy policy) in the South.

137. The southern and border states: Alabama, Arkansas, Florida, Georgia, Kentucky, Louisiana, Missouri, Mississippi, North Carolina, South Carolina, Tennessee, Texas, Virginia, West Virginia.

138. Hedrick Smith, "Reagan Easily Beats Carter," *New York Times,* 5 November 1980, A1; Clymer, "Displeasure with Carter Turned Many to Reagan."

139. Clymer, "The Collapse of a Coalition."

140. Adam Clymer, "Poll Shows Iran and Economy Hurt Carter Among Late-Shifting Voters," *New York Times,* 16 November 1980, A1.

141. Ibid.

142. Gallup polls found all adults in favor of Carter by about four points, while the subset of adults likely to vote favored Reagan by three points. *New York Times/* CBS polls reported similar findings. E. J. Dionne, "1980 Electorate Seen As Older, Whiter, and More Inclined to Vote for Reagan," *New York Times,* 5 November 1980, A23, and Steven Roberts, "Nonvoters Played Key Role in Election," *New York Times,* 5 November 1980, A23.

143. Steven Weisman, "Mondale Considers Democrats' Future," *New York Times,* 6 November 1980, A27.

144. Arkansas, Missouri, North Dakota, and Washington.

145. The number of states with Republican control of both chambers increased by two (Pennsylvania and Montana), and the number with divided control increased by two. Still, these gains were moderate compared with gains in past elections. "GOP Makes Modest Gains in State Legislative Contests," *Congressional Quarterly Weekly Report,* 15 November 1980, 3374.

146. Bill Brock, in Moore, *Campaign for President,* 254.

147. Vice President-elect George Bush repeatedly assured reporters and voters that conservative religious groups would not have too much influence over President Reagan. "Groups of Religious Conservatives Won't Control Reagan, Bush Says," *New York Times,* 11 November 1980, B8; Adam Clymer, "Bush Says No Single Group Gave Reagan His Victory," *New York Times,* 18 November 1980, B10; "New Right Wants Credit for Democrats' Nov. 4 Losses but GOP, Others Don't Agree," *Congressional Quarterly Weekly Report,* 15 November 1980, 3372.

148. Robert Teeter quoted by Hedrick Smith, "Reagan Buoyed by National Swing to Right," *New York Times,* 6 November 1980, p. A24.

149. Paul Kirk, in Moore, *Campaign for President,* 255.

150. "Mr. Reagan's Scary Mandate," *New York Times,* 8 November 1980, 22. On November 6, the editors wrote that the message of the election was, "We're desperate

to try a new approach." "The November Surprise," *New York Times,* 6 November 1980, A34.

151. "Transcript of Reagan News Conference," *New York Times,* 7 November 1980, A15.

152. Ronald Reagan, in his first press conference, when asked if he felt wedded to positions such as the anti-abortion stance of the Republican platform. "Transcript of Reagan News Conference."

153. A. O. Sulzberger, "Bush, in Victory Talk, Says Reagan Will Lead U.S. Back to Greatness," *New York Times,* 5 November 1980, A21.

154. Edwin Meese III, Reagan aide, cited by Douglas Kneeland, "Reagan Cut in Budgets Forecast; Federal Hiring Freeze Is Planned," *New York Times,* 6 November 1980, A24.

155. "Carter Post-Mortem: Debate Hurt But Wasn't Only Cause for Defeat: The Economy, 'Rose Garden Strategy' and Blunder on United Nations Vote Among Many Issues Cited," *New York Times,* 9 November 1980, A1.

156. See in particular, Caddell, "The Democratic Strategy," 278. He cites a January 1981 *Time* survey in which 63 percent of polled voters felt the election was "a rejection of President Carter," and only 24 percent labeled it "a mandate for more conservative policies." Only 30 percent of self-defined conservatives and 34 percent of Republicans surveyed labeled the election a mandate.

157. Moore, *Campaign for President,* 259.

158. Hunter, "Democrats Keep Control of the House." See also Smith, "Reagan Buoyed by National Swing to the Right."

159. "Voters Mandate Big Changes in Senate Panels," *Congressional Quarterly Weekly Report,* 8 November 1980, 3305.

160. Marjorie Hunter, "Conservative House Democrats Seek Bigger Voice," *New York Times,* 8 November 1980, 8; R. Lyons, "Conservative Democrats Press for Power in the House," *New York Times,* 21 November 1980, A21. On November 20, thirty-three representatives from southern and western states formed the "Democratic Conservative Forum."

161. M. Tolchin, "Baker and Conservatives Viewed as New Leaders," *New York Times,* 6 November 1980, A1. See also "National Mood for Change Boosted Republican Ticket," *Congressional Quarterly Weekly Report,* 15 November 1980, 3370–3371.

162. Moore, *Campaign for President,* 290–294.

163. S. Roberts, "Low Turnout Trend Hurts Democrats," *New York Times,* 10 November 1980, D8.

164. See, for example, Francis Clines, "A New Tide of Fortune in the Halls of Congress," *New York Times,* 13 November 1980, B11, and S. Roberts, "Democratic Legislators, Shaken by Losses," *New York Times,* 15 November 1980, 10.

165. "Congressional Factions Seek Power Balance," *Congressional Quarterly Weekly Report,* 15 November 1980, 3362.

166. Benjamin Rosenthal (D–NY), liberal member of the House, in Martin Tolchin, "Congress: Time for all Good Liberals to Cool It," *New York Times,* 9 November 1980, E2.

167. "Congressional Factions Seek Power Balance."

168. Adam Clymer, "A Chance to Govern," *New York Times,* 6 November 1980, A24. Democrats also started to rethink their fundraising and campaign organization techniques.

169. He later added that "it's somewhat consoling to go out in such good company." Judith Miller, "Church, Chief of Senate Foreign Relations Panel, Defeated," *New York Times*, 6 November 1980, A29.

170. S. Roberts, "Democratic Legislators, Shaken By Losses, Hoping to Rebuild Ties with Middle Class," *New York Times*, 15 November 1980, 10.

171. Reagan had pledged to "reinstitute this nation as a federation of sovereign states." John Herbers, "G.O.P. Governors Submit Proposals to Help States," *New York Times*, 19 November 1980, A30. The National Governors Association (both Democrats and Republicans) had voted in favor of similar proposals during the summer. John Herbers, "Governors Press for New State Powers," *New York Times*, 16 November 1980, 36.

172. A detailed description of the 1981 legislative year may be found in *1981 Congressional Quarterly Almanac; Congress and the Nation, Vol. 6, 1981–1984* (Washington, D.C.: Congressional Quarterly Inc., 1985); or Norman Ornstein, ed., *The President and Congress: Assessing Reagan's First Year* (Washington, D.C.: American Enterprise Institute, 1982).

173. *The Public Papers of the Presidents*, Ronald Reagan 1981, p. 222, March 10.

174. John Burke, "Presidential Influence and the Budget Process," in *The President and Public Policy Making*, ed. George Edwards, Steven Shull, and Norman Thomas (Pittsburgh: University of Pittsburgh Press, 1985), 81.

175. Samuel Kernell, *Going Public*, 3d ed. (Washington, D.C.: Congressional Quarterly Press, 1997), 149.

176. *The Public Papers of the Presidents*, Ronald Reagan 1981, p. 519, June 16; "The President's News Conference," June 16, 1981.

177. The bill passed 88 to 10 in the Senate. Fifty-one Republicans voted for the bill. Only one Republican voted against it. Thirty-seven Democrats voted for the bill and nine Democrats voted against it. All of the Democrats voting against the package were from northern states.

178. The bill passed in the House, with 217 votes for and 211 against. One hundred eighty-eight out of 200 Republican votes were cast in favor of the bill. Only twenty-nine Democrats supported the bill. Two hundred nine voted against it. While almost all of the northern Democrats voted against the bill (157 out of 160), only two-thirds of the southern Democrats voted against it (52 out of 78).

179. The final version passed in the Senate 89 to 11 and in the House 238 to 195. All House Republicans but one supported the final bill. While most Democrats voted against the bill, the proportion of northern Democrats who opposed the bill (151 out of 163) was much higher than the proportion of southern Democrats who opposed the bill (43 out of 79).

180. Outlined in Caddell, "The Democratic Strategy," and Richard Wirthlin, "The Republican Strategy and Its Electoral Consequences," in *Party Coalitions in the 1980s*, ed. Seymour M. Lipset (San Francisco: Institute for Contemporary Studies, 1981), 235–266.

181. Roosevelt's First Inaugural Address, in *Inaugural Addresses of the Presidents* (Washington, D.C.: U.S. Government Printing Office, 1989), 273.

182. *The Presidential Papers of Franklin D. Roosevelt, 1936*, item 217, "Greeting to the Third National Conference on Labor Legislation," November 7, 1936.

183. Ronald Reagan, Second Inaugural Address, in *Inaugural Addresses of the Presidents*, 340.

184. *The Public Papers of the Presidents*, Richard Nixon 1972, p. 832–833, item 276, August 29.

185. For instance, "we feel that we have a mandate, a mandate not simply for approval of what we have done in the past, but a mandate to continue to provide change that will work in our foreign policy and in our domestic policy." *The Public Papers of the Presidents*, Richard Nixon 1972, p. 1151, item 421, November 27; "Last November, the American people were given the clearest choice of this century. Your votes were a mandate, which I accepted, to complete the initiatives we began in my first term and to fulfill the promises I made for my second term." *The Public Papers of the Presidents*, Richard Nixon 1973, p. 697, item 233, August 15.

186. *The Public Papers of the Presidents*, Lyndon B. Johnson 1963–1964, p. 1200, item 619, October 3, 1964.

187. *The Public Papers of the Presidents*, Gerald R. Ford 1976, p. 830, item 264, March 27.

188. See, for example, *The Public Papers of the Presidents*, Gerald R. Ford 1976, p. 2652, item 948, October 23.

189. *The Public Papers of the Presidents*, Dwight D. Eisenhower 1954, p. 221, item 22, January 28.

190. *The Public Papers of the Presidents*, Lyndon B. Johnson 1966, p. 885, item 403, August 24.

191. *The Public Papers of the Presidents*, Ronald Reagan 1982, p. 554, May 4.

192. Doris Kearns Goodwin, *Lyndon Johnson and the American Dream* (New York: St. Martin's Press, 1976), 216.

CHAPTER SIX

1. "Bush and Clinton Pull No Punches in Holiday Rallies," Robin Toner, *New York Times*, 8 September 1992, A1. The vengeance with which the Republicans pursued the analogy prompted Margaret Truman to write an op-ed piece in which she criticized Bush as "no Harry Truman." Margaret Truman, "Mr. President, I Knew Harry Truman," *Washington Post Weekly Edition*, 31 August–6 September 1996, 28.

2. "Furious and Bittersweet End to President's Quest," Michael Wines, *New York Times*, 3 November 1992, A1.

3. On the election of 1948, see Richard S. Kirkendall, "Election of 1948," in *History of American Presidential Elections*, ed. Arthur Schlesinger Jr. and Fred L. Israel, vol. 4 (New York: Chelsea House Publishers, 1971), 3099–3211; Irwin Ross, *The Loneliest Campaign* (New York: New American Library, 1968); Harry S. Truman, *Memoirs* (Garden City, N.Y.: Doubleday, 1955–1956); Gary Donaldson, *Truman Defeats Dewey* (Lexington: University Press of Kentucky, 1999); Jules Abels, *Out of the Jaws of Victory* (New York: Henry Holt, 1959).

4. Elmo Roper, *You and Your Leaders* (New York: William Morrow and Company, 1957), 134.

5. The thirteen states were Alabama, Arkansas, Florida, Georgia, Kentucky, Louisiana, Mississippi, North Carolina, North Dakota, South Carolina, Tennessee, Texas, and Virginia.

6. Donaldson, *Truman Defeats Dewey*, 168–169.

7. *The Public Papers of the Presidents*, Harry S. Truman 1948, p. 881, item 259, October 27.

8. Roper, *You and Your Leaders*, 136–138.

9. *The Public Papers of the Presidents*, Harry S. Truman 1948, p. 881, item 259, October 27.

10. *The Public Papers of the Presidents*, Harry S. Truman 1948, p. 886, item 260, October 27, campaign speech in Boston.

11. *The Public Papers of the Presidents*, Harry S. Truman 1948, p. 147, item 32, February 19.

12. "Transcript of Truman's Address in Chicago," *New York Times*, 26 October 1948, 18.

13. *The Public Papers of the Presidents*, Harry S. Truman 1948, p. 886, item 260, October 27.

14. Donaldson, *Truman Defeats Dewey*, 169.

15. Sidney Shallett, quoted in Irwin Ross, *The Loneliest Campaign*, 2.

16. The *Louisville Courier-Journal* summed it up this way: "No presidential candidate in the future will be so inept that four of his major speeches can be boiled down to these historic four sentences: Agriculture is important. Our rivers are full of fish. You cannot have freedom without liberty. Our future lies ahead." Donaldson, *Truman Defeats Dewey*, 173.

17. "Dewey Advocates Broad Expansion of Social Benefits," *New York Times*, 29 October 1948, A1.

18. Donaldson, *Truman Defeats Dewey*, 167–183.

19. Later, Truman revealed that he trusted his feelings about the crowds he saw while campaigning, and his own sorts of "polls." In one such poll, the Senate secretary posed as a "chicken peddler" in rural areas, asking people their preferences. He found they supported Truman. In another, a milling company in Kansas City took a "pullet poll" among farmers buying feed in sacks labeled "Democratic" or "Republican." Democratic feed sold better. See David McCullough, *Truman* (New York: Simon and Schuster, 1992), 704, and Truman's own description in Merle Miller, *Plain Speaking* (New York: Berkley Books, 1974), 281.

20. "Truman Confident of Big Victory," *New York Times*, 30 October 1948, 7.

21. George Gallup quoted in "Gallup Defends Polls," *New York Times*, 28 October 1948, 22.

22. "Homestretch," *New York Times*, 24 October 1948, sec. 4, p. 1; Arthur Krock, "President Leads Dewey in Late Returns," *New York Times*, 3 November 1948, A1.

23. For example, A. Henning, "Landslide Predicted for Dewey-Warren: Expect Electoral Vote of 400 in 35 states," *Chicago Daily Tribune*, 1 November 1948, 1; James Hagerty, "Final Survey of Nation Gives Dewey Commanding Lead," *New York Times*, 31 October 1948, A1.

24. Hagerty, "Final Survey."

25. Thurmond won in Louisiana, Mississippi, Alabama, and South Carolina. His electoral college count included one faithless elector from Tennessee. Dewey won five western or midwestern states—Oregon, North Dakota, South Dakota, Nebraska, and Kansas—plus most northeastern states.

26. William White, "Sweep in Congress," *New York Times*, 4 November 1948, 1.

27. Kenneth Campbell, "Election Prophets Ponder in Dismay," *New York Times*, 4 November 1948, 8; Robert Whalen, "Our Forecast: What Went Wrong," *New York Times*, 7 November 1948, E4; Cabell Phillips, "And the Polls: What Went Wrong," *New York Times*, 7 November 1948, E4; "Roper Still Seeks Answer on Polls," *New York Times*, 8 November 1948, 13. The failure of polls was later explained as a function

of 1) combining early and late polls, thus ignoring trends; 2) oversampling of higher income voters, who were more likely to be Republican; 3) no accounting for the likelihood to vote; and 4) inconsistent allocation of undecided voters to the candidates. See Norman Bradburn and Seymour Sudman, *Polls and Surveys* (San Francisco: Jossey-Bass, 1988), 28–30.

28. McCullough, *Truman*, 712–713; public papers of Dewey, cited in Donaldson, *Truman Defeats Dewey*, 212.

29. James Reston, "Truman Victory Is Found to Contain Four Elements," *New York Times*, 4 November 1948, 8.

30. "Truman Sweep," *New York Times*, 7 November 1948, E1.

31. "Press Comment on the Presidency," *New York Times*, 4 November 1948, 9.

32. Ibid.

33. Ross, *The Loneliest Campaign*, 262.

34. A prominent Republican activist quoted in Donaldson, *Truman Defeats Dewey*, 213.

35. Louis Stark, "Labor Chiefs Hail Vote as Mandate," *New York Times*, 4 November 1948, 9.

36. "Press Comment on the Presidency."

37. John Morris, "Key Post Changes Shakeup Congress," *New York Times*, 4 November 1948, 6; C. P. Trussell, "Shift in Congress," *New York Times*, 3 November 1948, 1.

38. Morris, "Key Post Changes Shakeup Congress." Some, like Eleanor Roosevelt, argued that the rebellious southerners should be permanently ousted from the party. "Democrats Urged to Drop Dixiecrats," *New York Times*, 9 November 1948, 22.

39. L. Stark, "President to Seek Labor Act Repeal on Two-Sided Basis," *New York Times*, 5 November 1948, A1.

40. Harry S. Truman, Inaugural Address, in *Inaugural Addresses of the Presidents of the United States* (Washington, D.C.: U.S. Government Printing Office, 1989), 286.

41. *The Public Papers of the Presidents*, Harry S. Truman 1949, p. 558, item 253, November 10.

42. On the 1992 election, see P. Abramson, J. Aldrich, and D. Rohde, *Change and Continuity in the 1992 Elections* (Washington, D.C.: Congressional Quarterly Inc., 1993); Michael Nelson, ed., *The Elections of 1992* (Washington, D.C.: Congressional Quarterly Inc., 1993); Gerald Pomper, ed., *The Election of 1992* (Chatham, N.J.: Chatham House Publishers, Inc., 1993); Charles T. Royer, ed., *Campaign for President: The Managers Look at '92* (Hollis, N.H.: Hollis Publishing Company, 1994).

43. He would never have such a high share of the vote in any state again, and he had only 76 (of 2,210) delegates to the national convention by the end of the primary season.

44. Robin Toner, "Fractured GOP Meets as Public Voices Disfavor: Survey Shows President Far Behind Clinton as Party Convenes," *New York Times*, 17 August 1992, A1.

45. Text of the president's speech accepting the nomination for another four years, *New York Times*, 21 August 1992, A10. He refers to Bill Clinton's record on taxes as governor of the state of Arkansas.

46. Patrick J. Buchanan, speech at the 1992 Republican National Convention, Houston, Texas, 17 August 1992. http://www.buchanan.org/pa-92-0817-rnc.html.

47. "Excerpts from Vice-President's Speech," *New York Times*, 21 August 1992, A11.

48. David E. Rosenbaum, "G.O.P. Moderates from Congress Don't Feel at Home" *New York Times*, 17 August 1992, A7; R. W. Apple, "G.O.P. Is Flirting with the Dangers of Negativism," *New York Times*, 19 August 1992, A7.

49. R. W. Apple Jr. "Behind Bush's Mixed Abortion Signals," *New York Times*, 15 August 1992, 1; Alessandra Stanley, "First Lady on Abortion: Not a Platform Issue," *New York Times*, 14 August 1992, A1.

50. CNN/USA today poll, cited in "A Bush Bounce: Comparing Polls," *New York Times*, 25 August 1992, A11. See also, Andrew Rosenthal, "Bush Pulls Close in Poll, But Not with Women," *New York Times*, 22 August 1992, 1. In that poll, Bush went from seventeen points behind to only three points behind, within the margin of error.

51. Virginia governor Douglas Wilder declared for the nomination in September 1991 and then withdrew in early January 1992 before the primaries began.

52. Tsongas's criticism was aimed at Clinton's promise of a middle-class tax cut.

53. Jerry Brown and Paul Tsongas had the support of 14 percent and 5 percent of the delegates, respectively.

54. Text of address by Clinton accepting the Democratic nomination, *New York Times*, 17 July 1992, A12.

55. The Clinton campaign used the convention as an arena to address concerns about Clinton's character by reintroducing voters to the personal side of Bill Clinton. In prime time, right before his acceptance speech, they showed a short film describing the turbulent family life of Clinton's youth and his achievements despite his humble background.

56. Robin Toner, "Perot Quits Race, Leaving Two-Man Field; Clinton Vows Change and New Covenant as He and Bush Court Abandoned Voters," *New York Times*, 17 July 1992, A1.

57. Perot, quoted by Steven Greenhouse, "Hardly Laissez-Faire," *New York Times*, 27 June 1992, A9.

58. "Running against His Ambivalence: Five Months of a Not-Quite Campaign," Michael Specter, *New York Times*, 17 July 1992, A16.

59. "Excerpts from Perot's News Conference on Decision Not to Enter Election," *New York Times*, 17 July 1992, A16.

60. Ibid.

61. John Mintz and David Von Drehle, "The Day Perot Pulled the Plug," *Washington Post National Weekly Edition*, 27 July–2 August 1992, 9–10; Steven A. Holmes, "Advisors Describe Perot Disillusion," *New York Times*, 18 July 1992, 1; Michael Kelley, "Perot's Epic Failure," *New York Times*, 18 July 1992, 11.

62. Robin Toner, "Perot Re-enters the Campaign, Saying Bush and Clinton Fail to Address Government 'Mess,'" *New York Times*, 2 October 1992, 1. At the time, 72 percent of voters said he should not have reentered the race. Robin Toner, "Survey Finds Hostility to Perot and No Basic Shift in Race," *New York Times*, 6 October 1992, 1.

63. Richard L. Berke, "Perot Leads in $40 Million TV Ad Blitz," *New York Times*, 27 October 1992, A11; Steven A. Holmes, "Perot Wraps up His Campaign Where He Mostly Ran It: On TV," *New York Times*, 3 November 1992, A1.

64. Ross Perot, *United We Stand: How We Can Take Back Our Country* (New York: Hyperion, 1992).

65. Campaign flier, paid for by Illinois Victory '92; authorized by Clinton/Gore '92.

66. Marion Just et al., *Crosstalk* (Chicago: University of Chicago Press, 1996), 74–75.

67. R. W. Apple, "The Economy Falters, A President Falls," *New York Times*, 4 November 1992, 1.

68. Just et al., *Crosstalk*, 44–47.

69. All three candidates participated in three debates: October 11, 15, and 19. The three vice presidential candidates held a debate on October 13.

70. Robin Toner, "Issues, Not Attacks, Dominate as Audience Guides 2d Debate," *New York Times*, 16 October 1992, 1.

71. Maureen Dowd, "A No-Nonsense Sort of Talk Show," *New York Times*, 16 October 1992, 1.

72. Article by Andrew Rosenthal, *New York Times*, 12 October 1992, A1.

73. Gwen Ifill, "Clinton, Gazing Beyond Nov. 3, Outlines Vision," *New York Times*, 28 October 1992, A8.

74. "Surveys Vary," *New York Times*, 31 October 1992, 6.

75. Robin Toner, "Polls Say Clinton Keeps Lead Despite Furious GOP Fire," *New York Times*, 1 November 1992, A1.

76. Adam Clymer, "After the Election, A Certain Revolution in Congress," *New York Times*, 28 September 1992, A8.

77. Theodore Roosevelt won 27 percent of the popular vote and eighty-eight electoral college votes (six states) as the candidate of the Bull Moose Party in the election of 1912; Robert La Follette won 16.6 percent of the popular vote and thirteen electoral college votes (Wisconsin) as the candidate of the Progressive Party in 1924; George Wallace won 13.5 percent of the popular vote and forty-six electoral college votes (five southern states) as the candidate of the American Independent Party in 1968.

78. Howard Gleckman, "Job One: The Economy," *Business Week*, 16 November 1992, 31.

79. This includes K. B. Hutchinson, who won in a Texas runoff later in 1993.

80. Adam Clymer, "Democrats Promise Quick Action on a Clinton Plan," *New York Times*, 5 November 1992, B1.

81. Michael deCourcy Hinds, "Elections Change Face of Lawmaking Bodies," *New York Times*, 5 November 1992, B9.

82. Ibid.

83. R. W. Apple Jr., *New York Times*, 4 November 1992, A1; Steve Daley, *Chicago Tribune*, 4 November 1992, sec. 1, p. 1.

84. *New York Times*, 4 November 1992, B1; *New York Times*, 5 November 1992, B9.

85. Laurence I. Barrett, "A New Coalition for the 1990s," *Time*, 16 November 1992, 47.

86. "Portrait of the Electorate," *New York Times*, 5 November 1992, B9.

87. Barrett, "A New Coalition," 48.

88. Apple, "The Economy Falters."

89. Robin Toner, "Clinton Controls Key States and Big Margins in Poll," *New York Times*, 4 November 1992, B3.

90. David Broder, "A Turning Point—Or Just a Twist in the Road," *Washington Post Weekly Edition*, 9–15 November 1992, 12.

91. *Congressional Quarterly's Guide to U.S. Elections*, 3d ed. (Washington, D.C.: Congressional Quarterly Inc., 1994), 422.

92. Charles M. Madigan, "Clinton Elected President," *Chicago Tribune*, 4 November 1992, 22.

93. Ibid.

94. R. W. Apple, "Clinton, Savoring Victory, Starts to Size Up Job Ahead," *New York Times*, 5 November 1992, B2.

95. Helen Dewar, "George Bush's Loss Is Bob Dole's Gain," *Washington Post Weekly Edition*, 16–22 November 1992, 13.

96. Richard Berke, "Chastened GOP Leaders, Wary of Intolerant Image, Call for a Party of Inclusion," *New York Times*, 17 November 1992, A13.

97. "Excerpts from President-Elect's News Conference in Arkansas," *New York Times*, 13 November 1992, A8.

98. Toner, "Clinton Controls Key States."

99. David Broder, "Clinton Will Be Welcome in the House: But the Senate May Be Another Story," *Washington Post National Weekly Edition*, 14–20 December, 15–16.

100. Steven Mufson and Eric Pianan, "Changing of the Guard: The Economy and Congress Are Awaiting Clinton's Initiative," *Washington Post National Weekly Edition*, 9–15 November, 1992, 6.

101. Helen Dewar, "The Acid Test of Clinton's Skills: Congress," *Washington Post National Weekly Edition*, 9–15 November, 1992, 8.

102. Richard Morin, "Message: The New Congress Cares," *Washington Post National Weekly Edition*, 14–20 December 1992, 36.

103. Adam Clymer, "House Democrats Proclaim Unanimity for Next Year's Session," *New York Times*, 11 November 1992, A13.

104. Ibid.

105. Ibid.

106. Adam Clymer, "Avoiding Gridlock by Wooing Both Sides of the Aisle," *New York Times*, 17 November 1992, A12.

107. Thomas Friedman, "Clinton and Top Legislators Pledge Amity on Economy," *New York Times*, 17 November 1992, A12.

108. Broder, "Clinton Will Be Welcome in the House."

109. Text of Clinton's 1992 Inaugural Address, *Congressional Quarterly Weekly Report*, 23 January 1993, 193.

110. For a detailed account of the tensions between Clinton's economic and political advisors over the specific content of his policy, see Bob Woodward, *The Agenda* (New York: Pocket Books, 1994).

111. Adam Clymer, "Three Congressmen Say Deficit May Delay Clinton's Tax Cut," *New York Times*, 11 January 1993, A1.

112. R. W. Apple, "Democrats Unease May Slow Clinton On Economic Plan," *New York Times*, 21 February 1993, 14.

113. *The Public Papers of the Presidents*, William J. Clinton 1993, p. 30, February 1, remarks at the Democratic Governors' Association dinner.

114. Phil Duncan and Steve Langdon, "When Congress Had to Choose, It Voted to Back Clinton," *Congressional Quarterly Weekly Report*, 18 December 1993, 3427–3431. Success is measured by how often the president won his way on roll call votes on which he took a clear position.

115. Kitty Cunningham, "With Democrat in the White House, Partisanship Hits New High," *Congressional Quarterly Weekly Report*, 18 December 1993, 3432–3434.

116. Bob Benenson, "Clinton Keeps Southern Wing on His Team in 1993," *Congressional Quarterly Weekly Report*, 18 December 1993, 3435–3438.

117. See, for example, Ronald Elwing, "GOP's Field of Dreams Sows Nightmares for Democrats," *Congressional Quarterly Weekly Report*, 22 October 1994, 2991–2994.

118. Jim Gimpel, *Legislating the Revolution* (Boston: Allyn and Bacon, 1996), 3.

119. This includes Alabama senator Richard Shelby, who announced he was switching from the Democratic to the Republican Party the day after the election.

120. Robert Merry, "Voters' Demand for Change Puts Clinton on Defensive," *Congressional Quarterly Weekly Report*, 12 November 1994, 3207–3209.

121. "New House Speaker Envisions Cooperation, Cuts, Hard Work," *Congressional Quarterly Weekly Report*, 12 November 1994, 3296.

122. Ibid., 3295.

123. "Clinton Reaches out to GOP, Assesses Voters' Message," *Congressional Quarterly Weekly Report*, 12 November 1994, 3293–3294.

124. Ibid., 3294.

Chapter Seven

1. For more details on the 1960 election, see Theodore C. Sorensen, "Election of 1960," in *History of American Presidential Elections*, ed. Arthur Schlesinger Jr. and Fred L. Israel, vol. 4 (New York: Chelsea House Publishers, 1971), 3449–3562, and Theodore White, *The Making of the President, 1960* (New York: Atheneum House, 1961).

2. White, *The Making of the President*, 288.

3. Sorensen, "Election of 1960," 3467–3468.

4. Only the party and campaign chairmen forecasted comfortable victories for their candidates. The most confident forecast was that of Lyndon Johnson, who told one crowd, "The victory is going to be greater than any we have known in our lifetime except maybe the Roosevelt–Landon landslide of 1936." Bill Becker, "Johnson Foresees Landslide," *New York Times*, 25 October 1960, 30.

5. "Kennedy in Lead in Final Survey," *New York Times*, 7 November 1960, A1. In 1960, a majority was 269 of a total of 537 electoral college votes. In 1964 the total was readjusted to 535.

6. The number of undecided voters was larger than Kennedy's margin. Elmo Roper, director of the Roper Poll, commented, "It can go either way. This has been the most volatile campaign since we began taking samplings in 1936. I have never seen the lead change hands so many times." Charles Grutzner, "3 of 4 Major Election Polls Give Kennedy the Edge in Close Vote," *New York Times*, 8 November 1960, 18.

7. Claude Sitton, "Gains by Kennedy in the South," *New York Times*, 30 October 1960, 60.

8. "Deadlock in Vote a Possibility," *New York Times*, 25 October 1960, 28.

9. Russell Baker, "Democratic Edge in Senate Likely," *New York Times*, 27 October 1960, 32.

10. Leo Egan, "Record Vote Forecast for Today," *New York Times*, 8 November 1960, A1. Republicans were expected to gain seats because they had suffered such massive losses (forty-seven seats) in the House in the 1958 midterm elections.

11. Russell Baker, "Democratic Edge in States Seen," *New York Times*, 26 October 1960, 30.

12. James Reston, "Kennedy's Victory Won by Close Margin," *New York Times*, 10 November 1960, A1.

13. Reston, "Kennedy's Victory Won by Close Margin," and "Kennedy Is Apparent Victor," *New York Times*, 9 November 1960, A1; Philip Benjamin, "Other Elections Have Been Closer," *New York Times*, 10 November 1960, 36; "Now Kennedy," *New York Times*, 13 November 1960, sec. 4, p. 1.

14. "The 1960 Election Results," *1961 Congressional Quarterly Almanac*, 1025.

15. The half state for Kennedy was Alabama, whose delegates split their votes between Kennedy and Senator Harry Byrd of West Virginia.

16. Nixon won Indiana, Kentucky, Ohio, Tennessee, and Wisconsin.

17. Democrats lost one more seat in late May 1961 when Republican John Tower defeated Lyndon Johnson's appointed successor in Texas.

18. Reston, "Kennedy's Victory Won By Close Margin."

19. Claude Sitton, "Kennedy Scores Heavily in the South," *New York Times*, 9 November 1960, A1; Tom Wicker and Homer Bigart, "Nixon and Kennedy Aides Analyze Election Patterns," *New York Times*, 13 November 1960, A1.

20. Wicker and Bigart, "Nixon and Kennedy Aides," 52.

21. Homer Bigart, "Democrats Criticize Foes Campaign—Describe Result as Miracle," *New York Times*, 13 November 1960, A1.

22. Tom Wicker, "Vice President's Defeat Laid to City Machines," *New York Times*, 13 November 1960, A1.

23. "Now Kennedy."

24. Reston, "Kennedy Is Apparent Victor."

25. *San Francisco Chronicle* editorial in "Editorial Comments by Nation's Press on Victory for Kennedy," *New York Times*, 11 November 1960, 24.

26. *Hartford Courant* editorial, quoted in "Editorial Comments," 24.

27. The *Atlanta Constitution* editorial, quoted in "Editorial Comments," 24.

28. John Morris, "Liberals Suffer Setbacks in the House," *New York Times*, 10 November 1960, A1.

29. Ibid.

30. Russell Baker, "Liberals Retain Majority in Senate," *New York Times*, 10 November 1960, 36.

31. "The 1960 Election Results," 1025–1026.

32. "I went to the country with a very clear view of what the United States ought to do in the Sixties. I have been elected and therefore I'm going to do my best to implement those views and meet my responsibilities." Transcript of president-elect's news conference, *New York Times*, 11 November 1960, 20.

33. Ibid.

34. "Kennedy Boxscore," *1961 Congressional Quarterly Almanac*, 91.

35. "Congress—1961," *1961 Congressional Quarterly Almanac*, 63; "Kennedy Boxscore," *1961 Congressional Quarterly Almanac*, 91.

36. For more details about the 1976 election, see Betty Glad, "The Election of 1976," in *History of American Presidential Elections*, ed. Arthur Schlesinger Jr. and Fred L. Israel, vol. 5 (New York: Chelsea House Publishers, 1971), and Gerald Pomper, ed., *The Election of 1976* (New York: David McKay Co., 1977).

37. Carter's nationwide competition: Henry Jackson, senator from the state of

Washington; Morris Udall, representative from Arizona; George Wallace, former governor of Alabama; and Frank Church, senator from Idaho. Favorite-son candidates in the race included Adlai Stevenson from Illinois, Jerry Brown from California, Lloyd Bentsen from Texas, and Robert Byrd from West Virginia.

38. Humphrey was not a declared candidate at any time during the primary season. He was a write-in candidate and led only in the caucuses in his home state of Minnesota. Gallup polls showed Humphrey was more popular than Carter from January through May 1976. As late as June 4, Humphrey said he would be ready at the convention if Carter encountered difficulties. "Humphrey Ready If Carter Falters?" *New York Times*, 4 June 1976, A1.

39. See, for example, James Naughton, "Ford Vows Effort to Trim Taxes; Carter Hints but Bars Pledge," *New York Times*, 29 October 1976, A1, or Charles Mohr, "President and Carter Grow More Alike as Nov. 2 Nears," *New York Times*, 21 October 1976, 44.

40. Mohr, "President and Carter Grow More Alike."

41. For example, Joseph Lelyveld, "Has Campaign Cheated Voters?" *New York Times*, 1 November 1976, 44.

42. John Chancellor, "Fans, Unable to Tell David from Goliath, Doze in Arena," *New York Times*, 25 October 1976, 29.

43. R. W. Apple, "Presidential Rivals in a Very Tight Race," *New York Times*, 31 October 1976, A1; "Presidential Race Called Very Close on Eve of the Vote," *New York Times*, 1 November 1976, A1; "Ford and Carter Give Final Appeals in Race Still Viewed as Close," *New York Times*, 2 November 1976, A1.

44. Apple, "Presidential Race Called Very Close."

45. For example, Apple "Presidential Rivals," and Robert Reinhold, "Independent Swing Spurs Ford Comeback," *New York Times*, 31 October 1976, A1.

46. David Rosenbaum, "A Nominee Could Win with Small Popular Vote," *New York Times*, 2 November 1976, 20.

47. Richard Madden, "Parties Differ on Forecasts for Changes in House Seats," *New York Times*, 24 October 1976, 32; David Rosenbaum, "Analysts Predicting Little Change in Partisan Makeup of Congress," *New York Times*, 1 November 1976, 45; "Signs Point to a Congress Like the Last One," *Congressional Quarterly Weekly Report*, 30 October 1976, 3072–3078.

48. One faithless elector from the state of Washington would ultimately cast a ballot for Ronald Reagan, making the final tally 297 to 240 to 1.

49. James M. Naughton, "A Victory, but Not a Mandate," *New York Times*, 4 November 1976, 21.

50. Alan Ehrenhalt, "Carter and Democrats Move into Control," *Congressional Quarterly Weekly Report*, 6 November 1976, 3115; Rhodes Cook, "A New Candidate Wins with an Old Coalition," *Congressional Quarterly Weekly Report*, 6 November 1976, 3115; R. W. Apple, "Carter, In Victory, Hails 'New Spirit,'" *New York Times*, 4 November 1976, A1.

51. Ibid. See also Apple, "Carter, In Victory." Apple writes that "having won no more than 303 electoral votes and perhaps as little as 272, Mr. Carter failed to win the mandate he had appealed for in the waning days of the 22 month campaign."

52. Joseph Lelyveld, "The Tentative Thinking Behind the Close Vote," *New York Times*, 7 November 1976, sec. 4, p. 3.

53. Rhodes Cook, "A New Candidate Wins With an Old Coalition," 3116–3117; "The Easy Part," *New York Times*, 7 November 1976, sec. 4, p. 1.

54. See, for example, R. W. Apple, "The Presidential Election: One Week Later, the Politicians Tell How it Happened," *New York Times*, 10 November 1976, A22; Robert Reinhold, "Carter Victory Tied to Democrats Back in Fold, Plus Independents," *New York Times*, 4 November 1976, A25; James Naughton, "Survey Shows Union Households Giving Carter 60% of Their Votes," *New York Times*, 3 November 1976, 22.

55. James Wooten, "Carter Says He Won Because of Exposure Gained in Three Debates," *New York Times*, 7 November 1976, A1.

56. For example, David Rosenbaum, "Democrats Solidify Congress," *New York Times*, 4 November 1976, 22.

57. David Rosenbaum, "Carter, Kennedy, and Congress," *New York Times*, 12 November 1976, A1.

58. "Presidential Coattails of Little Benefit," *Congressional Quarterly Weekly Report*, 6 November 1976, 3135.

59. Mercer Cross, "Carter and Congress: 'Good Atmosphere,'" *Congressional Quarterly Weekly Report*, 15 December 1976, 3361–3364.

60. Rosenbaum, "Carter, Kennedy, and Congress"; Cross, "Carter and Congress."

61. "Transcript of News Conference Held by President-Elect Carter in Plains, Georgia," *New York Times*, 5 November 1976, A14.

62. Ibid.

63. Ehrenhalt, "Carter and Democrats Move into Control."

64. "Rebates Dropped as Honeymoon Spirit Ebbs," *Congressional Quarterly Weekly Report*, 16 April 1977, 691.

65. "Carter Support Score Low for Democrat," *1977 Congressional Quarterly Almanac*, 21–23B.

66. For details see "Congress Adjourns Without an Energy Bill," *1977 Congressional Quarterly Almanac*, 11–13, and Barry Hager, "Carter's First Year: Setbacks and Successes," *1977 Congressional Quarterly Almanac*, 65–70A.

67. On the election of 1988, see P. Abramson, J. Aldrich, and D. Rohde, *Change and Continuity in the 1988 Elections* (Washington, D.C.: Congressional Quarterly Press, 1990); Richard Ben Cramer, *What It Takes* (New York: Random House, 1992); Jack Germond and Jules Witcover, *Whose Broad Stripes and Bright Stars?* (New York: Politics Today, Inc., 1989); Gerald Pomper, ed., *The Election of 1988* (New Jersey: Chatham House, 1989); David Runkel, ed., *Campaign for President: The Managers Look at '88* (Dover, Mass.: Auburn House, 1989).

68. Gary Hart, the runner-up in 1984, withdrew after news of his affair with Donna Rice. Senator Joseph Biden withdrew after charges of plagiarism. New York governor Mario Cuomo simply refused to run.

69. Runkel, *Campaign for President*.

70. Bush's response to Dukakis's acknowledgment: "Miracle of miracles. Headlines. Read all about it. My opponent finally, after knocking me in the debate, called himself the big L, called himself a liberal." Maureen Dowd, "Bush Ridicules Dukakis," *New York Times*, 1 November 1988, A26.

71. R. Hershey, "Unemployment Declines to 5.2%," *New York Times*, 5 November 1988, A1.

72. E. J. Dionne, "Bush Still Ahead as End Nears but Dukakis Gains in Survey,"

New York Times, 6 November 1988, A1. Bush's margin ranged from a high of twelve points (Gallup poll) to a low of five points (NBC/*Wall Street Journal* poll).

73. Ibid.

74. Ralph Blumenthal, "Dukakis or Bush on November 8?" *New York Times*, 6 November 1988, 43; R. W. Apple, "Journey's End," *New York Times*, 6 November 1988, sec. 4, p. 1.

75. Albert Scardino, "Choice of the Dailies Is for None of the Above," *New York Times*, 4 November 1988, A20.

76. E. J. Dionne, "Race for the White House: How the Candidates Are Doing State by State," *New York Times*, 6 November 1988, 36.

77. David Rosenbaum, "Democrats Appear to Have a Lock on Congress," *New York Times*, 7 November 1988, B16.

78. One faithless elector in West Virginia ultimately cast a vote for Lloyd Bentsen for president, reducing Dukakis from 112 to 111 in the final tally.

79. Dukakis won Hawaii, Iowa, Massachusetts, Minnesota, New York, Oregon, Rhode Island, Washington, West Virginia, and Wisconsin.

80. Thus there were 260 Democrats and 175 Republicans in the House of Representatives, and 55 Democrats and 45 Republicans in the Senate.

81. See, for example, R. W. Apple, "The G.O.P. Advantage," *New York Times*, 9 November 1988, A1; G. Boyd, "How Bush Won," *New York Times*, 12 November 1988, 8; R. Toner, "Dukakis Aides Acknowledge Bush Outmaneuvered Them," *New York Times*, 12 November 1988, A1.

82. E. J. Dionne, "Bush Elected by a 6-5 Margin," *New York Times*, 9 November 1988, A25. As Reagan told one crowd the weekend before the election: "Although, come January, I'm going to be riding off into the sunset, I feel a little like I'm on the ballot myself this year." "Reagan Sees Election as Referendum on Himself," *New York Times*, 6 November 1988, A8.

83. Toner, "Dukakis Aides Acknowledge Bush Outmaneuvered Them." Dukakis said his advice to a future candidate would be "Smile a lot and respond somewhat more quickly to attacks against you." R. Toner, "Wistful Dukakis Sees No Mandate," *New York Times*, 10 November 1988, B5.

84. Warren Weaver, "Bentsen, in Texas, Hints That Loss by Democratic Ticket Is Possible," *New York Times*, 4 November 1988, A20.

85. "Baker Assails Democrats," *New York Times*, 4 November 1988, A20.

86. Jon Hale, "Shaping the Conventional Wisdom," *Political Communication* 10 (1993): Table 1, 292.

87. Ibid., Table 4, 295.

88. R. W. Apple, "Challenges for Bush: Agenda and Congress," *New York Times*, 10 November 1988, B1.

89. Toner, "Wistful Dukakis."

90. David Rosenbaum, "Democrats Take Solace as Party Defies History and Adds to Majority," *New York Times*, 10 November 1988, B7.

91. "Transcript of President-Elect's News Conference in Houston," *New York Times*, 10 November 1988, B2.

92. Gerald Boyd, "A Victor Free to Set His own Course," *New York Times*, 9 November 1988, A1. Boyd does mention Bush's burning desire to install a horseshoe pit on the White House grounds.

93. See, for example, "Legislative Agenda: No Clear Direction," *1989 Congres-*

sional Quarterly Almanac, 12, and "Bush Has Frail First-Year Hill Support," *1989 Congressional Quarterly Almanac*, 22B.

94. "Legislative Agenda," 12.

95. Ibid.

CHAPTER EIGHT

1. See, for instance, William Riker, *Liberalism Against Populism* (San Francisco: W. H. Freeman, 1982).

2. Nelson Polsby and Aaron Wildavsky, *Presidential Elections*, 10th ed. (New York: Chatham House Publishers, 2000), 261–266.

3. Adam Przeworski, Susan C. Stokes, and Bernard Manin, *Democracy, Accountability, and Representation* (Cambridge: Cambridge University Press, 1999), 10.

4. For an excellent discussion of elections as policy signals, see Bruce Buchanan, "Presidential Campaign Quality: What the Variance Implies," *Presidential Studies Quarterly* 29 (1999): 798–819.

5. Bruce Ackerman, *We the People 2: Transformations* (Cambridge, Mass.: Harvard University Press, 1998), 187.

6. See also Hanna Pitkin, *The Concept of Representation* (Berkeley: University of California Press, 1967). On pages 220–221, Pitkin argues that "political representation is primarily a public, institutionalized arrangement involving many people and groups, and operating in the complex ways of large-scale social arrangements. What makes it representation is not any single action by any one participant, but the overall structure and functioning of the system, the patterns emerging from the multiple activities of many people."

7. Quoted in George C. Edwards III, *At the Margins* (New Haven: Yale University Press, 1989), 149.

8. For example, see Robert Dahl, "The Myth of the Presidential Mandate," *Political Science Quarterly* 105 (1990): 355–372, and Theodore J. Lowi, "Presidential Democracy in America: Toward the Homogenized Regime," *Political Science Quarterly* 109 (1994): 401–415.

9. Woodrow Wilson, *Leaders of Men*, ed. T. H. Vail Motter (Princeton: Princeton University Press, 1952), 42.

10. This is similar to the argument that the president facilitates change, "exploiting opportunities to help others go where they want to," rather than directing change. Edwards, *At the Margins*.

11. *The Presidential Papers of Franklin D. Roosevelt, 1944*, item 109, statement urging employers to allow workers time off to vote, November 3, 1944.

12. Calvin Coolidge, Inaugural Address, March 4, 1925, in *Inaugural Addresses of the Presidents* (Washington, D.C.: U.S. Government Printing Office, 1989).

13. Stanley Kelley, *Interpreting Elections* (Princeton: Princeton University Press, 1983).

14. "Truman Asserts Vote Is Mandate," *New York Times*, 14 November 1960, A1.

15. V. O. Key Jr., *The Responsible Electorate* (Cambridge: Harvard University Press, 1966), 7.

Index

abortion, 94, 100, 127, 131
Abscam, 101
Ackerman, Bruce, 171
African Americans, 119, 135, 148, 151
agenda setting: basic model of, 18–20; elections and presidential, 11–31; elections manipulated by, 5; logic of, 15–20; as predictable, 167–68; presidents' concern with consequences of, 53. *See also* policy
agreement and difference, method of, 45–46
Anderson, John: and congressional races of 1980, 102; and debates of 1980, 100, 190n.113; defeat of 1980, 103, 105; in general election of 1980, 99–100; in primaries of 1980, 93, 94, 187n.66; on Reagan's 1980 victory, 107
"ANOVA" paradigm, 181n.32
Apple, R. W., 203n.51
Arrow's theorem, 4
Arthur, Chester, 59
Articles of Confederation, 172

Babbitt, Bruce, 160, 161
Baird, Zoe, 140
Baker, Howard, 93, 101, 187n.66
Baker, James, III, 163, 165, 187n.71
balanced budget amendment, 141
bargained mandates, 21, 117
Barkley, Alben, 118
Bayh, Birch, 104
behavioral tradition, 4
Bentsen, Lloyd, 161, 163, 202n.37
Biden, Joseph, 204n.68
Borda count, 5
Boren, David, 139

Boyd, Gerald, 205n.92
Brademas, John, 103
Brady bill, 140, 143
Brock, Bill, 96, 187n.71
Brown, Corinne, 138
Brown, Jerry: as candidate for 1976 nomination, 154, 202n.37; as candidate for 1980 nomination, 92, 186n.59; as candidate for 1992 nomination, 127, 129, 198n.53
Buchanan, James, 54, 58, 62
Buchanan, Patrick, 125–27, 197n.43
budget (spending) cuts, 109–10
Bush, Barbara, 127
Bush, George H. W.: comparing himself with Truman, 116, 195n.1; concurrence with own partisans, 74; congressional response to, 76, 164–65; defeat of 1992, 134; first-year success score of, 74, 165; in general election campaign of 1988, 161–62; in general election campaign of 1992, 132–34; Gulf War approval rating of, 125; interpretations of 1988 victory of, 163–65; interpretations of 1992 defeat of, 135, 136, 137; on magnitude of 1980 victory, 106–7; major policy changes not sought by, 21, 165, 166; mandate claim not made by, 4, 21, 164; party minority in Congress, 66; policy agenda of, 164–65; presidential nomination of 1988, 160; presidential nomination of 1992, 125–27; in primaries of 1980, 93, 94, 187n.66; "Read my lips: No new taxes," 125, 160; in second presidential debate